Korean Wild Geese Families

Korean Communities across the World

Series Editor: Joong-Hwan Oh, Hunter College, CUNY

Korean Communities across the World publishes works that address aspects of (a) the Korean American community, (b) Korean society, (c) the Korean communities in other foreign lands, or (d) transnational Korean communities. In the field of (a) the Korean American community, this series welcomes contributions involving concepts such as Americanization, pluralism, social mobility, migration/immigration, social networks, social institutions, social capital, racism/discrimination, settlement, identity, or politics, as well as a specific topic related to family/marriage, gender roles, generations, work, education, culture, citizenship, health, ethnic community, housing, ethnic identity, racial relations, social justice, social policy, and political views, among others. In the field of (b) Korean society, this series embraces scholarship on current issues such as gender roles, age/aging, low fertility, immigration, urbanization, gentrification, economic inequality, high youth unemployment, sexuality, democracy, political power, social injustice, the nation's educational problems, social welfare, capitalism, consumerism, labor, health, housing, crime, environmental degradation, and the social life in the digital age and its impacts, among others. Contributors in the field of (c) Korean communities in other foreign lands are encouraged to submit works that expand our understanding about the formation, vicissitudes, and major issues of an ethnic Korean community outside of South Korea and the Unites States, such as cultural or linguistic retention, ethnic identity, assimilation, settlement patterns, citizenship, economic activities, family relations, social mobility, and racism/discrimination. Lastly, contributions relating to (d) transnational Korean communities may touch upon transnational connectivity in family, economy/finance, politics, culture, technology, social institutions, and people.

Titles in the Series

Korean Wild Geese Families

Gender, Family, Social, and Legal Dynamics of Middle-Class Asian Transnational Families in North America

Se Hwa Lee

LEXINGTON BOOKS

Lanham • Boulder • New York • London

Published by Lexington Books
An imprint of The Rowman & Littlefield Publishing Group, Inc.
4501 Forbes Boulevard, Suite 200, Lanham, Maryland 20706
www.rowman.com

6 Tinworth Street, London SE11 5AL, United Kingdom

British Library Cataloguing in Publication Information Available

Library of Congress Cataloging-in-Publication Data Available

ISBN 978-1-4985-8347-3 (cloth : alk. paper)
ISBN 978-1-4985-8348-0 (electronic)

To my daughter,
Victoria Sheeyun Chung

Contents

Acknowledgments

I am filled with great joy and gratitude to many people who have helped me throughout this long journey to complete this book. First of all, I would like to express my deep gratitude to my advisors at the University at Albany, State University of New York: Christine Bose, Angie Chung, and Glenna Spitze. They not only read my book manuscript from the very early stage and gave me constructive feedback and comments on it. They were also always on my side and gave me invaluable advice and endless encouragement throughout my academic, professional, and personal life. I am also very grateful to Glenn Deane and Jaime Galusha at the Department of Sociology and Tara Evans at the International Student and Scholar Services at the University at Albany for their amazing institutional services and support for me, which were essential for me to complete this book.

I would like to give my special thanks to Joong-Hwan Oh, a book series editor of *Korean Communities across the World*, for his excellent advice and constant encouragement and support throughout this book project. I owe many thanks to Courtney Morales and Shelby Russell for their kind guidance and support throughout the editorial and publication process of this book. I am also thankful to the anonymous reviewers of this book for the detailed and constructive comments and suggestions.

I am deeply indebted to many people whom I met throughout my academic career for their helpful comments and feedback on my book project at different stages as well as their intellectual, practical, and emotional support, including Pyong Gap Min, Min Zhou, Yen Le Espiritu, Arnold Pan, Cathy J. Schlund-Vials, Rachael Joo, Paul Statham, Minjeong Kim, Hyunjoon Park, Hyeyoung Woo, Jun Yoo, Suk-Young Kim, and Doo-Sub Kim.

This book has been completed thanks to generous funding and honorary awards from: the Global Society of Korea and America Dissertation

Scholarship from the Research Center for Korean Community at Queens College of City University of New York, Korean Studies Dissertation Workshop from the Social Science Research Council (SSRC), Distinguished Student Paper Award from the Association of Korean Sociologists in America (AKSA), Research and Development Grant from Dickinson College, Annual Meeting Travel Fund Award from the American Sociological Association (ASA), as well as the Distinguished Doctoral Dissertation Award, Allen E. Liska Dissertation Award, Dissertation Research Fellowship Award, Benevolent Association Research Award, Initiatives for Women Award, Graduate Student Association Professional Development Grant, and Graduate Student Association Research Grant from the University at Albany.

I sincerely appreciate those who helped my fieldwork for a year in three different countries: the United States, Canada, and South Korea, including those in my family, academic, and professional networks. Many thanks to my interviewees who opened their mind and shared their valuable time, life stories, and perspectives with me.

Finally, my greatest thanks go to my family. My husband, Rakkoo Chung, is the best companion who has stood by me through the ups and downs of my life. Without his sacrifice, patience, and support, I would have not completed this book project. Thank you very much. I also would like to thank my parents, Kyungsim Bang and Changsik Lee, for their constant support throughout my life. I am particularly grateful for their transnational virtual grandparenting for my daughter. Finally, this book is especially dedicated to my daughter, Victoria Sheeyun Chung, who has always shown me her deepest love, support, encouragement, respect, and patience. She inspired me to grow as a mother, scholar, and human. I love you and thank you so much.

Introduction

Korean Wild Geese Families— Backgrounds and Motivations

This book explores the gender, family, social, and legal dynamics of Korean "wild geese" families (aka *kiroki* families) throughout their transnational family separation: before separation, during separation, and after family reunification. They are known as wild geese families, because they live apart for a lengthy period of time and occasionally fly back and forth across oceans to meet each other between Korea and the destination country. This book primarily focuses on Korean wild geese families whose mothers and children live in, or used to live in, North America.

As one of the rapidly increasing middle-class Asian transnational families who live apart for their children's education abroad, Korean wild geese families are similar to Hong Kong and Taiwanese "astronaut families"[1] and Chinese "study mothers."[2] That is, all three groups of families have mothers accompany and take care of their children who study abroad, while fathers remain alone in their home country and economically support their families abroad. There has been less scholarship on Korean wild geese families. This is probably because they are a relatively newer migrant group that has emerged since the late 1990s.[3] However, Korean wild geese families call for more scholarly attention. Note that Korean immigrants in North America have rapidly increased over time, and Korean nationals have been among the top three largest groups of international students enrolled in U.S. higher education institutions, followed by Chinese and Indian nationals.[4] Moreover, previous studies on Chinese astronaut families and study mothers have overlooked men's voices,[5] as if gender is only a women's issue. This book on Korean wild geese families examines both women's and men's perspectives and presents a more comprehensive picture of the gender and family relations of contemporary middle-class Asian transnational families.

1

Wild geese families are known to have strong familism[6] and prioritize parental obligations over spousal relationships for the sake of their children.[7] They also view children's education as a critical means for the family to achieve upward social mobility.[8] Thus, wild geese parents tend to equate their children's educational success with their own success.[9] In this regard, wild geese families' transnational living arrangement is initiated as a family strategy to pursue the collective goals and interests of all wild geese family members, as the *household strategy model* has suggested.[10] Under this model, every wild geese family member is also expected to equally share the outcomes (possibly, benefits) of transnational family separation.[11]

However, the household strategy model may not be useful to explain the dynamics among individual wild geese family members through and after transnational family separation. The outcomes of transnational family separation often differ from what wild geese families have originally expected, and the benefits and disadvantages may not be equally distributed among the individual family members. Through transnational family separation, wild geese mothers and fathers come to encounter different challenges and opportunities in host and home countries, and they eventually undergo substantial transformations in their gender and family relations, which often involve spousal confrontations and ongoing renegotiations.

Instead, such experiences of wild geese families are rather consistent with an alternative view on transnational family separation. That is, transnational family separation is a *gendered institution,*[12] which brings about different outcomes to women and men of transnational families, as Hondagneu-Sotelo has suggested. Her perspective also acknowledges that women and men of transnational families may develop different interests and goals, even if they initially shared the same goal, and that there may be serious gender struggles in the entire process of transnational migration. Therefore, my discussions in the following chapters are built on Hondagneu-Sotelo's framework, and I offer empirical evidence to further elaborate and test it.

Korean wild geese families have unique characteristics that distinguish them from so-called traditional working-class transnational families in North America.[13] First, the rationales for their migration differ: unlike traditional transnational families who often aim to enhance the parent's economic abilities, Korean wild geese families seek to improve their children's future socioeconomic status by providing them with better educational opportunities abroad. Second, they differ in terms of who stays in the home country and who migrates abroad: while traditional emigration is often led by men, for Korean wild geese families, it is not fathers but mothers and children who migrate abroad. Third, the directions of remittances differ: while traditional migrants usually send remittances from North America to their country of origin, remittances are sent from Korea to North America within wild geese families. Finally, unlike traditional migrants who plan to permanently settle down in the destination countries, a majority of wild geese families plan to reunite in Korea after a temporary transnational family separation, and only a few of them happen to permanently settle down in the host countries.

Due to these unique situations, wild geese families are faced with challenges that are qualitatively different from what permanent immigrants, undocumented immigrants, or working-class immigrants go through. However, or accordingly, the experiences of wild geese families have not been well explained, because contemporary middle-class Asian transnational families are not adequately discussed by previous studies, which have mainly focused on the experiences of working-class Latino[14] or working-class Asian[15] transnational families. Thus, this book offers the readers a unique venue to enhance their understanding of the increasingly diverse transnational families in North America through an analysis of Korean wild geese families, a group of middle-class Asian transnational families. Because this book aims at providing deeper insights into middle-class Asian transnational families, it takes an intersectional approach[16] and examines the intertwined impacts of race/ethnicity, social class, gender, and legal status (particularly, temporary visas, as well as permanent residency and citizenship) on the experiences of wild geese families. Given that the intersectional approaches in existing studies mostly focus on race, class, and gender, I seek to extend its scope by adding another layer: legal status.

This book explores the following themes: (1) the changes in women's and men's relative gender statuses, housework patterns, and the quality of spousal relationships through transnational family separation, (2) the changes in parenting practices (i.e., intensive mothering of wild geese mothers and transnational fathering of wild geese fathers) and intergenerational relationships (i.e., intimacy and conflict between children and parents), and (3) wild geese families' settlement and integration experiences in the host societies and their re-adaptation experiences after family reunification in the home country.

This book provides answers to the following questions: Why do some of the middle-class Korean families become wild geese families? What kind of changes do they experience throughout the transnational family separation and reunification processes? How and why do men and women in these families respond differently to such changes? How and why do wild geese families' transnational migration experiences vary between the United States and Canada? And how and why do their migration experiences differ from those of other transnational families such as Latino and/or Asian working-class migrant families in the United States?

I pay particular attention to the following factors of wild geese families' divergent gender, family, social, and legal dynamics: transnational family separation as a triggering moment that leads to the significant changes in family relationships; Korean wild geese mothers' resources in the host societies including legal status, economic activities, and additional education; significance of wild geese children's educational achievement; wild geese mothers' social isolation and discrimination in the mainstream host societies; functions and dysfunctions of co-ethnic immigrant communities; and Korean wild geese fathers' level of income, type of employment, use of advanced communication technologies, and the quantity and quality of their visits to families abroad.

DATA

I gathered the data for this book through qualitative face-to-face in-depth interviews with sixty-four Korean wild geese parents (thirty-one women and thirty-three men) over the course of 2013 and 2014 in three main research sites: (1) Tenafly, New Jersey, the United States, (2) London, Ontario, Canada, and (3) Seoul, Korea. I interviewed current wild geese mothers and a few fathers in the United States and Canada, and also former wild geese mothers and fathers as well as mostly current wild geese fathers in Korea. I recruited the initial interview participants via my personal networks, including my family, community, professional, academic, and religious networks, and then recruited the rest of participants by snowball sampling through referrals.

While previous studies of Korean wild geese families tend to be based on the accounts of only one gender,[17] because researchers choose to interview either wild geese mothers or wild geese fathers based on the location of researcher's residence, I traveled overseas to interview fathers in Korea, as well as mothers in the United States and Canada. Balanced numbers of both women and men in my research helped produce more comprehensive and balanced pictures of complex transnational family and gender dynamics. In addition, I interviewed not only current wild geese parents but also former wild geese parents so as to better portray the short- and long-term effects of transnational family separation on wild geese families' lives. Finally, my interviews with wild geese mothers in two different countries in North America (i.e., the United States and Canada) allowed me to compare and better explain the distinctive effects of immigration and settlement policies on transnational migrants' lives. In sum, the analysis of the carefully collected data helps the readers obtain a more gender-balanced and comprehensive understanding of emerging but understudied Korean wild geese families in North America. More detailed descriptions of data and methodology are presented in the appendix.

ORGANIZATION OF THE BOOK

Let me introduce the chapters of the book. Chapter 1 investigates the changes in wild geese parents' gender roles and relative gender statuses through transnational family separation. It describes wild geese parents' traditional gender roles and unequal relative statuses within their families when they lived together in Korea, and then discusses how the event of transnational separation has triggered significant changes in their spousal power dynamics. It further demonstrates that wild geese mothers' gender statuses after migration tend to be significantly diversified based on the way they utilize their new sources of gender empowerment, such as (1) legal status, (2) employment, and (3) education in the host societies. Chapter 1 highlights the significance of various legal statuses either as a foundation of, or obstacles to, migrant women's employment and education opportunities in the host societies. It also compares wild geese mothers' experiences between the United States and Canada and further discusses the implications of immigration and settlement policies for migrant women's reconfiguration of gender statuses within their transnational households, as well as their adaptation processes in the host societies.

Chapter 2 analyzes how patriarchal housework patterns of wild geese parents have been challenged through their lengthy transnational spousal separation. It shows that wild geese mothers feel liberated as their housework has considerably decreased after migration, whereas left-behind wild geese fathers are struggling greatly due to their increased domestic duties. This chapter demonstrates the strong effect of leaving "coresidential unions" on married couples and describes how they reconstruct their existing housework patterns in the transnational context. This chapter applies three theories of the division of household labor (i.e., the time availability perspective, the relative resources perspective, and the gender perspective) to the experiences of wild geese families and finds empirical evidence that the gender perspective has better explanatory power than the other theories.

Chapter 3 explores how transnational spousal separation impacts the quality of conjugal relationships over time and discusses the changing meanings of marriage, emotional intimacy, and sexual intimacy to Korean wild geese parents. While existing studies tend to focus on the negative impacts of transnational spousal separation on Asian middle-class transnational families,[18] this chapter alternatively highlights how Korean wild geese parents manage to maintain intimate transnational marital relationships with varying degrees of success.

Chapter 4 compares the intensive mothering practices of wild geese mothers between the two periods: prior to migration and after migration. It describes how wild geese mothers, who used to be an ambitious and competent educational manager for their children in Korea, struggle for achieving their educational goals after migration, because of their newly obtained structural marginality in the host societies as racial/ethnic minority women without much information of the education system in North America. It also explains how wild geese mothers, who are excluded from the main-stream social networks of the host countries, alternatively resort to Korean immigrant communities to achieve their goals of migration but have to pay special costs for maintaining their co-ethnic membership.

Chapter 5 examines wild geese fathers' transnational fathering practices and their changing relationships with their children. This chapter provides an in-depth analysis of both economic and emotional aspects of transnational fatherhood, as it explores how wild geese fathers not only try to fulfill their traditional role as economic providers but also implement new ideologies of involved and intimate fatherhood in their fathering practices so as to over-come their lengthy separation from children. This chapter focuses on (1) remittances, (2) transnational communication, and (3) face-to-face encoun-ters, which are three critical tools of transnational fathering, and shows the heterogeneous patterns of transnational father-children emotional ties by the ways wild geese fathers utilize these parenting tools.

Chapter 6 turns to the stories of former wild geese families and explores what has happened to them after family reunification. This chapter analyzes the experiences of former wild geese families around the key themes of the book, which include (1) diverging gender paths by wild geese mothers' employment/education and by children's educational outcomes, (2) sexual intimacy between couples, (3) spousal conflicts over the leadership and the division of household labor, and (4) children's educational outcomes and re-adaptation. This chapter is brief but offers a valuable opportunity to gain insights into the long-term effects of transnational separation on gender and family relations.

TREND IN KOREAN WILD GEESE FAMILIES

As mentioned earlier, wild geese families have rapidly increased in number since the 1990s.[19] However, there are no official statistics regarding them. Alternatively, the Korean educational statistical data show the numbers of Korean students at the age of elementary, middle-school, and high school (i.e., grade 1–12) who are studying abroad since 1995. Because these num-bers are closely related to the numbers of wild geese children, the overall trend in wild geese families can be estimated.

As table I.1 shows, the number of Korean elementary, middle school, and high school students studying abroad significantly increased from 2,259 in

Table I.1   Students Studying Abroad[a] by Year[b]

Year[b]	Elementary School[c]		Middle School[c]		High School[c]		Total
	Number[d]	Ratio[e]	Number[d]	Ratio[e]	Number[d]	Ratio[e]	Number[d]
1995	235	0.6	1,200	4.8	824	3.8	2,259
1996	341	0.9	1,743	7.3	1,489	6.6	3,573
1997	241	0.6	978	4.5	2,055	8.8	3,274
1998	212	0.6	473	2.4	877	3.8	1,562
1999	432	1.1	709	3.7	698	3.1	1,839
2000	705	1.8	1,799	10	1,893	9.1	4,397
2001	2,107	5.2	3,171	17.3	2,666	13.9	7,944
2002	3,464	8.4	3,301	17.9	3,367	18.8	10,132
2003	4,052	9.7	3,674	19.8	2,772	15.7	10,498
2004	6,276	15.2	5,568	28.8	4,602	26.3	16,446
2005	8,148	20.8	6,670	33.2	5,582	31.7	20,400
2006	13,814	35.2	9,246	44.6	6,451	36.3	29,511
2007	12,341	33.6	9,201	44.6	6,126	33.3	27,668
2008	12,531	36.1	8,888	43.6	5,930	31.1	27,349
2009	8,369	24.1	5,723	28.5	4,026	20.5	18,118
2010	8,794	26.7	5,870	29.7	4,077	20.8	18,741
2011	7,477	23.9	5,468	28.6	3,570	18.4	16,515
2012	6,061	20.5	4,977	26.9	3,302	17.2	14,340
2013	5,154	18.5	4,377	24.3	2,843	15.0	12,374
2014	4,455	16.3	3,729	21.7	2,723	14.8	10,907
2015	4,271	15.7	3,226	20.3	2,432	13.6	9,929
2016	3,796	14.2	2,700	18.5	2,247	12.8	8,743

Sources: Korean Educational Development Institute (KEDI), "2005 Educational Statistics Analysis" & "2017 Educational Statistical Analysis" (in Korean). Last accessed at http://cesi.kedi.re.kr/ on June 27, 2018.

Notes: (a) Students who went abroad to accompany their parents stationed in foreign countries and those emigrated to foreign countries are excluded; (b) Academic year in Korea (from March to February in the following year); (c) elementary school = grade 1–6, middle school = grade 7–9, high school = grade 10–12; (d) Number of students abroad; (e) Number of students abroad per 10,000 Students = (number of students abroad/number of total students registered) ×10,000.

1995 to 29,511 in 2006, and then decreased to 8,743 in 2016. In addition, these statistics exclude the students who went abroad to accompany their parents stationed in foreign countries and those students who emigrated permanently to foreign countries. When these students are included in the statistics, the actual number of total Korean elementary, middle school, and high school students studying abroad in 2016 is 18,024,[20] which is far greater than 8,743 in table I.1. Given that a substantial number of wild geese children in my study initially migrated abroad as dependents of their parents who stationed in foreign countries for their work,[21] the actual numbers of wild geese children may be much greater than the numbers of educational statistics presented in table I.1.

Table I.1 also reflects that studying abroad is more popular among younger children than older children. My study also confirms the domination of elementary school students among those who study abroad. Among the total 115 wild geese children in the sample, 58 percent were kindergarteners and elementary school students, 26 percent were middle-school students, and 17 percent were high school students when they became wild geese children.[22] Prior to migration, many wild geese parents in my study strongly believed that the best timing to start their children's foreign education was their elementary school period,[23] and that they could reunite soon after a short period of transnational family separation, such as one year or two.

However, once wild geese families started transnational family separation, it has often become much longer than their original plan. At the time of interview, wild geese parents in my study have been transnationally separated from their spouses for about four years on average, ranging from six months to thirteen years, and the majority of them plan to finish (or finished) their transnational spousal separation and reunite in Korea after their children (particularly the oldest child regardless of their gender) finish the high school education and enter prestigious universities either in Korea or in the host countries. This prolonged transnational family separation has occurred as wild geese parents recognize how it will be challenging for their foreign sojourning children to re-adapt into and survive in the competitive Korean education system. In particular, wild geese parents of teenagers tend to be very concerned about the possibility that their children may fall behind in the course subjects that are important for admissions to Korean colleges and universities, such as Korean literature, Korean social studies, and mathematics. Even if their children are competitive enough, some wild geese parents strategically decide to extend their transnational spousal separation until their children reach twelfth grade, hoping that their children can take advantage of the special college admission system arranged for overseas Koreans.[24]

Table I.2 illustrates that English-speaking countries were the most popular destinations for Korean students as of 2016. For example, 60 percent of elementary school, 55 percent of middle school, and 62 percent of high school students studying abroad went to English-speaking countries, such as the United States, Canada, New Zealand, Australia, and the United Kingdom. In particular, the United States and Canada were the most preferred destinations for young Korean students. In addition, the Philippines and China were emerging popular destinations for Koreans, as 18 percent of elementary school, 28 percent of middle school, and 21 percent of high school students studying there. Recently, the Philippines and Singapore have become cheaper alternative destinations of English-speaking countries for many Korean students, because they are closer to Korea and use English as their official language.[25]

Table I.2 Number of Students Studying Abroad[a] by Country, 2016[b]

Country and Region[c]	Total	Elementary School	Middle School	High School
All	8,743	3,796	2,700	2,247
United States	2,456	896	731	829
Canada	1,560	847	432	281
Philippines	952	417	373	162
China	942	254	384	304
New Zealand	444	229	134	81
Australia	374	189	96	89
Japan	187	61	49	77
United Kingdom	114	51	28	35
Latin America	54	25	17	12
Other Asia	694	361	231	102
Other Europe	205	53	66	86
Others	612	384	127	101
Unidentified	149	29	32	88

Source: Korean Educational Development Institute (KEDI), "2017 Educational Statistical Analysis" (in Korean). Last accessed at http://cesi.kedi.re.kr/ on June 27, 2018.
Notes: (a) Students who went abroad to accompany their parents stationed in foreign countries and those emigrated to foreign countries are excluded; (b) Data as of 2016 academic year; c. Countries and regions are sorted on the total number of students.

SAMPLE CHARACTERISTICS: WILD GEESE MOTHERS, FATHERS, AND CHILDREN

This section describes the backgrounds of wild geese parents that I interviewed, including the number of interviewees by gender, destination country,

Table I.3 Sample Characteristics: Wild Geese Mothers and Wild Geese Fathers

	United States	Canada	Australia	Singapore	Philippines	China	Total
Gender/Status							
Women							
Current	15	8	0	0	0	0	23
Former	7	1	0	0	0	0	8
Women Total	22	9	0	0	0	0	31
Men							
Current	13	4	3	0	1	1	22
Former	8	1	0	2	0	0	11
Men Total	21	5	3	2	1	1	33
All							
Current	28	12	3	0	1	1	45
Former	15	2	0	2	0	0	19
Grand Total	43	14	3	2	1	1	64

age, marital status, education, occupations, income, and the number and gender of their children.

As table I.3 shows, I interviewed sixty-four wild geese parents in total: thirty-one women and thirty-three men. About three-fourths of women and two-thirds of men were current wild geese mothers and fathers, whereas the others were former wild geese mothers and fathers at the time of interviews. Approximately two-thirds of women lived in the United States, while the other one-third lived in Canada. Men in the sample were more diverse in terms of destination countries: Two-thirds of wild geese fathers sent their families to the United States, and the others sent their families to Canada, Australia, Singapore, the Philippines, and China. I recruited wild geese mothers in the United States and Canada: the most popular destination countries for Korean students (see table I.2). On the other hand, the recruited wild geese fathers show a wider variation in their families' destination countries. Because I paid attention to the changes in left-behind fathers' lives in Korea, I did not limit my sample of wild geese fathers to certain destination countries.

To explore the backgrounds of wild geese parents, I asked my interviewees to report not only their own but also their spouse's demographic information. Thus, from the interviews with 64 wild geese parents, I obtained information on 126 people in total (Of note, among thirty-one wild geese mothers interviewed, one referred her husband for an interview. Among thirty-three wild geese fathers, no one referred their wives for an interview). The rest of this section summarizes the backgrounds of these 126 wild geese parents.

Wild geese parents in my study were middle-aged at the time of interview. Wild geese mothers were, on average, forty-six years old with a range from thirty-five to sixty years old. Wild geese fathers were, on average, forty-nine years old with a range from thirty-seven to sixty-three years old. Most wild geese parents were in their forties or fifties, while some were in their thirties or sixties. Wild geese parents had been married on average nineteen years, ranging from ten to thirty years. Most wild geese parents were maintaining an intact marriage at the time of interview, while a few parents were experiencing marital crises: separated (two), divorce proceedings (two), divorced (one), widowed (one), and remarried (one).

Wild geese parents had upper-middle social class status in Korea prior to transnational family separation, given their level of education, type of occupation, and annual household income. To begin with, wild geese parents show high levels of educational attainment: All but five had a bachelor's degree or higher. Wild geese mothers, in general, had a lower educational level than fathers: 20 percent of wild geese mothers and 40 percent of wild geese fathers had a master's degree or higher; two wild geese mothers and thirteen wild geese fathers had a doctoral degree; and the relative education levels of wild geese couples show that only seven out of sixty-two women[26] in the sample achieved a higher educational level than their husbands, whereas twenty-four men were holding a higher degree than their wives. This gendered asymmetry of educational attainment reflects the patriarchal marital pattern of hypergamy, a practice that women tend to *marry up* with men of a higher socioeconomic status. This pattern is partly related to the unequal spousal relationship prior to transnational family separation.

At the time of interview, all wild geese fathers held professional jobs, such as businessman, entrepreneur, professor, public official, doctor, journalist, banker, chief executive officer (CEO), lawyer, accountant, architect, programmer, research scientist, and teacher. On the other hand, a half of wild geese mothers were full-time homemakers prior to migration. Among the other wild geese mothers who worked before migration, a majority had professional positions, such as public official, businesswoman, lecturer at university, nurse, banker, journalist, computer programmer, research scientist, entrepreneur, and artist, while some had typical female-typed teaching jobs such as teacher and private tutor. A further description of wild geese mothers' employment after migration is provided in chapter 1 that discusses the changing gender status of wild geese parents.

Wild geese families' average annual household income before transnational family separation was about $128,000 with a range between $60,000 and $400,000.[27] According to the Korean Statistical Office,[28] the average annual household income in Korea in 2014 was $47,670; the annual household income of $71,000 or higher indicated the upper 20 percent income bracket; and the annual household income of $95,000 or higher indicated the upper 10 percent income bracket. Given this, the majority of the wild geese families in my sample fell in the upper 10 percent income bracket in Korea.[29]

Before they became wild geese families, many wild geese parents (not as families but as individuals) had prior experiences of living abroad (e.g., the United States, Canada, New Zealand, Australia, the United Kingdom, France, or Japan), mainly to pursue their own employment or educational opportunities, while only a few had experiences of emigration as a family unit for their children's education. Some wild geese parents even lived abroad as permanent immigrants. Others used to live abroad when they were younger as the 1.5 generation of Korean immigrants. A few parents had prior experiences of being wild geese families, and when I met them for the interview, it was their second or third time of being wild geese families since their marriage.

A significant discrepancy between wild geese mothers' emigration period and their transnational spousal separation period was observed. That is, while wild geese mothers lived in the host countries about six years on average with a range from eight months to twenty-five years, their actual transnational separation from their husbands was shorter as about four years with a range from six months to thirteen years. This confronts the common image of wild geese families: mothers and children migrate abroad while fathers remain alone in Korea. Rather, in reality, one-third of the wild geese mothers in my study originally migrated to their host countries as the whole family, following their husbands who pursued their professional career opportunities abroad, but then they became wild geese mothers by remaining with children in the host countries after their husbands returned to Korea. This pattern was especially common among the wild geese mothers whom I recruited in the United States, because many of their husbands were dispatched employees of the overseas branches of Korean global corporations or Korean government offices. In the following chapters, this phenomenon is discussed with respect to the legal and economic status of Korean wild geese mothers in the host countries.

Wild geese parents in my sample show variations in the number of their children. Nineteen wild geese parents had only one child, and thirty-nine had two children. Only six wild geese parents had three children. On the one hand, this reflects the alarmingly lowering fertility rate in Korea[30] and the increasing value of children among middle-class Korean families.[31] On the other hand, it also indicates how difficult and costly it is even for middle-class Korean parents to provide their children with educational opportunities abroad.

In regard to the gender of children, among the nineteen parents with only one child, twelve had a son and seven had a daughter. Among the thirty-nine parents with two children, twenty-one had both a son and a daughter, twelve had only sons, and six had only daughters. Among the six parents with three children, four had both sons and daughters and two had only three sons. Overall, sons outnumbered daughters among the wild geese families in my sample.

Wild geese children generally started their foreign education when they were young. Among the total 115 wild geese children in the sample, 58 percent were kindergarteners or elementary school students, 26 percent were middle-school students, and 17 percent were high school students when they became wild geese children.[32] However, two different patterns were observed in the timing of family reunification based on the age of children. When children were younger and still elementary- or middle-school students, wild geese mothers tended to return to Korea with their children as they had originally planned. However, when children became high school students, many wild geese mothers extended their stay in the host countries until their children (particularly the oldest child regardless of their gender) finished the high school education abroad and entered prestigious universities either in Korea or host countries. For instance, two-thirds of the former wild geese children in my study were either high school seniors or college students at the time their mothers finished transnational spousal separation and reunited with their husbands in Korea.

Finally, out of the sixty-four cases, wild geese parents' gender roles were reversed in two families. That is, most wild geese mothers in the sample (and in general) migrated abroad to accompany their children, while their husbands remained in Korea to economically support their families abroad. However, in two families in the sample, mothers remained in Korea and fathers accompanied their children abroad.

MOTIVATIONS OF WILD GEESE FAMILIES

Why did middle-class Korean parents choose to become transnational families? Did they make a decision of transnational family separation only for their children's education? Weren't there any other reasons? Motivations of wild geese families are more complex than commonly known and are deeply related to the changing cultural, economic, and social contexts in contemporary Korean society.[33]

Certainly, wild geese parents' decision of transnational family separation was for the sake of their children's education. Culturally, Korean society is built upon a strong Confucian tradition that highly emphasizes younger generation's upward social mobility through education.[34] Under this tradition, many middle-class Korean parents (particularly mothers) tended to equate their children's educational attainment with their own life's success and organize their family lives around their children's schooling and extracurricular activities even before they became wild geese families.[35]

In addition, middle-class Korean parents' educational zeal for enhancing their children's English skills has significantly increased as Korean society has experienced rapid economic and social transformations since the mid-1990s. First, the Kim Young-Sam administration (1993–1997) joined the Organisation for Economic Co-operation and Development (OECD) in 1996,[36] and actively pursued its main economic and social agenda under the slogan of globalization and extended English education to elementary school in 1997 as a part of its globalization projects.[37]

Furthermore, around the Asian financial crisis in 1997, many Korean employees suffered from massive layoffs and forced retirement in the name of labor market flexibility, which was requested by the International Monetary Fund (IMF) as one of the conditions of the bailout program.[38] Even if wild geese fathers in my study did not lose their jobs during this difficult time, many of them recognized that there would be no guarantee of lifetime or permanent employment anywhere in Korean society as they witnessed heightened economic insecurity and employment uncertainty.

Some wild geese fathers, during the interview, mentioned that after the IMF crisis in the mid-1990s they encountered new challenges in their workplace because of significantly increased importance of English skills. Some companies asked these fathers to get higher scores in English fluency tests as the minimum qualifications for promotion and other work-related evaluations.[39] Some wild geese fathers also had to use English in their daily work when communicating with foreign supervisors and colleagues, as their companies were merged with foreign ones. A story of Changsung, a 45-year-old businessman who works for a global IT company, well shows how wild geese fathers' imminent insecurity in their professional jobs becomes a reason for their strong support for their children's overseas education:

> I studied English as much as I could in Korea and then entered this company. [. . .] Here, I had to have teleconference [in English with colleagues abroad] from the beginning. My colleagues were from India and from England, and they all spoke in English. We also had to use English names. So, I really did my best to enhance my English skills. [. . .] I feel that my English is not so bad based on the Korean standard, but I am definitely not a native English speaker. If I had spoken English in a native tone, I would have gotten much more opportunities in this company and could have accomplished much more as I wanted. Thus, I have always thought that my children must have experience in English-speaking countries.

Confronted with the unprecedented economic pressures and increased importance of English in their own lives, many wild geese parents (particularly fathers) in my study not only heavily invested in their children's English education in Korea but also willingly made a decision of transnational family separation to promote their children's English capability. For them, English fluency was believed as the most crucial social capital for their children to secure their profitable and stable future career and thus survive in the competitive global world, as well as an important cultural symbol of a higher social status and education.[40] Wild geese parents also expected foreign educational experiences would help their children broaden perspectives and enhance cultural competency, which they believed to be essential qualifications of competent cosmopolitan professionals who would be successful in the global market across the national boundaries.[41]

Moreover, a majority of wild geese parents in the study were quite dissatisfied with the current Korean education system, because they thought it emphasized cramming for exams while killing children's creativity.[42] They also pointed out that entrance to a college was so competitive to the level that private educational expenses were unreasonably high in Korea.[43] Some wild geese parents who already had spent a huge amount of money for children's education in Korea even felt that sending their children abroad would not be more expensive than educating them in Korea.[44] In addition, according to many wild geese parents, it was heartbreaking to see that their children were so burnt out as they spent (or expected to spend) most of their adolescent period just studying to prepare for the university entrance exam. Moreover, if their children were not so well adapted to the standardized education system in Korea or if they had some conflicts with teachers and/or friends at schools, parents in my study were more eager to migrate abroad in search of alternative education that could provide their children with more freedom and creativity. Three wild geese mothers' accounts below well demonstrate that their frustration with the Korean education system was an important motivation for their emigration:

We did not want our child to be educated by the Korean system, which disregards individual students' personality. Because we all live life only once, we do not have to necessarily live that way [putting the greatest value of education on entering the top university]. We came to the United States because we thought that studying hard under great stress was not the goal of real education. (Sujin, 43-year-old wild geese mother of a tenth grade son)

In Korea, education does not allow students' independence nor creativity. I thought that American education would give a better opportunity to my child to be independent and creative, which would be important qualities in her future life, so I came to the United States. And my child was not fitted to the Korean education system, which emphasizes college admission. Neither did she well adapt to her school nor get along with her friends. (Hyojin, 44-year-old wild geese mother of a seventh grade daughter)

My first son is very smart. So, even though he had stayed in Korea, he must have been one of the top students. However, I did not want my child to be the one who just studied well. I did not like the Korean education system, which asks students to study too hard and is too competitive. I am sure that my son must have entered the specialized high school [elite high school in Korea] and then Seoul National University [top university in Korea]. However, until that moment, how hard time would he have to endure? He must be mentally exhausted. When I organized his schedule [in Korea], he had to study from Monday to Sunday by midnight combining his schooling and his private tutoring. He likes sports but he did not have time to do it [in Korea] even on Sunday because he was so exhausted. How would he feel? I did not want to keep doing that way. I felt really sorry to him. Living that way was not the only way of life. So, I came here [Canada]. (Sohee, 45-year-old wild geese mother whose older son was about to enter the top university in Canada with full scholarship at the time of interview)

Finally, as described earlier, the transnational living arrangement of wild geese families could neither be initiated nor be sustained without their strong familism,[45] which means child-centeredness,[46] combined with the patriarchal gender ideology that relegates nurturing exclusively to women.[47] Many wild geese parents in my study tended to prioritize their role of parents over their spousal relationships, and they readily sacrificed their current marital relations for their children's (bright) future. Furthermore, when they made a decision of transnational family separation, fathers were not considered the right person to accompany their children abroad.[48] It was almost always wild geese mothers who had to accompany their children abroad, even if both spouses had well-paid professional careers and contributed equally to the family economy.[49] In the same vein, wild geese fathers were expected to remain alone in Korea to accomplish the gendered role of competent economic providers for their families.[50] Accordingly, during the interviews, many wild geese parents asserted that their marriage and their conjugal relationship were intact as long as each spouse successfully fulfilled their expected gender roles (i.e., wife as a nurturer and husband as a breadwinner) despite their prolonged transnational spousal separation.

Nonetheless, I have found that many wild geese mothers also pursue their own goals and interests through transnational migration, although their own goals are often hidden or disguised. First, a substantial number of wild geese mothers in the sample migrated abroad in order to pursue their own education or career development, while their children's education abroad was regarded as an extra benefit that would come with it. Some mothers wanted to achieve another postgraduate degree in the destination countries, hoping to have better employment after returning to Korea. For example, Mina, an adjunct lecturer at a university prior to migration, came to the United States with her elementary-school-age daughter, mainly because she desperately wanted to earn another degree in the strong hope to get a tenure-track faculty position. Other mothers, like Minju (public official), Eugene (public official), and Soyoung (businesswoman), migrated with their children abroad because they were assigned to an overseas office of the Korean government or global corporations with better salaries and/or promotion opportunities. Some mothers, like Dohee (entrepreneur) and Eunwha (entrepreneur), emigrated in order to open their new business abroad.

In addition to their goals of education or career development, wild geese mothers pursued diverse interests. Some women felt exhausted from their work in Korea and wanted to migrate abroad to take a rest. Others had long desired to live abroad, particularly in the United States, hoping to fulfill their so-called American dreams.

Some women, like Jiwon, migrated abroad in order to be freed from their conflicting in-law relations or burdensome familial obligations as daughters-in-law.[51] Before migration, Jiwon had worked for a long time as a nurse in Korea, but she had been sick of her job. As an associate degree holder, Jiwon felt that her promotion opportunity was severely blocked and limited. Jiwon also had serious conflicts with her mother-in-law who lived together and took care of her children. As a solution to all of these problems in both work and family, Jiwon migrated to Canada, which was her dream country of destination, and was studying in a nursing program at a college at the time of interview. Jiwon was very happy with the expectation that she would become a registered practical nurse in Canada after passing the qualification test. She was also delightful that she no longer suffered from the in-law relationships. Jiwon says:

> I hate Korea because of conflict with in-laws. I don't want to return to Korea, frankly. I had a really hard time there because of emotional distress. I am very comfortable now because I don't see them [in-laws] anymore and I am also very happy because I no longer hate them.

Intriguingly, however, wild geese fathers who were so supportive of their children's foreign education tended to change their attitudes when they thought transnational family separation was mainly for their wives' career rather than for their children's education. Many husbands turned to be quite reluctant and/or even hostile against their wives' emigration when they found their wives' interest in their career opportunities, while a few husbands were still supportive. This may imply that the traditional Confucian family system is still powerful in Korea and does not allow full gender equality between spouses[52] despite women's increased educational achievement over time.[53] Even if both spouses were working and making an equal contribution to the household economy, many wild geese parents (both husbands and wives) in my study tended to value men's work and career more than women's, and wild geese fathers did not want to relinquish their comfortable life, which was cared by their wives, for the sake of their wives' career development.

As a result, it took more than a year for some wild geese mothers to persuade their begrudging husbands and parents-in-law to agree to transnational family separation. To overcome the confrontations with their husbands and parents-in-law, these women often emphasized the educational benefits to their children over their own goals or interests.

The story of Chaerim, a wild geese mother who had worked in a global company in Korea prior to migration, shows that hiding women's own goals is a very effective gender strategy, which is "a plan of action through which a person tries to solve problems at hand, given the cultural notions of gender at play" defined by Hochschild:[54]

Chaerim: Before migration, I worked for ten years and went on many overseas business trips. As I was promoted, I had more new staff under my supervision. When I went on overseas business trips with them, I recognized that they spoke

English much better than I did. Of course, they had experiences of studying abroad. Nonetheless, I felt very insecure in my position, and wanted to study abroad. If not now, I thought, there seemed to be no more chances . . . .

Sehwa: So, when you first suggested the idea of migration, how was your husband's response?

Chaerim: In fact . . . if I had frankly told him that I wanted to go abroad for my English education, most people would have opposed it.

Sehwa: What do you mean by "most people" here?

Chaerim: My husband, my parents-in-law, and my own parents as well. They would have not liked it if I had told them I would live apart from my husband for my own education. However, my child became a good excuse for me at that time. In Korea, we had spent about $2,000 monthly only for our daughter's English kindergarten. So, I argued that it would be better for her to migrate abroad to learn real English, rather than spending such an amount of money ineffectively in Korea. As my husband agreed to her study abroad, I additionally could obtain a chance to study abroad.

In sum, wild geese parents' decision of transnational family separation is certainly initiated by their strong educational enthusiasm to provide their children with better educational opportunities abroad with the vision that their children will survive in the rapidly changing Korean society as well as competitive global economy. Nonetheless, while pursuing this officially agreed-upon goals of the entire family, substantial numbers of wild geese mothers also pursue their own goals and interests. To overcome actual and potential spousal conflict around their emigration, many wild geese mothers also employ a gender strategy of hiding their own goals but emphasizing educational benefits for their children.

NOTES

1. For Hong Kong and Taiwanese "astronaut families," see Man Wai Chang and Yvonne Darlington, "Astronaut Wives: Perceptions of Changes in Family Roles," *Asian and Pacific Migration Journal* 17, no. 1 (2006): 61–77; Maria W. L. Chee, "Migrating for the Children: Taiwanese American Women in Transnational Families," in *Wife or Worker? Asian Women and Migration*, ed. Nicola Piper and Mina Roces (New York: Rowman and Littlefield, 2003), 137–156; Johanna L. Waters, "Flexible Families?: 'Astronaut' Households and the Experiences of Lone Mothers in Vancouver, British Columbia," *Social and Cultural Geography* 3 (2002): 117–134.

2. For Chinese "study mothers" in Singapore, see Shirlena Huang and Brenda S. A. Yeoh, "Transnational Families and Their Children's Education: China's 'Study Mothers' in Singapore," *Global Networks* 5, no. 4 (2005): 379–400.

3. Yean-Ju Lee and Hagen Koo, "'Wild Geese Fathers' and a Globalised Family Strategy for Education in Korea," *International Development Planning Review* 28, no. 4 (2006): 534.

4. Allison O'Connor and Jeanne Batalova, "Korean Immigrants in the United States," *Migration Policy Institute* (April 10, 2019), accessed October 1, 2020, https ://www.migrationpolicy.org/article/korean-immigrants-united-states-2017.

5. Chang and Darlington, "Astronaut' Wives," 61–77; Chee, "Migrating for the Children," 137–156; Huang and Yeoh, "Study Mothers," 379–400; Waters, "Flexible families," 117–134.

6. Lee and Koo, "Wild Geese Fathers," 539.

7. Hakyoon Lee, "'I Am a Kirogi Mother': Education Exodus and Life Transformation among Korean Transnational Women," *Journal of Language, Identity & Education* 9, no. 4 (2010): 250–264.

8. Yang-Suk Choi, "The Phenomenon of 'Geese Families': Marital Separation between Geese-fathers and Geese-mothers," *Family and Culture* 18, no. 2 (2006): 37–65 (in Korean); Se Hwa Lee, "Closer or Estranged: Transnational Spousal Relationships between Korean Wild Geese Parents," in *Companion to Korean American Studies*, ed. Rachael Joo and Shelley Lee (Boston, MA: Brill, 2018), 505; Jeehun Kim, "'Downed' and Stuck in Singapore: Lower/Middle Class South Korean Wild Geese (Kirogi)," *Research in the Sociology of Education* 17 (2010): 271–311; So Jin Park and Nancy Abelmann, "Class and Cosmopolitan Striving: Mothers' Management of English Education in South Korea," *Anthropological Quarterly* 77, no. 4 (2004): 645–672; Joseph Yi, "Tiger Moms and Liberal Elephants: Private, Supplemental Education among Korean-Americans," *Society* 50 (2013): 190; Min Zhou and Susan S. Kim, "Community Forces, Social Capital, and Educational Achievement: The Case of Supplementary Education in the Chinese and Korean Immigrant Communities," *Harvard Educational Review* 76, no. 1 (2006): 2–8.

9. Se Hwa Lee, "Only If You Are One of Us: Wild Geese Mothers' Parenting in the Korean Immigrant Community," *Amerasia Journal* 42, no. 2 (2016): 74; Juyeon Park, "Public Fathering, Private Mothering: Gendered Transnational Parenting and Class Reproduction among Elite Korean Students," *Gender & Society* 32, no. 4 (2018): 563–586; Yi introduces the stories of Asian American parents who "live vicariously through their children, viewing them as extensions of themselves." See Yi, "Tiger Moms," 193.

10. Patricia R. Pessar, "The Role of Households in International Migration and the Case of U.S.-Bound Migration from the Dominican Republic," *International Migration Review* 16 (1982): 342–364.

11. Ibid.

12. Pierrette Hondagneu-Sotelo, *Gendered Transitions: Mexican Experiences of Immigration* (Los Angeles: University of California Press, 1994), 7.

13. See Lee, "Closer or Estranged," 503.

14. For literature on Latino families, see Joanna Dreby, "Honor and Virtue: Mexican Parenting in the Transnational Context," *Gender & Society* 20, no. 1 (2006): 32–59; Hondagneu-Sotelo, *Gendered Transitions*; Pierrette Hondagneu-Sotelo and Ernestine Avila, "'I'm Here, But I'm There': The Meaning of Latina Transnational

Motherhood," *Gender & Society* 11, no. 5 (1997): 548–571; David Kyle, *Transnational Peasants: Migrations, Networks, and Ethnicity in Andean Ecuador* (Baltimore, MD: Johns Hopkins University Press, 2000); Veronica Montes, "The Role of Emotions in the Construction of Masculinity: Guatemalan Migrant Men, Transnational Migration, and Family Relations," *Gender & Society* 27, no. 4 (2013): 469–490; Jason Pribilsky, "'Aprendemos a Convivir': Conjugal Relations, Co-parenting, and Family Life among Ecuadorian Transnational Migrants in New York City and the Ecuadorian Andes," *Global Networks* 4, no. 3 (2004): 313–334; Leah Schmalzbauer, "Family Divided: The Class Formation of Honduran Transnational Families," *Global Networks* 8, no. 3 (2008): 329–346; Leah Schmalzbauer, "Temporary and Transnational: Gender and Emotion in the Lives of Mexican Guest Worker Fathers," *Ethnic and Racial Studies* 38, no. 2 (2015): 211–226.

15. For literature on Asian families, see Evelyn Nakano Glenn, "Split Household, Small Producer and Dual Wage Earner: An Analysis of Chinese-American Family Strategies," *Journal of Marriage and Family* 45, no. 1 (1983): 35–46; Mirca Madianou and Daniel Miller, "Mobile Phone Parenting: Reconfiguring Relationships between Filipina Migrant Mothers and Their Left-Behind Children," *New Media & Society* 13, no. 3 (2011): 457–470; Deirdre McKay, "'Sending Dollars Shows Feeling': Emotions and Economies in Filipino Migration," *Mobilities* 2, no. 2 (2007): 175–194; Rhacel Salazar Parreñas, "Long Distance Intimacy: Class, Gender, and Intergenerational Relations between Mothers and Children in Filipino Transnational Families," *Global Networks* 5, no. 4 (2005): 317–336; Rhacel Salazar Parreñas, "Transnational Fathering: Gendered Conflicts, Distant Disciplining and Emotional Gaps," *Journal of Ethnic and Migration Studies* 34, no. 7 (2008): 1057–1072.

16. For the in-depth discussion of an intersectional approach, see Patricia Hill Collins, "Toward a New Vision: Race, Class, and Gender as Categories of Analysis and Connection," *Race, Sex & Class* 1, no. 1 (1993): 25–45.

17. For exceptions, see Choi, "Geese Families," 37–65 (in Korean); Kim, "'Downed' and Stuck," 271–311. Yet, these two studies still have limitations in producing comprehensive knowledge on transnational family dynamics, because of significant gender imbalance in their samples. Specifically, Kim J. conducted in-depth interviews with eighteen mothers in Singapore, but conducted interviews with only eight fathers in Korea. While Choi conducted twenty face-to-face interviews with husbands in Korea, her data on wives abroad were quite limited: It was based on only five face-to-face interviews, combined with five phone and four email interviews.

18. Chang and Darlington, "'Astronaut' Wives," 65–69; Chee, "Migrating for the Children," 151–152; Huang and Yeoh, "Study Mothers," 392–393; Sung-Sook Kim, "The 'Kirogi' Fathers' Changes of Lives and Adaptation Problems," *Journal of Korean Home Management Association* 24, no. 1 (2006): 141–158.

19. Lee and Koo, "Wild Geese Fathers," 534.

20. Korean Educational Development Institute (KEDI), "2017 Educational Statistical Analysis" (in Korean), accessed June 27, 2018. http://cesi.kedi.re.kr/.

21. If children accompanied their mothers who worked abroad, they became wild geese children from the beginning of migration. If children migrated abroad as legal dependents of their fathers who worked abroad, they became wild geese children after

their fathers returned to Korea alone and they remained in the host countries with their mothers.

22. Due to the rounding error, the sum of percentages is 101 percent. Kim, Choi, and Lee also find a similar outcome in the study of wild geese mothers in New Zealand. See Young-Hee Kim, Myung-Seon Choi, and Jee-Hang Lee, "Actual State of Korean "Geese Mothers" in New Zealand," *Journal of the Korean Home Economics Association* 43, no. 11 (2005): 141–152 (in Korean).

23. Kim, Choi, and Lee, "Geese Mothers," 145–146 (in Korean).

24. Advantages for overseas Koreans are differently arranged by the number of years a student has spent outside of Korea. See Overseas Korean Education Portal, "Guideline for Overseas Koreans' College Admission" (in Korean), accessed October 1, 2020, http://okep.moe.go.kr/html/page.do?htmlId=18&menu_seq=21.

25. According to Kim, not only Philippines and Singapore but also India is also emerging Asian destination countries for wild geese families, because they also speak English as one of their official languages. See Kim, "'Downed' and Stuck," 276–277.

26. In my sample, all thirty-three wild geese fathers reported both their own and their wives' education level achieved. However, out of thirty-one wild geese mothers who were interviewed, two women who were widowed and divorced reported their own education level, but not their husbands'.

27. Out of sixty-four wild geese parents interviewed, forty provided a usable answer for the question on their annual household income prior to migration. Some refused to report their annual household income; some dual-earners knew only their own income, not knowing their spouse' income; and some full-time homemakers only knew their monthly living expenses given by their husbands.

28. Korean Statistical Office, "2015 Korean Household Finance and Welfare Survey Result," 27–28 (in Korean), accessed July 7, 2018, http://kostat.go.kr/porta l/korea/kor_nw/2/4/4/index.board. Some wild geese parents reported their annual household income in Korean won (KRW), while others reported in U.S. dollars (USD). For consistency, I asked them to convert their household income into dollars. When asked, wild geese parents converted their annual household income based on the exchange rate of 1,000 KRW equals to 1 USD. Therefore, throughout this book, I also use the same exchange rate to convert the Korean Statistical Office's 2015 average annual household income in KRW into USD.

29. Out of forty wild geese parents who provided information on their annual household income, thirty-two had income higher than $100,000.

30. OECD, "Society at a Glance 2016: A Spotlight on Youth" (October 5, 2016), 4, accessed July 10, 2018, http://www.oecd.org/korea/sag2016-korea.pdf. The average number of children per Korean woman was 1.21 in 2014. This is not only the lowest fertility rate among the OECD countries but also far lower than the rate necessary to keep the population constant, 2.1.

31. Lee, "Only If," 73.

32. Due to rounding, the sum of percentages is 101 percent. Kim, Choi, and Lee also find a similar outcome in the study of wild geese mothers in New Zealand. See Kim, Choi, and Lee, "Geese Mothers," 145 (in Korean).

33. Se Hwa Lee, "'I Am Still Close to My Child': Middle-Class Korean Wild Geese Fathers' Responsible and Intimate Fatherhood in a Transnational Context," *Journal of Ethnic and Migration Studies* (2019), https://doi.org/10.1080/1369183X .2019.1573662.

34. Choi, "Geese Families," 44 (in Korean); Lee, "Closer or Estranged," 505; Kim, "'Downed' and Stuck," 271–311; Park and Abelmann, "Class and Cosmopolitan Striving," 534–672; Yi, "Tiger Moms," 190; Zhou and Kim, "Supplementary Education," 2–8.

35. Lee, "Only If," 74; Park, "Public Fathering, Private Mothering," 563–586; Yi introduces the stories of Asian American parents who "live vicariously through their children, viewing them as extensions of themselves." See Yi, "Tiger Moms," 193.

36. Kim, "'Downed' and Stuck," 274–275; Lee, "Closer or Estranged," 505; Lee and Koo, "Wild Geese Fathers," 534.

37. Bok-Rae Kim, "The English Fever in South Korea: Focusing on the Problem of Early English Education," *Journal of Education & Social Policy* 2, no. 2 (2015): 118; Park and Abelmann, "Class and Cosmopolitan Striving," 649.

38. Se-il Park, "The Labor Market Policy and Social Safety Net in Korea: After the 1997 Crisis" (Washington, DC: The Brookings Institution, September 1, 1999), accessed July 21, 2018, https://www.brookings.edu/research/the-labor-market-policy -and-social-safety-net-in-korea-after-the-1997-crisis/.

39. Similarly, in Cho's study, some wild geese fathers had experiences of discrimination in their workplace because of their lack of foreign education, which highly motivated them to send their children abroad. See Uhn Cho, "Korean Families on the Forefront of Globalization," *Economy and Society* 64 (2004): 164–165 (in Korean).

40. Similar rationales were resonated in other literature on wild geese families. See Cho, "Korean Families," 163–166 (in Korean); Lee, "Only If," 71; Kim, "'Downed' and Stuck," 283; Choi, "Geese Families," 44–45 (in Korean); Kim, "English Fever," 119–121; Kim, "'Downed' and Stuck," 283; Lee, "Kirogi Mother," 251; Lee and Koo, "Wild Geese Fathers," 541–542, 552; Park and Abelmann, "Class and Cosmopolitan Striving," 646, 650.

41. Wild geese parents' such high cosmopolitan desire was also discussed in Park and Abelmann, "Class and Cosmopolitan Striving," 646–648.

42. Cho, "Korean Families," 165 (in Korean); Kim, "'Downed' and Stuck," 283.

43. Cho, "Korean Families," 165 (in Korean); Doohyoo Lee, "A Study of Kiroghee Fathers' Hopes and Struggles about Children's Education," *Research in Educational Issues* 32 (2008): 24–26 (in Korean); Lee and Koo, "Wild Geese Fathers," 542–544.

44. The stories of two wild geese mothers, Jina and Damso, in chapter 4 provide good examples.

45. Lee and Koo, "Wild Geese Fathers," 539.

46. Cho, "Korean Families," 161–162 (in Korean); Lee, "Kirogi Mother," 254.

47. Arlie Hochschild, with Anne Machung, *The Second Shift* (New York: Viking Press, 1989), 15–16; Seungsook Moon, "Immigration and Mothering: Case Studies from Two Generations of Korean Immigrant Women," *Gender & Society* 17, no. 6 (2003): 852–853.

48. Lee, "I am Still Close."

49. Ibid.

50. Ibid.

51. Other studies also document in-law conflicts as one of the reasons of wild geese mothers' migration abroad. See Choi, "Geese Families," 47 (in Korean); Kim, "Kirogi Fathers," 178, 185 (in Korean).

52. Chong also points out Korean society has successfully preserved core traditional Confucian values within its family and gender system in spite of its rapid modernization and economic development. See Kelly H. Chong, "Negotiating Patriarchy: South Korean Evangelical Women and the Politics of Gender," *Gender & Society* 20, no. 6 (December, 2006): 704–705.

53. Women's enrollment for universities and graduate schools has significantly increased from 26.8 percent and 18.3 percent in 1985 to 41.0 percent and 49.6 percent in 2017, respectively. See KEDI, "2017 Educational Statistical," 55, 98 (in Korean).

54. Hochschild, *Second Shift*, 15.

Chapter 1

Women's Empowerment and Three Resources

What are the impacts of transnational family separation on the gender roles and relative gender statuses of wild geese mothers and fathers in their households? In this chapter, I explore how wild geese couples' patriarchal gender relations are contested and renegotiated through transnational family separation and how wild geese mothers' paths to gender empowerment are diversified based on the way they utilize the three new resources in the host societies, such as legal statuses, employment, and re-education.

GENDER AND POWER IN TRANSNATIONAL FAMILIES

Academic literature has noted the three distinctive patterns of transnational spousal power dynamics based on the migrants' gender, social class, and goal of migration. First, working-class Chinese, Filipino, Mexican, and Ecuadorian transnational families, whose fathers have migrated abroad to earn money, show that transnational family separation leads to more egalitarian conjugal relations. During the long spousal separation, left-behind wives have gradually increased their power and authority over the family decisions and household economy as they have assumed expanded tasks and responsibilities beyond the domestic arena.[1] Wives' strengthened ties with their children as the sole resident parent also have increased their leverage within the transnational family arrangement.[2] After family reunification in the host countries, many working-class migrant wives tend to have paid jobs and build extended personal networks within their immigrant communities, which further strengthens their status within the households.[3]

At the same time, working-class migrant husbands tend to perform more housework during transnational family separation because they no longer live with their wives who used to take care of them.[4] Some migrant men are also more willing to share domestic tasks with their wives even after they reunite, because they have learned how to perform housework during lengthy spousal separation.[5] Other migrant husbands gladly share housework with their wives whenever they come back to visit families in their home countries, because they do not feel that their masculinity is threatened by sharing housework with their wives as they make greater financial contribution to the household economy than they did before transnational spousal separation.[6]

Yet, it is also acknowledged that women's empowerment through their working-class husbands' emigration may be mitigated by gendered confrontations between transnational couples. From men's side, migrant men try to maintain their patriarchal power over their wives by utilizing the "code of silence"[7] (i.e., restricting information about their lives in the host countries to their wives who remain in the home countries) and/or delaying sending remittances.[8] From women's side, left-behind wives are concerned that their migrant husbands may have extramarital relationships abroad and/or that they may be abandoned by their husbands as their transnational separation is prolonged.[9] Thus, some wives are highly motivated to migrate to the host country despite their migrant husbands' reluctance and opposition.[10] Other women attempt to wrest power from their migrant husbands despite their increased economic dependence on husbands as these women have assumed a new role of a "remittance manager" and managed their household economy.[11]

Second, working-class Filipino, Mexican, and Honduran transnational families, whose mothers migrate abroad as migrant (domestic) workers, have not shown significant changes in patriarchal conjugal relationships. Left-behind husbands' share of the housework and childcare has not conspicuously increased despite their wives' absence and despite their migrant wives' increased economic contribution to the family.[12] Rather, these migrant wives continue to retain their traditional responsibility as the primary caregiver of the families despite their physical distance from their families and remain responsible for seeking help to substitute their nurturing role from other women such as their own mothers, extended female kin, and eldest daughters, as well as paid female domestic workers.[13] This demonstrates a strong effect of patriarchal gender ideology that hinders the working-class migrant women's leverage from being promoted by their increased economic contribution to the family economy.

Third, middle-class Asian transnational families, whose mothers and children have migrated abroad for children's education, such as Chinese *astronaut families,*[14] *parachute children,*[15] and *study mothers,*[16] imply that women's domestic statuses in their transnational households are likely to be lowered. In contrast to their working-class counterparts, these middle-class wives tend to suffer from their diminished economic power through transnational migration. They often lose their professional careers after migration, partly because of the difficulty of transferring their prior educational and occupational qualifications from the home countries to the labor market of the host societies[17] and partly because of the host countries' restrictive immigration policies that forbid migrant women from finding gainful (or any) jobs.[18] These women also have to take full responsibility for child rearing as a sole resident parent, while losing their parental support and the social networks they used to enjoy prior to migration.[19] On the other hand, their husbands, who remain in the countries of origin, keep their professional careers and relationships with relatives and friends intact.[20] Therefore, even if middle-class Chinese migrant women enjoy the increased decision-making power and a sense of freedom and independence through physical separation from their husbands,[21] many of them still feel that their domestic status is rather weakened through migration.

Then, what happens to the Korean wild geese mothers' bargaining power and relative gender status after transnational family separation? Given their structural similarity (in terms of gender, social class, and the goal of migration) with Chinese middle-class women who live apart from their husbands for their children's education, people may expect that Korean wild geese mothers also suffer from the lowered gender status through transnational family separation. Interestingly, however, wild geese mothers in my study tend to be empowered through transnational family separation and their paths to empowerment are much more complex and diversified than those documented in the studies of Chinese transnational mothers.

To better understand what causes such different gender paths between Chinese transnational families and Korean wild geese families, let me examine previous studies on Chinese transnational families as well as some of the differences between Korean wild geese families and Chinese transnational families.

First, in the descriptions of the gender relations of Chinese transnational couples, existing studies have primarily focused on women's perspectives and largely overlooked men's voices. While these studies presume that men who remain in the home countries may not undergo any notable changes in their lives through transnational family separation, I argue that it is not always the case. Rather, transnational family separation is a significant turning point for many left-behind fathers, who happen to reflect on their taken-for-granted traditional roles and patriarchal relationships within their families and to start reshaping their marital relations in the transnational context.[22] I further argue that men's accounts, as well as women's, are also an important source of insights into many of the changes married couples experience through transnational spousal separation. Therefore, my research incorporates not only women's perspectives but also men's views and is able to produce a more nuanced and comprehensive picture of the changing spousal power dynamics among the married couples in the transnational context.

Second, Korean wild geese families are quite different from Chinese transnational families in many respects. According to the studies of Chinese transnational families, transnational mothers tend to be described as passive victims of migration who forcibly sacrifice their lives for the sake of the family. However, as I have explained in the Introduction, Korean middle-class wild geese mothers are an active agent of transnational migration who strategically migrate abroad and pursue not only their children's education but also their own goals and interests. In the similar vein, Chinese transnational mothers tend to lose paid employment through migration, whereas many of Korean wild geese mothers are not necessarily confined to domestic sphere after migration but continuously hold paid employment or newly seek job opportunities in the host countries despite the restrictive immigration laws. There is another interesting difference: While most Chinese astronaut mothers used to have paid help (e.g., domestic workers and nannies/babysitters) prior to migration, a majority of Korean wild geese mothers in my study did not have such luxuries before migration. This difference has important implications for their postmigration life experiences, because both Chinese astronaut mothers and Korean wild geese mothers can rarely afford paid help after migration to North America.

In the following sections, I explore how wild geese couples' patriarchal gender relations are challenged and reconstructed through transnational family separation. Specifically, I first describe wild geese couples' unequal domestic statuses in Korea before separation. Next, I explain how the event of transnational family separation has triggered significant changes in their existing spousal power dynamics. Then, I present wild geese mothers' diverse patterns of gender empowerment according to the way they utilize their three new resources in the host societies: (1) legal status, (2) employment, and (3) additional education.

PATRIARCHAL GENDER RELATIONS
BEFORE SEPARATION

Before migration, many wild geese parents in my study had quite patriarchal spousal relationships, although a few maintained egalitarian relationships. Mothers generally managed child- and husband-centered lives, as if their primary goals of life were assisting their husbands and nurturing children, whereas many fathers maintained career-oriented lives. Mothers had to arrange major family events, such as memorial services for ancestors and family gatherings on national holidays, as well as take care of their aging parents-in-law, whereas their husbands were usually exempted from such familial responsibilities, because their busy work schedule and professional career were regarded as valid excuses.

In addition, spouses were not so equal in the decision-making process for their households. About two-thirds of wild geese parents in my study reported that husbands had greater power in their spousal relationships and made the final decisions for their households. Both parents internalized the traditional gender ideology and accepted the role division between spouses, which defined husbands as the head of the household, primary breadwinner, and decision-maker, and wives as a secondary breadwinner, nurturer, and follower. Therefore, even if many wild geese mothers managed their monthly household income and expenditure as the primary financial manager of their households and exerted substantial discretion in their decisions on minor, domestic, and daily issues (including their children's education), most of them always discussed with their husbands before making major, important, and official decisions, as if husbands were their supervisors. Such unequal decision-making power was particularly the case for most full-time homemakers. For instance, an account of Mikyung, who used to be a full-time homemaker in Korea, well illustrates how she was deeply dependent on her husband in all aspects of her life before spousal separation:

> I feel that I was always protected by my husband. He is little bit older than me, and thus always took care of me. He also helped me a lot with childcare. For instance, he always dropped off and picked up my child. I even did not have to drive. . . . He did everything for me. When I went on a long-distance excursion with my kid, he always gave us a ride, regardless of how far it was . . . I did not receive any living expenses [in cash] from him, because he managed all the household economy. We always went to grocery shopping together. If I needed to buy something else, I always bought it with his credit card. I didn't mind letting him know what I bought, because he was not the type of person to say "no."

Many wild geese fathers also confirmed their dominant status within their households during the interviews. For example, a wild geese father named Changmin said, "I let her [his wife] do minor things as she wished, but I made the big decisions." Another wild geese father named Kyusik claimed, "If I mostly made decisions, my wife just always followed." A third wild geese father named Dongkun enjoyed his exclusive power within the household:

> We did not have power struggle. It is because I was always the number one. I was always in the superior position to her [his wife] to the extent that my power [compared to hers] was 100:0.

Wild geese parents did not equally share household labor including childrearing when they were living together in Korea. For about three-fourths of wild geese parents in the study, it was women who performed almost all of the housework and childcare regardless of women's employment status, while their husbands were not only exempted from such responsibilities but also served by their wives. Because the division of household labor is one of the critical indicators of the power distribution between spouses,[23] I provide an in-depth discussion of the wild geese couples' changing patterns of household labor as a separate topic in chapter 2.

SPOUSAL SEPARATION: TURNING POINT FOR WOMEN'S EMPOWERMENT

Korean wild geese parents' decision of transnational family separation was originally an extension of their existing patriarchal spousal relationships. While it required both parents to sacrifice their current marital relationships, it additionally asked wild geese mothers to further sacrifice their own careers as well as social status and prestige attached to their jobs in order to accompany their children abroad and perform their role of so-called *ideal mothers*[24] who would provide the necessary emotional and physical care for their children.

Nonetheless, transnational spousal separation unexpectedly functions as a *turning point* for many wild geese mothers to be disillusioned with traditional patriarchy that normalized women's lower status and took women's sacrifice for their families for granted, as these women are freed from their former subordination to the traditionally assigned roles of good wives and filial daughters-in-law and happen to have a chance to ponder on their past lives. For example, a former wild geese mother named Youngmi defines her wild geese period as "liberating" time because it gave her great comfort and freedom as she was physically separated from her husband and parents-in-law. Similarly, a wild geese mother named Heeyoung, who had a hard time in Korea to juggle her competing obligations between work and family, well points out why she is greatly pleased after migration:

> The positive side [of migration] is I can just focus on my son. I don't have to pay attention to my husband. I don't have to take care of my parents-in-law. I am freed from all family events, and no longer have to read other people's countenance. So, I feel much relieved and freer now.

A wild geese mother named Miyoung used to be a full-time homemaker prior to migration. After migration, however, she has become a Korean language teacher at a local school board. Miyoung explains how she has deeply speculated about her previously taken-for-granted roles through migration and has ultimately pursued more independent life with her own career as her new path of life:

> Through migration, I have gotten many opportunities to contemplate myself. As I have been separated from the rest of the family, I have more time to reflect on myself. In Korea, I mainly lived as a member of family-in-law, my family, some gatherings, and parents' associations, rather than being myself. I chose my outfit to match my age. Whenever I met people, my [social] life just began as somebody's mom. However, in Canada, I am no longer named as somebody's mom. It seems that I have lived solely as one human-being. I have been able to use much of my time to reflect on myself. I have raised philosophical questions like who I am and how I should live. I have enjoyed the time to observe on myself.

Moreover, some wild geese mothers have become gradually estranged from the traditional ideology of motherhood that requires them to devote every moment to, and find joy in supporting, their children's growth and academic achievements, when they experience conflicts with their adolescent children or when their children have not achieved satisfactory academic outcomes after migration. As an alternative, these mothers start developing new identities: Some pursue more education while others seek employment opportunities in the home countries.

A wild geese mother named Eunji was a committed homemaker who was so busy giving her daughter a ride to various after-school activities in Korea. She strongly wanted her daughter to become the top student in the school and thus sent her to various private learning institutes to enhance her overall academic achievement. Yet, after migrating to the United States to fulfill her traditional role as a committed mother, she unexpectedly has greater free time because of the remarkably reduced amount of housework. She also has hard time after migration because of increased conflict with her adolescent daughter. As a result, Eunji is no longer satisfied with her role as a devoted mother. Rather, she comes to have her own wish, which is resuming her new life as a career woman. Eunji explains how her migration has transformed herself from a family-oriented homemaker to an ambitious woman who is preparing for her new career as a florist even after the long period of career disruption since marriage:

> I regret my past life [in Korea] . . . I was very busy, because I had to support my husband as a wife and take care of my young child as a mother. I was wholly focused on those two. While it was not totally meaningless, I had a sort of feeling that I was losing myself. Since I came here [America], my husband has

been there [in Korea] out of my sight, and my child has grown and needs less attention. With greater free time, I have come to deeply think of what kind of occupation I should have [in the future] and how I should live up to my seventies or eighties. While I used to be so focused on my child, through migration, I have looked backed on myself. Migration has become a turning point in my life.

To find her new path of life, Eunji has started a part-time job at a local flower business, while learning English in the ESL (English as Second Language) program. She also plans to enroll in a local professional school to get a florist certificate. Eunji finds great joy from her a new job, as it gives her not only a new identity but also a valuable venue for interacting with people in the host society and learning about its culture. Eunji delightfully describes her new life:

It has been eight months, since I worked at this store. And I am very happy to work here. The conversation I have at work is different from what I used to have with other moms in Korea. I can ask them [my Korean American boss and other employees] about the immigrant life and we can have some discussion on the various social issues, like presidential election. I am very happy that I can learn about the American culture and thoughts.

Similarly, Jaehee, a wild geese mother who enrolled at nursing program after migration and has become a registered nurse at a local hospital, well explains how her additional education and paid employment in the host country has given her a new kind of satisfaction that she did not find from her wifehood or motherhood:

[After migration] I liked that I could concentrate on my work, I mean, my study. I sometimes studied overnight. Because becoming an RN was as much difficult as becoming a doctor, I was under great pressure. I studied really hard because I did not want to lose as a person who studied later than others. I really liked that I was able to focus on studying. [. . .] After I started working as a nurse, as a professional, I earned a stable income that came with a good [health] insurance, and I also felt a great sense of fulfillment.

Living without husbands in a new environment has also increased wild geese mothers' independence and decision-making power and enhanced their confidence and autonomy, which is also found from the cases of many working-class women in the transnational households.[25] Most wild geese mothers in my study, whether they want or not, have gradually transformed into more independent decision-makers, as they handle everyday challenges they encounter in the host society by themselves. Because many wild geese fathers who remain in Korea are not so familiar with the culture and institution of the host countries, they are not the right consultants or advisors for their wives. Even if some wild geese fathers know a lot about the culture and system of the host society, it is still not so easy for these men to help with or do anything about what their wives are facing in the destination countries because of wild geese fathers' physical separation and distance. Consequently, despite many wild geese mothers' lack of familiarity with the host society and/or English proficiency, they have to make important decisions and handle everyday issues by themselves based on their own discretion. Furthermore, as the sole parent residing with their children in a foreign country, Korean wild geese mothers are authorized to exercise much greater leverage than their husbands when making decisions about their children, like Chinese women remaining in their home country.[26]

Interestingly, wild geese mothers are not always happy with their enhanced decision-making power, particularly at the beginning of their spousal separation. Some women are not so accustomed to independent decision-making, and thus undergo many trials and errors. Others find it quite burdensome to take full responsibility for the results from their decisions, especially for their children's educational outcomes. A wild geese mother named Jina describes the high pressure on her as a sole mother abroad:

> Because I live separately from husband, I have to take care of father's [my husband's] domestic jobs from minor thing, such as throwing away trash bags, to major things like purchasing a car and managing a house, which makes me feel overwhelmed. I am so busy and thus cannot relieve my tension at any time. I am highly sensitive even when I sleep so that I wake up even with a rustling sound. Sometimes, I really need to take a rest, but I cannot. I cannot. I am always anxious because I am not sure if what I am doing here is right.

Accordingly, some wild geese mothers are missing their husbands or even resentful about their husbands who do not seem to share the burden of decision-making in the host societies. A wild geese mother named Damso was a respected high school teacher with a busy work schedule in Korea. However, she gave up her career and eagerly came to the United States to better serve the role of ideal mother for her two children. Nonetheless, after migration, Damso feels increasingly frustrated as a sole parent who has to provide all the guidance and support for her children's growth and development in the right direction. She also struggles to make up for her husband's absence because her younger child is greatly missing him. It is also challenging for her to maintain a good relationship with her adolescent son who has become more defiant over time. Her constant struggles make her greatly infuriated because her left-behind husband does not share such a demanding parenting responsibility:

> When I first came here, I was under too much pressure and very mad at my husband. So, we fought many times on the phone. I reprehended him [on the phone] a lot because he did not help me at all while I was undergoing such a hard time. I felt that we both didn't know how to handle our new situation at the beginning [of transnational separation]. I felt stifled watching my husband who neither knew how to help me nor could actually help me. I even thought it would be better not to talk with him on the phone. As such, we had many troubles.

Despite such hardships, wild geese mothers have gradually started enjoying their enhanced decision-making power and its accompanying responsibilities. Moreover, as their autonomous decision-making and problem-solving experiences have accumulated, wild geese mothers become even more confident in themselves and more independent from their husbands. For example, it is interesting to see how independent decision-making experiences after migration has changed a wild geese mother named Mikyung from a highly dependent wife to an independent woman:

> My status is not the same [as before spousal separation]. Because I am now in charge of many things, my husband respects my opinions. I was passive in the past. I mean, I always discussed with my husband and followed his opinions, as if I did not have my own voice at all. But, I have become much more assertive [after spousal separation]. Now, he can figure out what is going on here only through me. Thus, he totally believes in me and follows what I say to him. Though I shifted all the responsibilities on him in the past, I now handle many things by myself and notify him of my decisions.

Transnational spousal separation also poses a challenge to the traditional gender role division between wild geese couples (i.e., husband as the leader and wife as the supporter), as many wild geese fathers do not successfully address the problems that their wives encounter in the host societies. Wild geese mothers, after migration, do not want their husbands to direct them what to do. Instead, they want their husbands to emotionally support them by expressing compassion and sympathy for their hardships in the foreign countries. Accordingly, the role of wild geese fathers has been gradually adjusted from the leaders or decision-makers of the family to the emotional (and economic) supporters after spousal separation. This transition in wild geese fathers' gender role has usually occurred slowly over the long period of time.

Nevertheless, some wild geese fathers are not ready to accept their wives' enhanced voices and authority, which, in turn, leads to new spousal conflicts over the leadership within their transnational households.[27] Furthermore, according to some former wild geese mothers, if wild geese couples fail to successfully re-arrange their changed roles during spousal separation, their spousal tensions can go even worse after family reunification, because wild geese mothers may not want to relinquish their enhanced status, while their husbands often want to recover their supremacy as the primary decision-maker.[28] Hence, wild geese mothers' enhanced domestic status tends to be maintained after spousal reunification if their husbands accept it or if their husbands' challenges and resistance are successfully subdued by their wives.

So far, this section has discussed how transnational spousal separation leads to wild geese mothers' empowerment and what this empowerment means to wild geese mothers and fathers and their relationships. This section has also revealed that wild geese mothers are more empowered when the separation is lengthier, because lengthier separation gives wild geese mothers more chances to assume expanded roles and make independent decisions. In addition to wild geese women's empowerment, the following sections explore how wild geese mothers' postmigration gender paths are substantially diversified by the way they utilize their newly obtained resources of the host society, including legal status, employment, and additional education. I also discuss how wild geese mothers' three resources differently shape their gender status not only during spousal separation but also after family reunification.

FIRST RESOURCE FOR WOMEN'S EMPOWERMENT: LEGAL STATUSES

Scholars have paid growing attention to legal status as one of the paramount factors that influence the lives of immigrant families. Menjívar's study of the Salvadoran and Guatemalan immigrants in the United States suggests that immigrants' legal instability negatively shapes their family relationships, as well as their social interactions and experiences with the institutions of the host society, including schools, healthcare systems, and police authorities.[29] Specifically, because of their legal uncertainties, Salvadoran and Guatemalan immigrants tend to endure indefinite family separation and cannot regularly meet their family members to the extent that they fail to recognize each other when they finally meet.[30] Moreover, Salvadoran and Guatemalan immigrants' children encounter barriers to obtaining educational information and resources that are essential for their upward social mobility due to their own and/or their parents' legal uncertainties.[31]

Dreby's study on the Mexican immigrant families with mixed legal statuses shows that different legal statuses among family members put migrant women with undocumented status in a vulnerable position within their own families and exacerbate the exiting power imbalance between migrant couples.[32] Dreby explains that undocumented Mexican migrant women perform more household labor than their partners and even endure abusive relationships, because they are highly dependent on their partners with documented legal status.[33]

These two studies demonstrate how Latino immigrants' undocumented legal status makes their lives precarious and unstable, compared to documented legal status. On the other hand, in this book, I focus on documented legal status. I discuss how different types of documented legal status have varying impacts on the experiences of Korean wild geese mothers in North America and argue that legal status is one of the critical resources for migrant women's empowerment. Yet, I do not mean that documented migrant women are free from challenges associated with their legal statuses. Rather, because of the different levels of temporality and instability attached to each type of legal status,[34] I suggest in the following discussions that legal statuses bring unique sets of challenges and opportunities to wild geese mothers in North America and eventually lead to heterogeneous patterns of women's empowerment within their transnational households.

Indeed, wild geese mothers in my study migrated to North America with diverse legal statuses such as international students, visitors, temporary workers, dependents of their husbands, permanent residents, or citizens of the destination countries. While wild geese mothers are known to have international student visas,[35] I have found that their legal statuses are much more diverse than people often imagine. Furthermore, wild geese mothers' legal statuses have not been constant throughout their migration process. Rather, wild geese mothers have flexibly changed their legal statuses over time. Therefore, in this section, I investigate the reasons why wild geese mothers choose such diverse legal statuses, how their bargaining power and settlement patterns are differently shaped based on their choice of legal statuses, and what opportunities and challenges each legal status poses to wild geese mothers.

Table 1.1 shows the diverse entry and final visa statuses of wild geese mothers in North America. Entry visa refers to the visa status when wild geese mothers first entered North America. For the current wild geese mothers, final visa refers to their current visa status at the time of the interview. For the former wild geese mothers, final visa refers to their visa status at the time they exited North America to reunite with their husbands in Korea. According to table 1.1, more than one-third of wild geese mothers held international student or visitor status when entering North America. It should be also noted that wild geese mothers with a visitor visa are mostly found in Canada, whereas those with an international student visa are often found in the United States. This is the outcome of their strategic decision-making to

Table 1.1   Entry and Final Visa Statuses of Wild Geese Mothers in North America (n=55)

	Student/Visitor	Resident/Citizen	Dependent	Temporary Worker
Entry Visa	20 (36%)	13 (24%)	19 (35%)	3 (5%)
Final Visa	24 (44%)	23 (42%)	3 (5%)	5 (9%)

Note: Out of sixty-four wild geese families that I interviewed, fifty-seven wild geese families migrated to North America (see table I.3 in Introduction for sample characteristics), and two of them are gender role reversed cases. That is, in these two families, not mothers but fathers migrated to North America with their children, and mothers continued to hold their professional careers in Korea after their families migrated to North America in order to support them economically. Thus, in order to discuss the implication of the legal status change of wild geese mothers, I use these fifty-five people's data.

maximize their migration benefits and cope with different immigration and citizenship policies between the United States and Canada. The opportunities and challenges of an international student and visitor statuses are discussed first, followed by the discussions of dependent, resident/citizen, and foreign worker statuses.

International Student Status in the United States

In the United States, if children migrate with a F1 international student visa, their mothers are not allowed to stay in the United States as their guardians but must go back and forth between the United States and Korea with a visitor visa in order to take care of children. In addition, children with a F1 international student visa are not allowed to enroll in an American public school but may attend a private school, which is much more costly. Accordingly, it is not such a good option for wild geese families to get their children a F1 international student visa, even if wild geese families migrate to the United States for their children's education. Instead, children can go to a public school, whose tuition is free of charge, if their parents hold a F1 international student visa. Therefore, many wild geese mothers in my study strategically choose to become international students with a F1 visa, while their children migrate to the United States as their dependents with a F2 dependent visa. In my study, these international students represent the majority of wild geese mothers who have migrated to the United States with their children for their children's education while leaving their husbands in Korea.

Then, what kinds of educational institutions do wild geese mothers attend as F1 international students? In order to provide their children with free public education, wild geese mothers in the United States can enroll either in academic or language programs. In my study, the majority of wild geese mothers with a F1 visa attend private language schools, although some enroll in university language programs or study at postsecondary academic programs such as colleges, universities, or graduate schools. Given that these women's primary goal is not pursuing their own education but supporting their children's education, maintaining their full-time international student status is quite burdensome, because they are required to spend a significant amount of their time, money, and energy that can be otherwise used for their children. Accordingly, many wild geese mothers with a F1 international student visa choose to attend private language schools, whose tuition is cheaper than that of university language programs and whose workload is much lighter than that of postsecondary academic programs. Even if some wild geese mothers attend university language programs at the beginning of their migration, they are likely to move to private language schools once they have learned of the cheaper option. By becoming international students by themselves, these wild geese mothers can legitimately justify their long residency in the United States and have their children receive free public-school education.

Furthermore, among the wild geese mothers who attend language schools, there are some women who genuinely enjoy learning English and feel a sense achievement by moving to the upper levels of language class. They even believe that their advancement in the language program offers good evidence that they do not just waste their precious time and the remittances sent by their husbands. Some of them even feel empowered with their student status itself. Sujin, a wild geese mother who used to be a full-time homemaker in Korea but has become an international student after migration, expresses her satisfaction with her new identity as a student:

Sujin: I feel freer here.
Sehwa: Can you explain why?
Sujin: It is probably because I go to school here. Here, in the U.S., if people ask me "What do you do?" I answer "I am a student." Because of my student status, I feel I am younger. I also like to learn. Moreover, in Korea, I used to be someone's mother and someone's wife, rather than being myself. However, here, I don't feel that way. Although I am still a mother, because I am a stranger, people don't care [about my mother side identity]. In my ESL school, I am standing by myself with my own name. So, I feel that I become more active.

Despite these benefits, wild geese mothers with a F1 international student visa still encounter many challenges in the United States due to their legal status. In particular, the vast majority of these women's challenges are related to their legal instability as temporary visa holders. Menjívar emphasizes that prolonged "liminal legality," which is transitional and ambiguous *in-between* status between documented and undocumented statuses, is a critical factor that negatively shapes the personal, social, and cultural lives of Salvadoran and Guatemalan immigrants in the United States.[36] Building on the Menjívar's findings, I further suggest that when immigrants hold a temporary visa for a lengthy period of time, it can also have negative influence on their lives in the host societies, even if they are documented immigrants because of many uncertainties involved with their temporary legal status.

The first common challenge mentioned by many wild geese mothers with a F1 international student visa is that their attendance in the language schools is strictly monitored on a regular basis, because all F1 international students are mandated to maintain the full-time student status. If they have missed too many classes, they can no longer maintain their international student status in the United States. Even though many wild geese mothers know a few private language schools that have a more lenient attendance policy, all women in my study report that they do not want to attend such schools. Some say that they hate to do anything illegal as foreigners. Others say that they do not want to take the risk of deportation. An account of Eunji, a wild geese mother who attends a private language school, well demonstrates this point:

> It is dangerous to attend an ESL school that allows you to often miss classes. If their practices are detected by an investigation office, such an ESL school will be shut down, and students who attended there will also lose their F1 student visa. So, we, who come here for our children's education, should be more careful in choosing our ESL program.

Therefore, regardless of whether they are satisfied with their language school programs or not, most wild geese mothers with a F1 international student visa go to their ESL class every weekday from the morning to the afternoon, which makes many of them feel that they have forfeited freedom to organize their daily schedule as they want.

Second, while enormous anxiety associated with visa applications and renewals is often noted among undocumented Latino immigrants,[37] my study also reveals that documented Korean wild geese mothers also experience similar anxiety. Because their F1 international student visa is temporary and thus must be renewed regularly, they worry about the chance, even if it is low, that their visa renewal application may be rejected due to unknown reasons. In particular, those who have attended a language school for a prolonged time are more concerned about the possibility that the U.S. consul may be suspicious of their true purpose of staying in the United States and reject the renewal of their F1 visa.

Minji is a former wild geese mother who was attending a private language school and then a local community college while she stayed in the United States with her F1 visa. She well describes her precarious situation as a temporary visa holder who had to renew her visa regularly:

In fact, one of the most crucial reasons that we decided to return [to Korea] was our visa. I was so tired of enduring such an insecure life. As foreigners, we were neither assimilated into the dominant society nor were we fairly treated. Reflecting on my past, anxiety about my temporary status was so critical in negatively shaping my experiences there. [. . .] I regularly had to renew my F1 visa. But, as time passed, I was even more anxious whether my visa could be renewed next time. Further, whenever I renewed my F1 visa, I had to pay for it. I continuously felt uneasy while living there. It was not like a real life.

Because wild geese mothers' F1 visa is not easily extended if they attend the same language school for a long time, many of them jump around to different language schools every two or three years. Some mothers even apply for (community) colleges, if their children are expected to stay in the United States much longer than they originally planned. Even if these wild geese mothers are not so interested in pursuing an additional postsecondary degree in the United States, they strongly believe that their enrollment at a higher level of education legitimately justifies their prolonged stay in the United States and relieves the immigration office's suspicions about them. However, in that case, because the tuition of (community) college is much more expensive than that of language school, wild geese mothers' (community) college enrollment puts extra financial burden on their transnational household economy, which has already been very constrained, and thus may become a new source of conflict between wild geese couples.

Moreover, after having transferred from a language school to a college, some wild geese mothers still feel frustrated, because they have to invest more time and energy in the subject that they cannot find any motivations for learning. The story of a wild geese mother named Yuri, who has recently transferred from an ESL program to a community college, also reflects this point:

> In order to study hard, I should have a goal. Of course, I like to learn. However, I am very doubtful how much my education here would be helpful for my career after return. If I had come here earlier when I was much younger, I must have had a goal such as getting a better job after graduation. If so, I must have studied harder. However, I now don't have any motivations at all. I am just busy trying to do homework. So, I become lazy [. . .]

As Yuri's case shows, when wild geese mothers have to enroll for any levels of educational programs after migration to the United States just to maintain their legitimate legal status, it has quite negative impact on their lives in the host society.

Third, in the United States, there are no generous employment or residency opportunities available for international students with a F1 visa. According to the Department of Homeland Security, international students are not allowed to work during their first academic year in the United States; they can limitedly have on-campus jobs during this period. After the first academic year, international students can seek off-campus employment with a temporary work permit, such as CPT (Curricular Practical Training),[38] which usually has to be renewed every semester by the U.S. Citizenship and Immigration Services (USCIS). However, their off-campus jobs must be related to their area of study and must be authorized prior to starting. Given that most wild geese mothers with a F1 international student visa attend private language schools, they can hardly benefit from such employment options available for international students. Even if some wild geese mothers find on-campus employment, they can work only part-time during the semester. Wild geese mothers who have stayed in the United States more than ten years note that visa regulations on international students have become much stricter after 9/11.[39] While some wild geese mothers find off-campus jobs other than their area of study, despite the regulations on international students, they often find it very unstable and insecure to have such employment that has illegality attached to it.

Minji is a former wild geese mother who had several under-the-table jobs while studying at a language school and a local community college during her migration period. She expresses her frustration with her legal status when she was an international student in the United States:

> I was frustrated when I found out that the employer I really wanted to work for would not hire me [. . .] Even if I got an interview opportunity, once they met me, they did not hire me because of my visa status. They told me that they needed a person with permanent residency. At that time, I desperately wanted to have a full-time job. However, I could not. I was screened out because of my legal status. Finally, I admitted that I could not work where I really wanted to work.

Moreover, international students are mandated to leave the United States within sixty days from their graduation. To search for gainful employment after graduation, they are required to apply for OPT (Optional Practical Training) program before graduation.[40] While the OPT is typically valid for a year, international students need to leave the United States if they have not found employment within ninety days since their OPT program became effective.[41]

Finally, the lack of a social security number adds further challenges to wild geese mothers' everyday life. In the United States, international students are not allowed to have a social security number unless they have paid employment. As mentioned above, most wild geese mothers who stay in the United States as F1 international students attend private language schools and thus are not allowed to have paid employment. That is, these women cannot have a social security number. The lack of a social security number, on top of their temporary international student status, makes their everyday life even more uncomfortable and challenging. Sujin, a wild geese mother holding an international student status, well describes her everyday hardships and challenges.

Sujin: International students do not have a social security number. Without a social security number, I realized, I really cannot do anything here.

Sehwa: What are the implications of living without a social security number for you?

Sujin: For example, if I needed to register for some places, they asked me to submit my social security number. So, I could not register. Even if I wanted to open a small credit card or a department store card, I could not. Further, because I am a F1 international student, my I-20 document[42] should be also re-issued regularly [less than a year period]. Whenever I have a new I-20, I also have to renew my driver's license. Do you know how annoying it is to go to the DMV [Department of Motor Vehicles] office here?

In sum, Korean wild geese mothers are very strategic in utilizing the American immigration law and education system to achieve their goal. By becoming international students themselves, they seek to provide their children with free public education and legitimately stay with their children for an extended period of time in the United States. However, because of their temporary international student status, wild geese mothers continuously encounter challenges and uncertainties in their everyday lives. Above all, wild geese mothers' opportunity to find official employment is blocked, as most of them are attending private language schools. Plus, their international student status inherently conflicts with their original goal of migration, which is supporting their children's education. Given these disadvantages of a F1 visa, holding a F1 international student visa in the United States is not so helpful for wild geese mothers to enhance their gender status in their households, compared to other legal statuses, which are discussed next.

International Student Status in Canada

In Canada, in contrast to the United States, children who migrate with a *study permit*[43] can go to the Canadian public school by paying cheap tuition, and their accompanying parents are allowed to stay in Canada with a visitor visa as their legal guardians. Canada also provides dependent children of international students with free public education, but only if these international students are enrolled in Canadian postsecondary education programs, such as colleges, universities, and graduate schools. That is, in contrast to the United States, dependent children cannot receive free public education in Canada if their parents are international students at private language schools. Therefore, if Korean wild geese mothers intend to provide their children with free Canadian public education, they have to attend postsecondary education, not ESL programs. However, mothers' college tuition is often more expensive than their children's public-school tuition. Furthermore, Canadian postsecondary education programs require their prospect students to submit an English language score as a pre-requisite, which is quite burdensome for many wild geese mothers who are not so fluent in English.

Consequently, many wild geese mothers in my study have migrated to Canada with a visitor visa as legal guardians of their children, while their children have mostly migrated with their own study permit. Only some wild geese mothers have migrated to Canada with their own study permit, because they want to study for their own goals. This pattern is quite different from that of the United States, where many wild geese mothers unwillingly become international students for their children's education.

Wild geese mothers who are international students in both countries share similar kinds of challenges because of legal instability as temporary visa holders. Nonetheless, those in Canada have reported interesting issues that are not mentioned by their American counterparts: serious conflict between their own interests (i.e., pursuing their own education) and obligation as mothers (i.e., pursuing their children's education). Because these women go to schools for their own sake, they tend to feel more frustrated than their American counterparts if they cannot spend enough time on their own study. As mentioned above, while many wild geese mothers with a F1 international student visa in the United States are attending ESL programs, all wild geese mothers with a study permit in Canada are taking higher education and thus need to invest more time and energy in their study. Unfortunately, in Canada, these mothers no longer have childcare and housework support from their children's grandparents that they used to enjoy in Korea. Chaerim, a wild geese mother who is studying in Canada with a seven-year-old daughter, expresses her frustration, as her reality after migration is quite different from what she originally expected:

> There are no wild geese mothers who came here with such a young child like me. If children are older, it is easier for mothers to study. They have more time for their own study. However, in my case, my child is too young to be cared by others. So, I cannot really concentrate on my study, because my day is mainly organized by her schedule. It is difficult for me to study.

Jiwon, a wild geese mother who migrated to Canada with her two adolescent children and is studying in a nursing program, also describes her work-family conflict:

> While I was preparing for my mid-term exam [in Canada], I could not cook for my children for a month. [. . .] In Korea, I did everything for them. They were just expected to study in Korea. However, after coming here, it is not the case anymore. They have to study and they are also expected to help me doing housework. So, my kids are confused of their roles. In Korea, I told them that I would have done everything for them after migrating to Canada. But, since we came here, they have found that their mom is even busier than she used to be. I neither cook well, nor do other housework [because I am so busy with my study]. So, my kids have a very hard time.

As these two women's accounts indicate, it is not so easy for wild geese mothers in Canada to pursue their own education while performing the ideology of *intensive mothering*.[44] Because their official goal of migration is supporting their children's education, wild geese mothers who pursue their own education continue to struggle with a sense of guilt about their children. They are also highly pressured to prove to their husbands and family-in-law that they keep providing sufficient care for their children while they are also studying abroad. Some mothers even give up their college education in the host society because of the difficulty of combining study and family obligations.

Despite such difficulties, I argue that the international student status in Canada gives more leverage to wild geese mothers to enhance their domestic status than that in the United States, because Canada provides its international students with more generous employment and residency options. In contrast to the United States, full-time international students studying at the Canadian postsecondary institutions such as colleges and universities can officially have part-time jobs both on-campus and off-campus without any working permit.[45] They can also have full-time jobs during breaks.[46] More importantly, in contrast to the United States, if international students graduate postsecondary education in Canada, they are eligible for a three-year work permit, and if they have one year of full-time work experience in Canada, they are eligible for permanent residency.[47]

As wild geese mothers in Canada have gradually realized this chain of permanent settlement through education and employment, those who are not students want to be students, those who are language school students want to transfer to postsecondary schools, and those who are attending postsecondary schools are highly motivated to complete their education.

Chaerim is a wild geese mother who graduated from a prestigious university in Korea and worked for a global company prior to migration. She originally migrated to Canada to study at a language school with a goal of enhancing her English skills. English fluency was deemed to be very important for her success in her career, because her job involved frequent overseas business trips and daily interactions with foreign partners and buyers. However, soon after her migration, Chaerim changed her plan. She applied for the culinary program in a Canadian college rather than continuing her language program. The following account of Chaerim demonstrates how the acknowledged chain of permanent settlement through education highly motivates many wild geese mothers in Canada to pursue additional postsecondary education, even though they already have a bachelor's degree or higher from Korea.

> I have planned to return to Korea after three years. However, because I don't know what will happen after returning, I would like to apply for the [Canadian] residency at the same time. For that, I will graduate [Canadian] college and then have a full-time job for some time. Then, even if my child fails to re-adapt to Korea, then we can come back here easily. I see my education as a steppingstone to settle down [in Canada]. If I graduate college here, when I come back here later, I will be able to find my job right away.

Similarly, another wild geese mother named Jiwon has been studying in a nursing program in Canadian college at the time of the interview, and she is very excited with her new future, in that she will become a registered practical nurse after passing the qualification test. Jiwon says:

> Once I graduate my program in two years, then I will get a working permit for three years. If I work full-time for one year, I am eligible for residency application. Just thinking about it makes me so happy. I am just so happy. Even if my current life puts me under serious budget constraint and I am always very anxious because of it, except that, I am very happy, very happy, and very happy.

Moreover, since they can dream of their future life in Canada after graduation, wild geese women who are international students in Canada are more willing to overcome their current challenges as temporary visa holders and make more efforts to incorporate into the mainstream Canadian society. At the time of the interview, some wild geese mothers have already achieved Canadian residency statuses through their education and employment, which greatly enhances their bargaining power and gender status within their family.

A wild geese mother named Sohee provides a good example from Canada. In Korea, Sohee used to be a full-time homemaker and lived as a subordinate to the extent that she described herself, during the interview, as her husband's maid. It was also mainly Sohee's husband who strongly wanted their children's foreign education and led the family's migration to

Canada. Sohee was just a follower during the migration decision-making process. However, interestingly, through migration, Sohee's relationship with her husband has tremendously changed. Sohee completed an esthetics program in a college and has been working for a local salon since graduation. Sohee's husband has been quite supportive of her study and employment, because he views them as good investment for the family to generate additional income and maintain two transnational households. Meanwhile, Sohee achieved Canadian residency through her employment and is now preparing to apply for Canadian citizenship with her new dream of opening her own business. Certainly, after migration, Sohee has extended her roles from a full-time homemaker to an international student and a worker. And her two new resources from the host society, such as additional education and employment, are critical for her empowerment and independence in the family. Sohee joyfully describes her enhanced status in her transnational spousal relationship:

> In the past, I was highly dependent on my husband. He did everything for me. I even didn't do the banking work alone. He did it. I just took care of kids. However, after coming here, I have become greatly independent. There are many tasks that I handle by myself, not depending on my husband. [. . .] As I have become independent from husband, he feels bittersweet. In the past, I always called him and said, "I love you. I miss you." But, now it has changed. Now, he says to me, "I love you. I miss you." Then, I serenely respond to him, "Oh, I see." [. . .] Even when I miss his text message, I don't feel sorry to him. I have been independent from him, while he has been increasingly relying on me. Now, our relationship is reversed.

In conclusion, although wild geese mothers with an international student status encounter similar difficulties and fluidities as temporary visa holders in both Canada and the United States, those in Canada have greater resources to contest male dominance and renegotiate patriarchal spousal relations based on the Canadian government's more generous employment and residency opportunities available for its international students.

Visitor Status in Canada

As I mentioned earlier, when children migrate to Canada with a study permit, their parents are allowed to stay with a visitor visa as their guardians. Moreover, children with a study permit can enroll in a Canadian public school while paying cheap tuition. Thus, visitor status in Canada is quite a viable option for wild geese families, and many wild geese mothers in my study hold a visitor visa while their children are studying with a study permit.

In the United States, in contrast, visitor status is the least preferred legal option for wild geese mothers. With a visitor visa, wild geese mothers are not allowed to constantly stay with their children. Accordingly, these mothers have to go back and forth between the United States and Korea. Furthermore, wild geese mothers' frequent shuttle between the United States and Korea as visitors/travelers invites suspicious looks from U.S. Customs and Border Protection (CBP) agents.

Miseon is a former wild geese mother who once held a visitor visa in the United States. Because her visitor visa was valid only for six months per visit, she had to go outside and come back to the United States every six months. She well illustrates how painful and traumatic it was when she was under the strict interrogation by a CBP officer who treated her as if she were a criminal offender or illegal immigrant:

> When I first entered the U.S. with a visitor visa, it was OK. But, at the second time, the immigration officer interrogated me so badly, asking, "Why are you going back and forth so often?" Since I was so scared I could not answer his questions well. I was just shivering and crying until he finally allowed me to go. He also told me that "I will keep an eye on you." So, I was extremely nervous until I finally returned to Korea. [. . .] [Before having such a bad experience at immigration] I had thought that such an ill-treatment was only for those who committed a crime or illegal immigrants.

Because of such disadvantages, none of the wild geese mothers in my study hold a visitor status for the entire period of their migration in the United States. They hold such a status for a very short time, only when there are no other options available, and then promptly switch to another legal status. Therefore, in this section, I discuss the opportunities and challenges of a visitor status primarily based on the experiences of wild geese mothers in Canada.

In general, compared to the international student status, the visitor status in Canada seems to better serve wild geese mothers' fulfillment of their official goal of migration, which is supporting their children's education through intensive mothering. Unlike their international student counterparts, mothers with a visitor visa in Canada are less likely to be distracted by other obligations, and thus they can devote most of their time, energy, and money to children.

One very unique pattern is observed among the wild geese mothers with a visitor visa in the City of London in Canada. That is, some of them are the permanent residency applicants. At the time of the interview, London was one of the few Canadian cities that allowed permanent residency applicants to come to their cities even before their application would be approved, and applicants' dependent children could get free public education while the application was being processed. Therefore, London was a quite popular destination for Korean wild geese families, although it was not a major city in Canada.

Interestingly, the migration goal of wild geese mothers who applied for Canadian residency is not so different from that of other wild geese mothers in my study: providing their children with education in English. Like the other wild geese mothers, they are also just strategic in utilizing the existing immigration law and educational opportunities available in Canada, in that their children's public education tuition is waived by their application for permanent residency. They pursue Canadian residency as a means to achieve their educational goal more efficiently while minimizing the educational costs, and thus they do not necessarily plan to permanently settle down in Canada. In fact, many wild geese mothers in my study applied for Canadian residency but still planned to return to Korea after their sojourns. Nevertheless, over time, wild geese mothers who applied for Canadian residency have gradually leaned toward permanent settlement in the Canadian society, particularly after their husband's retirement in Korea.

Nevertheless, wild geese mothers with a visitor visa in Canada also encounter many challenges based on their legal instability as temporary visa holders. In particular, those who came to Canada with a visitor visa while their permanent residency application was being processed are most vulnerable to the changes in Canadian immigration policies. According to the wild geese mothers that I interviewed, the Canadian federal government has recently decided to eliminate the backlog of immigration applications. Thus, many wild geese parents' applications for permanent residency have also been rejected. That is, their children are no longer eligible for free public educational benefits in Canada. Accordingly, many wild geese families whose permanent residency has been rejected have to make a critical decision: either returning to Korea or staying in Canada and paying tuition for their children's education. In the process of decision-making on returning, many wild geese parents have experienced serious spousal conflicts. Especially, when their children are attending high school, spousal conflicts on the timing to return to Korea tend to be very intense. Wild geese fathers often ask their families in Canada to return to Korea as soon as possible due to the increased economic burden, whereas wild geese mothers insist on staying until their children graduate Canadian high school.

A wild geese mother named Hyomin migrated to Canada five years prior to the interview as Canadian residency applicant with three adolescent children and has recently been informed of the rejection of her immigration application. Hyomin describes how she has experienced intense conflicts with her husband after that:

My husband asked me to return to Korea right away when our residency was rejected. However, I insisted on staying. [. . .] My youngest [son] is timid . . . And the most importantly, since he came here when he was in the seventh grade, he did not have any experiences in Korean middle school. So, if he returns to a Korean high school now, his academic record must be the lowest of all students. Then, how can my son cope with such frustration? As such a loser, what kinds of friends will he make? What if he continues to live as a loser? Because of such concerns, I have kept persuading my husband . . . I have insisted to stay . . . Even if my son does not study so hard here, he is doing OK at school. If he graduates with his OK grades, he will not feel that he is behind others. Further, if he returns to Korea when he enters the university, he will not experience any bullying issues. So, I have insisted to return to Korea after he graduates high school. However, I am not so sure whether my decision [to stay] is right. Furthermore, my family-in-law and my husband have not been so amicable to me during our decision-making process. They have been suspicious that I argue for staying, because I have lived here so comfortably.

In addition, when wild geese children return to Korea unexpectedly earlier than they originally planned, because their parents fail to achieve Canadian residency, there are a lot of tensions and conflicts between parents and children. Moreover, some wild geese children undergo serious maladaptation to Korean society. Stories of former wild geese parents who witness their children's maladaptation after family reunification are explored in detail in chapter 6.

Finally, the Canadian government's delayed immigration decisions (as well as the rejections of permanent residency) also negatively affect the career paths of wild geese fathers who remain in Korea. Generally, after their families' migration, many wild geese fathers have found that they can better concentrate on their work, as they are less distracted by the familial obligations. However, once wild geese fathers plan to reunite with their families abroad, they often lose their loyalty to their current jobs and are not so interested in their career advancement opportunities, as they expect to leave Korea and start a new life in another country in the near future (e.g., within a year). Consequently, if the immigration decision on their Canadian permanent residency is delayed for several years and then eventually rejected after a long waiting period, these wild geese fathers' careers are also negatively impacted. An account of Bora, a wild geese mother who migrated to Canada five years prior to the interview with her two adolescent children while leaving her professor husband in Korea, is exemplary:

Before making his mind [not to come to Canada], my husband refused so many good offers such as writing a book. He also could have been promoted earlier at his college. However, since he always expected to come to Canada [whenever the residency would be issued], he did not accept any good offers for his career. Only after giving up coming here, he devoted himself to his current job and was promoted. Now, we feel that he made a forethoughtful decision, because we finally failed to get residency.

In sum, a visitor status in Canada is like a double-edged sword. On the one hand, it allows wild geese mothers to focus on their primary goal of migration, while not being distracted by other obligations such as their own college education. Moreover, migration to Canada as a visitor even before the approval of their permanent residency application is a blessing for many wild geese families, because their children can receive free Canadian public education sooner. On the other hand, the opportunity of earlier arrival in Canada with a visitor visa, while waiting for permanent residency, can cause many unexpected familial problems if their immigration application is rejected. Thus, wild geese mothers have to be good negotiators adjusting conflicting interests among family members.

Dependents in the United States

It is quite interesting that one-third of wild geese mothers who migrated to the United States in my study were not originally wild geese mothers, but dependents of their husbands. Their husbands entered the United States with L1 visas (intracompany transferee executives or managers) or J1 visas (exchange professors), while some also had O1 visas (individuals with extraordinary ability or achievement), F1 visas (international students), and E1 visas (treaty traders). However, in my study, there are no wild geese mothers who migrated to Canada as their husbands' dependents. It is probably because my research site in Canada (London, Ontario) is a small city and may not be such an attractive location for overseas branches of big Korean companies or governmental offices. Thus, I discuss the implications of the dependent status based on the experiences of wild geese mothers in the United States.

Unlike wild geese mothers who migrated to North America with a student or visitor visa, this group of wild geese mothers with a dependent visa did not intend transnational family separation at the time of their initial migration. Rather, all of them admit that they originally came to the United States in order to live together with their husbands who migrated for their work or study. So, their original goal of migration was to keep their family together. This group of women has become wild geese mothers by remaining in the United States for their children's education even after their husbands returned to Korea.

Then, what kinds of legal statuses do these women choose when becoming wild geese mothers? As table 1.1 shows, nineteen women entered the United States with a dependent visa, but only three have kept the same dependent visa until the time of the interview or their return to Korea. The other sixteen women have obtained new legal statuses: one has a visitor visa, six have become international students, and nine have achieved permanent residency or citizenship. This legal status change is one of the distinct characteristics of this group, because such changes occur less frequently among the other wild geese mothers.

Why have such legal status changes occurred? When they first migrated to the United States as a whole family, these women (and their husbands) often over-emphasized the positive aspect of migration. They strongly upheld a belief that it would be a great opportunity for their children to learn English and experience diverse cultures. They also planned that the whole family would return to Korea all together. However, by the time that they were supposed to return to Korea, these families realized that their return was not as easy as they originally thought because of their children's education. These parents recognized how it would be challenging for their children to survive in the competitive education system in Korea. In particular, parents with teenagers were immensely concerned that their children might fall behind in the subjects that were important for the university admission, such as mathematics, Korean language and literature, and Korean social studies. Even if their children seemed to be competitive enough, some mothers strategically decided to remain in the United States in the hope that their children would enter a prestigious Korean university through a special admission program for overseas Koreans. Other mothers wanted their children to stay in the United States, enter a good university, find employment, and permanently settle down in the American society.

After their husbands' return to Korea, only a few wild geese mothers have continued to hold a dependent visa. There are two main issues involved with this legal status. First, wild geese mothers with a dependent visa need their husbands to come to the United States quite often so that they can legitimately maintain their dependent statuses.

The story of Sihoo, a former wild geese father, demonstrates how costly it is to have such frequent transnational commutes between Korea and the United States, which may put wild geese families under increasing financial pressure. Sihoo was a professor in Korea and came to the United States as a visiting scholar with a J1 visa while his family members were holding J2 dependent visas. After one year of sojourn, Sihoo returned to Korea. Yet, his family continued staying in the United States for children's education while keeping their J2 visas. They did not change their legal status because they planned to stay only one more year in the United States to enhance children's

English fluency. Instead, Sihoo had to frequently go back and forth between Korea and the United States to maintain his family's dependent legal status and justify their staying:

Sihoo: I went there as a visiting scholar and had a J1 visa. I went there with my family and then returned first. Then, my family stayed there one more year.

Sehwa: If you came back first [to Korea], how could your rest of family maintain their J visa in the United States? Did they change their legal status?

Sihoo: No, [They did not change their legal status]. To keep their [dependent] status, I did my best. So, I frequently went to conferences [held in the United States], such as twice per semester. While I lived apart from them, I was still commuting [between the two countries].

Sehwa: Do you remember how many times did you visit your family in the United States for a year?

Sihoo: As I have said, I visited [my family] twice per semester. So, in total, I went there six times [during transnational family separation], including once in the summer break and another in the winter break . . . When I went there for a conference, I stayed only five to seven days. However, during breaks, I spent most of my time with my family [in the United States]. It was about two months [per break].

Second, even if their dependent visa is maintained well, these wild geese mothers are still struggling to handle many problems without their husbands' presence. A dependent visa holder's legal ability in the United States is even more limited than that of an international student. For example, wild geese mothers with a dependent status are not able to open a bank account or credit card, sign on their leasing contract, or have paid employment.

Jiyoung is a wild geese mother who got through three different legal statuses (from F2 to H4 to permanent resident) throughout her migration in the United States. She offers an insightful account on the limitations of the dependent status. Prior to migration, Jiyoung was a successful career woman in Korea. However, eight years before the interview when her husband was admitted to an Ivy League MBA program, she gave up her job and accompanied her husband. At that time, she held a F2 visa as a spouse of a F1 international student. After her husband acquired an MBA degree and got a job in the United States, Jiyoung attained new dependent status as a spouse of a H1B temporary worker, and her visa was switched into a H4 visa. Then, her legal status changed again as a dependent, as her husband achieved permanent residency through his company's sponsorship. Three years prior to the interview, Jiyoung finally became a wild geese mother as she remained in the United States for her children's education while her husband returned to Korea to pursue his new career opportunity. Now, as a permanent resident,

Jiyoung reflects on the challenges associated with her various dependent statuses from F2 to H4.

Sehwa: You have experienced three different legal statuses. Then, do you find any differences among them?

Jiyoung: Of course!!! [laugh] When I was on the F2 visa, that is, international student's wife, everything was so uncomfortable to me. I even had a hard time to get a driver's license. I couldn't do anything. Everything was all so challenging. I couldn't do anything but to follow my husband. [. . .] H4 visa was a little better [than F1] in terms of extending driver's license. Nonetheless, it never meant that I could do something. In addition, it [H visa] was always unstable, because we would have to return [to Korea] right away in case my husband was laid off. I was always under great stress because H visa was extremely unstable.

While Jiyoung experienced the challenges associated with the dependent status while her husband was residing with her in the United States, other wild geese mothers who have maintained their dependent legal status even after their husband's return to Korea have faced so many challenges in their everyday lives that they cannot handle without their husbands, who are living across the oceans. For these reasons, the dependent legal status is not an ideal option for wild geese mothers who plan to stay in the United States for a longer period. Needless to say, wild geese mothers' dependence on their husbands despite their physical separation, as well as their inability to pursue further education or paid employment in the host society, does not help improve these women's leverage in their transnational households.

As mentioned above, most wild geese mothers who initially held a dependent visa in my study have changed their legal statuses to independent ones since they became transnationally split families. As table 1.1 shows, the majority have become permanent residents or citizens, which are the most preferred legal status. Unlike visitors or F1 international students who suffer from many predicaments as temporary visa holders, permanent residents and citizens are able to organize their everyday life as they want. They do not have to attend postsecondary education unless they want to do so. They are also able to legitimately find paid employment. As wild geese parents gradually learned such pros and cons of various legal statuses through their migration period, some wild geese fathers with professional jobs in the United States applied for permanent residency or citizenship prior to their return to Korea. In such cases, because wild geese mothers' (and their children's) permanent resident status was obtained through their husbands, it has been relatively easier for these fathers to maintain their patriarchal authority as the head of the transnational household with legal power.

In sum, in terms of the implications of the dependent legal status for wild geese mothers' empowerment, the positive implications do not outweigh the negative ones, based on my analysis. Of the wild geese mothers who started their lives in the United States as their husbands' dependents, those who have continued holding a dependent legal status even after their husbands' return to Korea are small in number (i.e., only three out of nineteen) in my sample. While their lives have become independent in some respects, due to their physical separation from their husbands, they at the same time have become more dependent on their husbands in other respects, with regard to maintaining the essential elements of their everyday lives, such as handling the issues with visa renewals, leasing contracts, credit cards, and bank accounts. The gender paths of the other sixteen wild geese mothers who have obtained independent legal statuses after their husbands' return to Korea are greatly diversified by their choice of the legal status. As mentioned earlier, the majority (i.e., nine out of sixteen wild geese mothers) have obtained permanent residency or citizenship. These legal statuses are discussed next.

Residents or Citizens

As table 1.1 shows, one-fourth of wild geese mothers in my study already had a resident or citizen status when they migrated to North America, and this number was almost doubled at the time of the interview (for current wild geese mothers) or when they returned to Korea (for former wild geese mothers). Some became residents through their families (husbands or parents), while others achieved the resident or citizen status through their own education and employment in their destination countries.

As mentioned earlier, Jiyoung is a wild geese mother who got through three different legal statuses (from F2 to H4 to permanent resident) throughout her eight years of migration in the United States. Her story highlights the benefits of permanent residency over other temporary dependent statuses. To Jiyoung, becoming a permanent resident is such an important event that has tremendously changed her life, because it not only gives her a sense of stability and the ability to set up a long-term plan but also highly motivates her to more adapt to American society:

Sehwa: Are there any reasons to apply for a green card [permanent residency]?
Jiyoung: Green card gives you stability. Because without it, you cannot stay here [in the United States] continuously. Stability from the [permanent resident] status has played a very positive role on me, particularly emotionally. For example, [when I held an H4 visa as a dependent of a temporary worker], I was continuously concerned about the possibility that we would pack and return to Korea in case my husband was laid off, and it also negatively

impacted children. Even if I wanted to arrange new educational activities for my children, I was hesitant because I kept thinking that we would have to return to Korea within two weeks after my husband got laid off. Whenever we got a new apartment or a house, our temporary status also kept negatively impacting us. [. . .] At that time, having a plan itself was like building a house on the sand. However, after getting residency, I am highly encouraged to make a more serious effort to settle down in this society, because I will live here permanently. For example, I can plan for my future, including the kinds of work that I want to do after the children are grown. I also can set up a more specific plan on how to raise my children here with more confidence. I really want to raise these children well in the United States. I extremely like that many of my concerns have been cleared [after achieving permanent residency].

In addition, compared to the others, wild geese mothers with a permanent resident or citizen status enjoy greater freedom and autonomy in their host societies. They organize their everyday life as they want. They do not have to attend postsecondary education unless they want to. They can legitimately contribute to the family economy through their employment, which is critical for enhancing their domestic status. Of note, diverse gender paths through wild geese mothers' education and employment are discussed later in this chapter.

Some women even plan to stay in the host societies permanently, even if it means that they may live separately from their husbands forever. Wild geese mothers' legal independence from their husbands also leads to their emotional detachment from their husbands, which further strengthens their relative gender status in their transnational households.

A wild geese mother named Sohee used to be a subordinate full-time home-maker in Korea and she was treated like a maid by her husband. However, after migration to Canada, she achieved Canadian residency through her education and employment and now plans to apply for Canadian citizenship with her dream of opening her own business. Through her six years of trans-national spousal separation, Sohee has become empowered and emotionally detached from her husband to the extent to say, "In fact, I no longer neces-sarily need my husband as a man, while I still like that he is a good father." Moreover, when her husband visits the family in Canada and criticizes the ways she performs housework, she no longer endures it but confronts him. Sohee describes:

I no longer can stand it [my husband's criticism]. It [my patience] might pass the Maginot Line. I don't care what he says now. While I used to be downhearted when he criticized me, I now respond to him, "Oh, you don't like it? OK. Then, let's divorce!" It seems that I have become stronger since I lived alone. . . . I now feel that we are equal.

Some wild geese mothers who have the citizenship of their host countries, like Minhee, feel that their domestic status has been heightened after migration because of their newly achieved legal power to sponsor the permanent residency of their children and/or husbands.[48] Minhee initially migrated to the United States ten years before the interview as a legal dependent of her husband who was a dispatched employee of the Korean company's American branch. She soon achieved permanent residency through her husband, and then has become a wild geese mother by remaining in the United States after her husband returned to Korea about three years before the interview. During the period of transnational spousal separation, Minhee acquired U.S. citizenship by herself. Minhee even asserts that her citizenship status offers her much greater advantages compared to her permanent residency with respect to her everyday life, mothering practices, and relative gender status within the transnational households:[49]

Sehwa: Could you explain how the change in your legal status has impacted your everyday life?

Minhee: After changing from a [American] resident to a citizen, I no longer have to wait [to get through immigration] in the long line [for foreigners] at the airport. [laugh]. And another thing that I really liked was, my first child [boy] was exempted from [Korean mandatory] military service [as he also achieved American citizenship]. [. . .] It is also much easier for him to find a job after college graduation, because you know that there are many restrictions for internationals.

Sehwa: Oh, I see. Then, how has your legal status change impacted the relationship with your husband?

Minhee: I feel that I have greater power because I have citizenship. I can bring him to this country. [laugh]. I mean I have power because I now have the right to sponsor my husband' citizenship application. And my life in America has become freer. Whenever I visit Korea, I am no longer under the [American immigration's] restriction of when I should return [to maintain my resident status]. I think that the best [advantage] is just my [legal] freedom.

As the stories of Sohee and Minhee demonstrate, compared to wild geese mothers with other legal statuses in my study, those with resident or citizen statuses have the strongest legal resources that can promote their relative gender status within their families.

At the same time, however, these wild geese mothers' enhanced status may aggravate spousal conflicts over the leadership of their transnational households. A wild geese mother named Yuna provides a good example. Interestingly, her family has mixed legal statuses[50]: she is a permanent resident; her eldest son is a U.S. citizen; and her youngest son is a F1 international student. When I met her for an interview, she had lived in the United States for twelve years, including the ten years as a wild geese mother. It was quite interesting why she would continue to stay in the United States, although her two sons were already fully grown up: one had a professional job on Wall Street and the other was an Ivy League university student. Yuna argues that she has to sponsor her younger son's permanent residency. To sponsor her child, she first has to achieve the citizenship status, which is the reason for her prolonged stay in the United States. While she has sacrificed her own life in Korea for her children, Yuna has also pursued her own interests as she extends her stay in the United States. For instance, she enjoys her enhanced decision-making power as an emerging leader of the family, as well as her promoted autonomy and freedom from her husband. In this process, Yuna also has to cope with conflicts with her husband:

> With children, I am the leader. I make decision and they follow. However, when my husband comes, he overthrows my authority [as a decision-maker]. Because he lives alone [in Korea], he likes to make all the decisions [even when visiting us]. He also wants to recover his status as the head of the family. He wants me to take care of him twice more than I used to do in Korea in order to make up for the loss of his status. He also asks me to run many errands for him. For the first few days of his visiting, I tried to endure it. But, soon, I could not stand it. I wondered why I had to ingratiate myself with him whenever he visited us.

In sum, the permanent residency and citizenship statuses are the best legal resources that can greatly empower wild geese mothers in the transnational context. This corroborates the significance of citizenship as it performs an "enormous legitimizing function"[51] in the lives of immigrants. Sometimes, however, their enhanced status can become a new source of spousal conflict. Thus, as a newly emerging leader of the household, wild geese mothers have to constantly negotiate with their husbands who are frustrated and resented because of their weakened dominant status as the head of the household.

Temporary Workers

Finally, there are a few wild geese mothers who do not fit the traditional definition of wild geese mothers: professional women who are working in North America with a temporary work visa for foreigners. As table 1.1 shows, only three out of fifty-five wild geese mothers in my study entered the United States with a temporary work visa. Two held an A1 visa (diplomats or foreign governmental officials) and one held a L1 visa (intracompany transferee executive or manager). They are high-profile professional women. Their main goal in becoming wild geese mothers is pursuing their career development, while providing their children with educational opportunities abroad is a secondary goal.

The number of wild geese mothers who have official employment in North America as foreigners has increased from three to five at the time of the interview (See table 1.1). Unlike the first three women who held a temporary work visa for foreigners from the beginning of their migration, these two women have achieved such work authorization through their education in the host societies: One has become a professor and the other has become a nurse. Since I discuss in more detail the impact of having additional education and employment in the host society on the empowerment of wild geese mothers in the later part of this chapter, the rest of this section is focused on the gender status of the three wild geese mothers who migrated to North America with a temporary work visa from the beginning of their migration.

Compared to the other wild geese mothers that I have discussed so far, these three wild geese mothers who came to North America with temporary work visas as foreigners have an advantageous status in various aspects. First, they are the only group of mothers who did not experience any period of career disruption, even for the short-term, for the sake of their children's education. Second, during transnational spousal separation, they are economically independent from their husbands who remain in Korea. They hardly receive remittances from their husbands in Korea but make an independent living on their own salary. Sometimes, they even send remittances to their husbands. Third, unlike the other wild geese mothers who take care of their children alone in the host societies, these three women brought their own mothers to North America to share the childrearing responsibilities. Accordingly, they are less burnt out by the responsibility of childcare than the other wild geese mothers. Finally, while most wild geese mothers send their children to public schools due to their budget constraints, these three mothers educate their children at expensive private schools thanks to their continued dual-earner systems during the wild geese period.

Notwithstanding their greater economic, familial, and legal resources, these three wild geese mothers with temporary work visas for foreigners still have encountered difficulties after migration, but these difficulties are qualitatively different from those of other wild geese mothers.

First of all, because they are distinct from other wild geese mothers who automatically assume the role of good mothers by sacrificing their lives (and careers if they had any) for the children, these three professional wild geese mothers are continuously challenged by their husbands and families-in-law about their motherhood. Their husbands, in particular, are not so supportive, because these men often think that they are making a huge sacrifice for their wife's career advancement opportunities. Accordingly, these husbands tend to be less sympathetic to their wives' hardships, even if their wives are struggling with the competing demands for work and family in the foreign countries.

Sungjae is a wild geese father who has a lucrative career in a global corporation in Korea, and his wife is also a highly ranked Korean public official who has been transferred to the United States. His account well represents the begrudged attitudes of wild geese fathers who are left behind in Korea toward their professional wives who are working abroad:

> When my wife said to me that she was exhausted, then I responded to her, "This is the trouble that you asked for. So, does it make sense if you say it is hard?" My wife also goes to school because she wants to study more. She works on weekdays and serves the role of the father on weekends [on behalf of me]. She always told me that she was so tired because she played triple roles [parent, worker, and student]. But, I then responded to her like this, "You should not say that you are tired. This is what you chose. Don't complain!"

More fundamentally, the experiences of these professional wild geese mothers well show how deeply the patriarchal gender ideology, which regards nurturing as exclusively women's work,[52] is still rooted even in the transnational arrangement with these professional women. As described earlier, when men have good career opportunities abroad, their wives are usually expected to give up (or pause if possible) their own careers in Korea and accompany their husbands abroad to be good wives. In contrast, as seen in the cases of professional wild geese mothers who have migrated to North America for their jobs, when women have good career opportunities abroad, they can hardly expect that their husbands will accompany them and provide support. Of course, no husbands in my study are willing to do so, because they are supposed to be the primary breadwinner. Those three professional wild geese women, because they share the same patriarchal gender ideology, often feel sorry for their husbands as if they abandoned their husbands for their own sake and grateful to their husbands for having allowed them to go abroad for their own careers.

Furthermore, these wild geese mothers are expected to continuously serve as the primary caretaker of their children even when they have migrated to a foreign environment and been very busy with their jobs. Because of the persisting gender inequality that relegates nurturing exclusively to women,[53] three professional wild geese women in my study try to share their heavy burden of childrearing with the other woman, in this case, their own mothers, rather than asking for their husbands' support. As Parreñas's research shows the international transfer of reproductive labor from the upper-middle-class women in industrialized countries to low-waged migrant Filipina domestic workers,[54] my study demonstrates the transfer of reproductive labor from professional Korean wild geese mothers to their own mothers.

In sum, wild geese mothers who migrated to North America with their own independent legal status to work as foreigners are in a quite advantageous position to promote their domestic status, because their economic power, legal independence, and the social prestige attached to their professional jobs are critical resources. Nonetheless, it is important to note that these women's empowerment is achieved through their own mothers' sacrifice and sharing of the childcare roles. Confronted by begrudging husbands who are not so happy with their wives' going abroad, accompanying their own mothers is the only viable solution for these women to overcome challenges and suspicions from husbands and families-in-law. This shows that even professional wild geese mothers are not free from the patriarchal pressure on their womanhood. Rather, because of their apparent deviance from the culturally approved gender roles, these women are constantly asked to prove that they are not off the track of traditional gender ideology that defines good motherhood (if not good wifehood).

SECOND RESOURCE FOR WOMEN'S EMPOWERMENT: PAID EMPLOYMENT

Wild geese mothers' employment, income, and financial contribution to their family economy are of great importance in shaping their relative power to their husbands. Immigration research has emphasized migrant women's increased economic contribution to the family as a pivotal source to challenge male dominance and renegotiate unequal domestic relations.[55] In the same vein, studies on the middle-class Chinese women who migrate abroad for their children's education, including *astronaut families* and *study mothers*, have noted that these women's gender status has been substantially lowered due to their increased economic dependence on their husbands after migration, often combined with their failure to address the continuous challenges and fluidity they encounter in the host society as *transient sojourners*.[56]

Nonetheless, previous studies on Korean wild geese families have overlooked the role of economic factors in their family power dynamics. Although a few studies have noted that some wild geese mothers have paid employment after migration,[57] they do not specify what kinds of jobs these women hold or how these women's contribution to their transnational family economy impacts their spousal dynamics. To fill this gap in the literature, I analyze the economic aspects of wild geese families in this section. Specifically, I investigate how wild geese mothers' economic dependence has changed through migration and how their employment in the host society have affected their gender status in the transnational households.

As figure 1.1 shows, among the fifty-five wild geese mothers who have migrated to North America, a half (twenty-eight) used to be full-time homemakers in Korea, whereas the other half (twenty-seven) had paid employment prior to migration. Of the twenty-seven wild geese mothers who worked prior to migration, ten had typical female-typed teaching jobs, such as a teacher or tutor, and the other seventeen had professional jobs such as a businesswoman, lecturer at university, public official, banker, nurse, accountant, computer programmer, journalist, researcher, and artist.

After migration to North America, as figure 1.1 shows, a majority of wild geese mothers (forty out of fifty-five) have become either international students or full-time homemakers regardless of their prior careers in Korea. Only fifteen women have been officially employed after migration: the majority have well-paid full-time positions including a professor, public official, businesswoman, entrepreneur, nurse, beauty professional, and cook, whereas a few have low-paying part-time positions, such as a cashier at a deli or laundry shop or a private tutor.

Importantly, international students (holding a F1 visa in the United States) and homemakers (holding a dependent visa in the United States) have very limited opportunities to have paid employment in the United States because

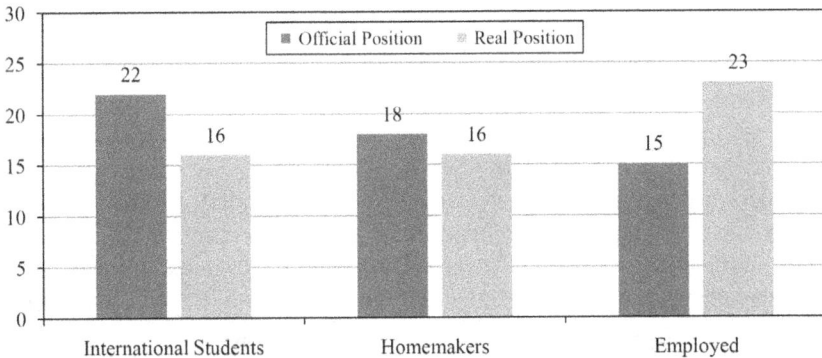

Figure 1.1 Wild Geese Mothers' Official and Real Occupations after Migration to North America (n=55). *Note:* Out of 57 wild geese families that migrated to North America, two of them are gender role reversed cases. That is, in these two families, not mothers but fathers migrated to North America with their children, and mothers continued to hold their professional positions in Korea after their families migrated to North America in order to support them economically. Thus, this figure shows the employment patterns of the 55 wild geese mothers.

of the restrictive immigration policies. Nonetheless, some of them still seek under-the-table jobs at Korean immigrant-owned shops, such as café, restaurant, laundry shop, and flower shop, and a few even work full-time. Thus, the number of wild geese mothers who actually work after migration is greater than the official number (see figure 1.1).

In this section, I examine how wild geese mothers' gender status is shaped primarily based on their real employment status, although I also compare the different impacts of official and unofficial employment on their empowerment.

Wild Geese Mothers without Employment after Migration

Let me first explore the gender status of wild geese mothers who are not employed after migration. They are divided into two groups: (1) those who do not work both before and after migration and (2) those who used to work prior to migration but no longer work after migration.

Wild geese mothers who do not work both before and after migration do not find much change in their economic dependence on their husbands, but their control over the household finance has greatly heightened through migration. When they were living together with their husbands in Korea, many wild geese mothers needed their husbands' permission or approval for their spending. Some of them further had to receive the exact amount from their husbands for each item they purchase. In contrast, after migration, once they have become separated from their husbands by the ocean, these wild geese mothers no longer need such permission on their expenditure. Moreover, they start receiving a lump sum of money as a remittance.

Wild geese fathers also acknowledge that they can no longer easily control their wives' spending from a long distance, as their wives have enhanced the economic autonomy by not sharing the specific details on their spending with husbands. While the *code of silence* has been noted in Kyle's study as a gender strategy that Ecuadorian male migrants employ to maintain their dominance over their wives remaining in the home country,[58] Korean wild geese mothers use this *code of silence* as an effective gender strategy to counterbalance their economic dependence on their husbands. Because wild geese mothers serve as the remittance manager of their transnational households, not only their decision-making power but also their domestic status has been significantly promoted, just like Ecuadorian women in Pribilsky's study who have managed remittances from their husbands abroad and formed their own autonomous households.[59]

A wild geese mother named Bora portrays her enhanced financial autonomy after migration, which also allows her to perform her role of mothering in her discretion:

I have greater decision-making power here. For now, I have children with me. Before migration, my husband had a final say on every household issue. However, now, I have to decide even minor issues by myself. Such minor decisions accumulated into a big decision. With respect to living expenditures, when I lived in Korea, I had to read his countenance and got his final approval for my spending. However, in here, he doesn't know how I spend, because I do not keep a household account. For example, my children are now playing instruments in the local youth orchestra. When we lived in Korea, I could not dare to ask him about the youth orchestra, because I knew that he would say that orchestra was a luxury for us. But, here, if I want my children to play in the orchestra, then I just can do it . . . He also knows that our children are orchestra members. But, it is OK with him. Why? It is because I do not tell him how much it costs. I just cut unnecessary information to him. That's the way I manage my spending here.

Furthermore, because these wild geese mothers live in a foreign country with their children, they are entitled to ask their husbands for remittances without feeling sorry or guilty. Some mothers even argue that they are not economically dependent on their husbands, even though they receive a huge amount of remittances from their husbands, because they portray their mothering in a foreign country as one of the most important economic activities for their entire family. A wild geese mother named Miyoung is exemplary:

I think the remittance [from my husband] is my money. I don't think that I am economically dependent on my husband. After getting married, spouses should build the economic community by both making contributions to it. In particular, because I brought a lump sum money [at the time of migration] and saved it in my bank account, I think that it is my money rather than my husband's money. I believe that I certainly have the right to claim it as my money. If I did not take care of children but someone did it instead, we would have spent much more money. I am sure that my mothering is deemed to be valuable economic activity.

It is quite interesting that many wild geese fathers in my study also agree to this argument and some of them even feel sorry if they cannot send as much as their wives request. Given this, Korean wild geese fathers are not effectively utilizing remittances as a means to maintain their patriarchal power over their wives, in contrast to Ecuadorian and Mexican transnational husbands in other studies.[60] Of note, Korean wild geese fathers' remittances and its implications are discussed in-depth in chapter 5.

Let's turn our attention to the second group of wild geese mothers. In contrast to those who did not work prior to migration, wild geese mothers who worked prior to migration but no longer work after migration tend to be quite sensitive to their increased economic dependence on their husbands. This is particularly the case for those who were economically independent and thus were not accustomed to receiving remittances from husbands. Some of these women even feel guilty of spending their husbands' money, and such a feeling is not so conducive to improving their leverage in their conjugal relationships.

In addition to their increased economic dependence, the loss of social status attached to their former employment also disempowers these wild geese mothers after migration. In particular, wild geese mothers who used to have prestigious professional careers in Korea tend to think of becoming full-time homemakers themselves as quite derogatory. Even after they have migrated to North America to pursue the ideology of intensive mothering and to fulfill the goal of children's education, these wild geese mothers still do not see full-time motherhood as a respected status for them.

A wild geese mother named Damso used to be a respected high-school teacher with a busy work schedule prior to migration. However, through migration, she has lost the job that she greatly enjoyed and was so proud of. Damso recounts her sense of loss after becoming a full-time mother:

> In Korea, I was extremely busy as a teacher. I always lived with a pride that I was a very smart and competent person. However, after migration, I am no longer a teacher respected by others. I feel that I have been downgraded to a mother whose mission is only cooking and doing laundry for children. I was very depressed particularly when I first migrated, because I could not find any value in the work I did as a full-time homemaker.

Moreover, some wild geese mothers who used to work in fast-changing industries, such as computer science and fashion, are seriously concerned about their future job prospects after returning to Korea, because it will be extremely difficult for them to be re-employed in these industries after the long career disruption. In sum, some wild geese mothers who have experienced the discontinuation of their employment through migration are quite sensitive to the loss of their own income and social status attached to their jobs, which in turn lowers their bargaining power as well as their self-esteem.

Interestingly, however, I have found that wild geese mothers' increased economic dependence and their loss of social status attached to their jobs do not always weaken their domestic power in their transnational households, in contrast to the previous studies' findings on middle-class Chinese women who migrated abroad for their children's education.[61] There are several reasons for this.

First, some wild geese mothers were extremely tired with their hardworking professional jobs in Korea and were looking for justification to themselves and their family for quitting their jobs, and thus they are quite satisfied with their jobless status after migration. For them, becoming wild geese mothers serves as a valid excuse to legitimately quit their jobs. Furthermore, some of them ironically feel liberated from the heavy burden of economically supporting their families after migration. They are relieved as they no longer have to worry about their household economy as much as they used to do. They can just inform their husbands of the total amount of money they need in order to survive in the host countries, and it is their husbands' duty to find financial resources and send remittances to them.

Second, wild geese mothers who have temporarily left their professional jobs through migration but plan to return to their original positions after returning to Korea do not feel that their domestic status is quite lowered, even if they do not work after migration. In particular, wild geese mothers who used to be teachers at public school prior to migration are quite sure that they can resume their career as teachers once they return to Korea, because teachers are protected, by law, to have a long family-related break (e.g., up to three years per child) and to return to their original positions.[62] Thanks to their strong job security, these women tend to evaluate their wild geese period more positively than the other wild geese mothers, for instance, as a time to recharge themselves, because their economic dependence on their husbands is only temporary.

It is also interesting that these professional wild geese mothers are likely to feel happier after migration, because they no longer compete with their husbands to do less housework, which is thoroughly discussed in chapter 2. Prior to migration, they and their husbands made an equal or similar contribution to their household economy. Nonetheless, they had to perform the majority of housework. When they challenged the unequal division of household labor and childrearing responsibilities, it often ended up with serious spousal conflicts and confrontations. For instance, some wild geese parents (both mothers and fathers) admit that they cursed their spouses and even threw stuff at each other. Others recall that they thought of divorce because of endless spousal conflicts on the division of household labor.

After spousal separation, however, their conflicts on the division of household labor have considerably decreased. Given that housework is a "symbolic enactment of gender relations,"[63] in the absence of their husbands, wild geese mothers are liberated from the pressure of traditional gender ideology that forced them to perform more housework. On the other hand, wild geese fathers, who were exempt from much of the housework when living with their wives, are now struggling with increased housework.

This changed situation gives a valuable opportunity to these men to better appreciate how it was onerous for their wives with professional jobs to handle both paid work and housework. Thus, these fathers have increasingly expressed greater compassion and gratitude to their wives for what they have done for the family, which in turn greatly improves their transnational spousal relationships and helps elevate wild geese women's domestic status.

In short, some wild geese mothers who had professional jobs in Korea do not think that their domestic status has been substantially lowered after migration, because their economic dependence on their husbands is only temporary and their spousal conflict on the household labor is considerably mitigated. Of note, the impacts of changing patterns of housework on wild geese mothers' gender status and the quality of their transnational spousal relationships are discussed in-depth in chapters 2 and 3.

Third, some wild geese mothers who are voluntarily enrolled in graduate schools or professional programs in the destination countries are not significantly dispirited by their increased economic dependence on their husband during their wild geese period. They are quite confident that their current loss of income is temporary and that they can find better occupations after completing their additional education. Their belief is corroborated by the job trajectories of former wild geese mothers who completed a degree program in North America and have found new (often better-paying) occupations after their return to Korea, which is discussed in-depth in the later part of this chapter.

Finally, some wild geese mothers who used to have professional jobs prior to migration contend that the loss of their own income is the outcome of their unwanted career disruption for children, and their husbands are also quite sympathetic with this argument. Thus, these women are not debased by their increased economic dependence on their husbands after migration. Rather, like their full-time homemaker counterparts, these women feel entitled to ask their husbands to send remittances, and their husbands, now as single earners, also accept it as their familial obligation.[64] In addition, like their full-time homemaker counterparts, former professional women also enjoy an increased level of leverage on household expenditure as a transnational remittance manager, which is quite helpful to complement their loss of income and social status attached to their jobs.

In sum, in the case of wild geese mothers who do not work in the destination countries, their new gender status tends to be more influenced by their prior employment status and future job prospects rather than by their current economic dependence on husbands. For wild geese mothers who used to be full-time homemakers in Korea, their economic dependence on their husbands is not an important factor to affect their transnational gender relations.

Rather, they have strengthened their domestic status by playing the role of remittance manager and by reframing their mothering as a fruitful economic activity for their transnational family. Wild geese mothers who worked prior to migration tend to be more sensitive to the loss of their income and social status after migration as well as their increased economic dependence on their husbands, compared to their full-time homemaker counterparts. Nonetheless, not all of them feel that their gender status has been destabilized after migration. In particular, those who plan to return to their original jobs or those who expect to find better jobs through their additional education in the host countries tend to evaluate their current domestic status more positively than those who do not have such optimistic job prospect. Moreover, by emphasizing their career disruption as a sacrifice for children, these women's economic dependence on their husbands are successfully justified and accordingly does not significantly lower their status within their transnational households.

Wild Geese Mothers with Employment after Migration

Now, let me discuss the gender status of wild geese mothers who have paid employment in the host countries. They are also divided into two groups: (1) those who have employment although it is not legally allowed and (2) those who are legitimately holding jobs. My previous research noted that middle-class Asian migrant women's leverage in their marital relationship was more impacted by social status and prestige attached to their jobs than their actual income.[65] Given that, I originally expected that low-tiered under-the-table jobs would not empower wild geese mothers as much as professional jobs did. On the contrary, I have found that both professional employment and under-the-table jobs help wild geese mothers have greater bargaining power after migration for the following reasons.

First of all, most wild geese families have encountered increased economic pressure as they maintain two middle-class households in the transnational context. Thus, wild geese mothers' additional income from their employment, regardless of its type, is deemed to be essential to maintaining their decent lifestyle in the destination countries. In my study, wild geese families' average annual household income is about $128,000. Wives and children abroad spend approximately 70 percent of their annual household income on average, and some of them even spend more than 100 percent of their household income. Given that wild geese fathers also have to make their own living in Korea, it is certain that their income is not sufficient for many wild geese families to keep maintaining their middle-class lifestyle in two transnational households.

Then, why do so many wild geese families spend more than they can afford? Wild geese parents admit that they failed to estimate how much they would spend in the host societies, and thus eventually have spent much more money than they originally planned. Unless they had their own families or close friends in the host societies, it would have been very difficult for most wild geese parents to accurately estimate their future living expenditure. Only a few wild geese families are able to spend in the host countries as they initially planned, thanks to consultation with their close friends or family members who were already living in the host countries.[66]

Wild geese families spend much more money than they expected for their initial settlement in the host countries, such as buying a car and/or purchasing a house. They also spend much more money to pay recurring expenses, such as rent, health insurance premiums, overseas trips, and college tuition. Wild geese families in my study pay $2,200 on average for their monthly rent (with a range between $1,300 and $3,500) in North America. Because most of them are homeowners in Korea, they are quite embarrassed by the fact that they have to pay expensive rent for housing of a lower quality compared to their home in Korea. Therefore, some wild geese families, who are richer and open to permanent settlement, buy a house in the destination countries although it was not what they originally planned.

In addition, health insurance premium is a surprise to most of wild geese mothers. Because they used to pay a very low premium for their health insurance thanks to the generous national healthcare system in Korea, health insurance costs they have to pay in the host countries as foreigners seem to be abnormally high. Moreover, most wild geese families did not consider carefully how frequently they would visit each other during the separation. In the case of wild geese families in my study, wild geese fathers visit North America more often than their families visit Korea. It is a decision to save the travelling costs while maintaining their familial intimacy across the ocean. Nonetheless, it is still costlier than they expected. Finally, some wild geese families have to pay for their children's college tuition. Although all wild geese children in my study migrated to North America when they were younger, some have entered universities later in North America, whose tuition is much more expensive than that of Korea.

To cope with their imminent financial pressure, wild geese parents try various strategies. Most wild geese fathers in my study have their house leased to pay their family's initial settlement costs, and then move to a smaller house. Some also move into the house of their parents or parents-in-law to save their living expenses. They also take advantage of bank loans to make up their monthly shortage and to pay for their children. Some fathers also plan to clear their increasing debt with their severance pay and/or pension after they are retired. Wild geese mothers who worked prior to migration often use their own financial resources such as savings, salary, and/or severance pay after migration. Some wild geese mothers even receive economic support either from their parents-in-law or their own parents. Most wild geese parents also have significantly decreased expenditures for themselves after spousal separation, such as shopping, socializing, and dining out.

Despite such cost-saving efforts, many wild geese parents in my study still suffer from severe economic pressure from maintaining two transnationally split households. Because they used to maintain a comfortable lifestyle or the upper-middle-class *habitus*[67] in Korea, wild geese parents are quite sensitive to the changes in the size and the pattern of their spending, even if they are minor ones. Some believe that the quality of their life has been greatly lowered after migration, for which some of them even suffer from serious depression. In addition, many wild geese parents commonly state that their overall family assets have significantly decreased during the wild geese period. Some even recognize that their debt has greatly increased in that period. Accordingly, many wild geese parents are very anxious about their future. Some are concerned that their stable and comfortable postretirement life is compromised and sacrificed by their heavy investment in their children's education. A narrative of wild geese mother named Younghwa well represents the financial concerns of many wild geese parents:

> It is not the family. My husband is really like a machine that earns money. In short, he is just an ATM machine. This is not the right way of family life. If we just focus on our children, this is a really good place to live. I like education here, which provides a solid foundation for my children to grow. On the other hand, it is based on such a huge parental sacrifice. We have to support our children, while not preparing for our elderly life. As we live in this way, not only our family economy has become unstable but also our spousal relationship has become estranged because we no longer share our lives as much as we did.

Confronted with the combination of such current economic pressure and concern about their own future, it may be imperative for some wild geese mothers to seek employment opportunities in the host countries.

Surprisingly, wild geese mothers in my study do not mind having low-tiered under-the-table jobs, and there are several reasons for that. First, wild geese mothers know well how challenging it is for them to find gainful employment after migration, because of the difficulty of transferring their prior educational and career backgrounds to the hosting society's job market, which is also noted by the studies of Asian middle-class migrant women.[68]

Second, wild geese mothers tend to adopt a "dual frame of reference" in evaluating their social class position. A dual frame of reference among immigrants suggests that they tend to view their current lives in the host countries quite positively, even if they are confined to low-paying marginal jobs, because they usually compare their present immigrant lives with their previous lives in their home countries prior to migration where they underwent greater economic hardships rather than with the lives of other people in the host countries.[69] Likewise, wild geese mothers in my study are less likely to be discouraged even if they have low-tiered under-the-table jobs in the host countries.

Interestingly, however, the dual frame of reference works for wild geese mothers for different reasons. Wild geese mothers, in general, view themselves as temporary migrants who eventually return to Korea after their sojourn. Therefore, their social class perception tends to be primarily based on Korea rather than North America. That is, wild geese mothers do not think their real social class is lowered notwithstanding their dead-end-jobs in the host countries, as long as their upper-middle-class location in Korea is safely secured by their left-behind husbands who are successful professionals.

Third, faced by current and/or future economic constraints, middle-class Korean wild geese mothers have expanded the definition of motherhood to incorporate not only nurturing but also economic provision, as many working-class migrant women do.[70] Although wild geese mothers can no longer devote all their time and energy to their children once they have paid employment, they try to balance between work and family duties by working part-time while their children are studying at school. Their employment enables wild geese mothers to provide their children with greater educational opportunities beyond the limit of remittances sent by their husbands, and also greatly enhances their leverage to make decisions on their children's education.

Fourth, and most importantly, paid employment, even if it is an under-the-table part-time job, greatly helps elevate wild geese women's bargaining power, autonomy, and domestic status. To begin with, under the tight budget, wild geese fathers in my study highly welcome their wives' decision to work. Some fathers even directly ask their wives to find jobs. Wild geese fathers are also very grateful for their wives' initiative to take dead-end-jobs in a foreign country for the families despite their high social class and prior careers. Some wild geese fathers who used to work in North America before becoming wild geese families know very well how difficult it is for foreigners to find any types of employment abroad. Thus, they express further compassion toward their wives who find paid employment in the host countries. As they happen to change their perspectives on their wives from dependents to equal earners or companions, wild geese fathers more readily accept their wives' enhanced status without much resistance.[71]

Furthermore, even if there is no imminent economic crisis, employment is still a crucial resource for wild geese mothers to enhance their bargaining power and contest male supremacy in their transnational households, as they have achieved greater economic and emotional autonomy from their husbands. After migration, many wild geese mothers often feel guilty to buy something even small for themselves, because they know how burdensome it is for their husbands to economically support their families abroad. Some women further think that their husbands do not like them to spend remittances for their own education or leisure. Because wild geese mothers are expected to spend most (if not all) of their time and energy for their children, spending remittances for their own goals or interests is deemed to be a violation of the ideological mandate for good mothers.

Given these, having a paid job is a great option for many wild geese mothers who need additional financial resources that they can spend in their own discretion while not feeling guilty or sorry for their husbands. Even some women do not tell their husbands that they have part-time jobs in the host countries. Yejin is a wild geese mother who used to be a full-time homemaker prior to migration, but now works as a part-time cashier at a local deli shop after migration. Her account well illustrates migrant women's empowerment through employment (even if it is a low-paid one).

[Before having a job] I didn't have much leverage on the remittances. It was quite transparent where I had to spend. However, after I have earned $800 a month as a cashier, I can more comfortably buy lunch for my friends or make an offering of money for my church's missionary work. Before working, I felt sorry to spend money for myself, because it was not the essential part of our living expenditure. But, now I treat others and make church offerings with my own income. This makes me feel less sorry for my husband and I have more leverage. I am much freer on my expenditures now. I can do what I want to do without asking my husband.

A little extra money at hand also gives wild geese mothers valuable opportunities of socializing, given that it is hardly feasible for many wild geese mothers to build and expand their social networks in a new society without investing time, energy, and money. A story of Damso, who used to be a high-school teacher prior to migration and has found a part-time job as a private tutor after migration, also shows how her small income from a new job helps her recover a social life:

We are economically better off than others. However, since I lost my job [due to migration] and was economically dependent on my husband, I was not able to spend money for me. So, when I first came, I rarely went out, which was so painful. Since I started teaching students and making money, I feel like I can breathe again. Before teaching, the money issue always weighed on me. But, after earning my own money, I can meet people more freely. I now have recovered my social life.

Finally, employment in the host countries encourages wild geese mothers to become more independent decision-makers. Through their employment, some wild geese mothers acquire invaluable opportunities to learn about their host societies while interacting and socializing with the mainstream citizens, even if they earn only the minimum wage from their unofficial employment. They also enjoy their low-paid employment as a good chance to practice and upgrade their English fluency. Interestingly, but not surprisingly, the more they are familiar with the host societies than their husbands, the less wild geese mothers discuss with their husbands when making decisions. Such independent decision-making experiences greatly empower wild geese mothers to challenge patriarchy in their transnational households. In sum, wild geese mothers' employment after migration enhances their domestic status, as they become more emotionally and economically independent from their husbands, which corroborates Hondagneu-Sotelo's findings in her study of Mexican migrant women.[72]

Nonetheless, it is noteworthy to mention that there are two critical differences between official and informal employment in their positive impacts on wild geese mothers' gender status. First, wild geese mothers who have official employment after migration not only contribute to their family economy but also have legal power to obtain their own permanent residency (and even citizenship) as well as to sponsor their children and husbands' permanent settlement in the host countries. In contrast, wild geese mothers with informal employment do not have such legal power, although they still can make an economic contribution to their family economy. In my study, many wild geese families are open to the option of permanent immigration to North America. Some even plan to reunite in the host countries after their fathers' retirement or quitting jobs in Korea. Hence, wild geese mothers' legal capability of supporting their family's permanent settlement in the destination countries serves as a very powerful resource for them to further enhance their status within their families.

Second, the positive impact of wild geese mothers' official employment can last even after the family reunification in Korea, whereas that of informal employment tends to be effective during the transnational family separation only. In my study, former wild geese mothers who had official employment in North America tend to find new (and sometimes better) employment soon after their return to Korea without career disruption. Their work experience abroad is often highly valued in Korean job market. Furthermore, although these women's income is no longer essential for making a living after their family reunification, they are still empowered by the fact that they can keep contributing to their family economy with their new job in Korea. Former wild geese mothers' continued employment after their return to Korea endows these women with respectful social status and helps them maintain their confidence and pride as a competent member of society. Former wild geese mothers also tend to feel more legitimate to request their husbands to share household labor more equally when they have a job after family reunification. Former wild geese fathers are also more willing to share housework when their wives are working after family reunification. Stories of former wild geese mothers are further discussed in chapter 6.

On the contrary, it is much more difficult for wild geese mothers to find gainful employment after their return to Korea, if they used to have informal jobs in the host countries. Furthermore, wild geese mothers who have informal jobs in the host societies tend to regard them as a temporary expedient to supplement their family income, not as their real careers. Therefore, these women do not eagerly seek for jobs but readily return to the full-time home-maker positions after having returned to Korea. Given that migrant women's economic contribution to the family economy is a pivotal resource for them to contest male dominance and reconfigure unequal gender relations in their households,[73] it makes sense that wild geese mothers without paid employment are less likely to maintain much of their enhanced sense of social power and autonomy after family reunification.

THIRD RESOURCE FOR WOMEN'S EMPOWERMENT: ADDITIONAL EDUCATION

Not only paid employment but also additional education in the host society is critical in helping wild geese mothers contest patriarchal spousal relationships. Substantial numbers of wild geese mothers in my study officially hold an international student status after migration so that they can legitimize their prolonged stay and provide their children with free public school education in the host countries. While most of them are enrolled in the ESL programs, some women are highly motivated to pursue their own education and thus voluntarily enrolled in postsecondary education. This latter group of wild geese mothers (i.e., those enrolled in postsecondary education) is further divided into two groups: (1) those who plan to settle down in North America and (2) those who plan to return to Korea. Wild geese mothers have chosen different educational options in their host countries based on their future plans.

Wild geese mothers who have dreamed of permanent settlement in the host countries tend to choose very practical programs, such as culinary work, esthetics, and nursing programs, which will help them find new jobs in the host society regardless of their prior education or careers in Korea. They have made such program choices because they acknowledge the difficulty of transferring their prior educational and occupational qualifications to the labor market of the host society, as noted by the studies of Asian middle-class migrant women.[74] It is also a strategic decision to overcome their weaknesses in the North American job market as newly migrated women who are not so fluent in English.

Chaerim is a good example. She is a wild geese mother who has a bachelor's degree in marketing and used to work as a successful businesswoman in a prestigious company prior to migration. Nonetheless, after migration, she is pursuing an associate degree in culinary arts at a community college. Chaerim provides a good explanation of why she has made such a choice:

> I majored marketing. So, I should have studied marketing after migration. However, there will be no job for me if I study marketing in this country. Thus, I chose to study culinary arts. If I complete the culinary program, it is relatively easy to find a job here. I also heard that culinary jobs do not ask for a high level of English proficiency. So, it is advantageous for Asian migrants who are not so fluent in English like me. . . . Studying culinary arts might not be helpful for me to find a job if I return to Korea. I chose this major on the premise that I would continue to live here. If I return to Korea, I need to find the type of marketing job that I used to work in.

Another wild geese mother named Miyoung points out that discrimination against Asian immigrants in the host society is such a critical barrier that she has given up her original dream of opening her own business. Miyoung used to be a full-time homemaker in Korea. She migrated to Canada nine years prior to the interview as a legal resident of Canada and then has achieved Canadian citizenship. Therefore, she did not have any legal problems of opening a business or finding a job. Nonetheless, in reality, it was still very challenging for her to find any job after migration (not to mention opening a business) because of her apparent foreignness as an Asian immigrant woman. Miyoung explains:

> Here, it is difficult to find a job that you want. When I used to live in a different city, I tried to find a part-time job at a [local] cafeteria. I thought opening a cafeteria would give me a good source of income to make a living while taking care of children. Thus, to learn the cafeteria work, I sought a part-time job [at a cafeteria] there. However, you know here is different from Korea. Even if it is a cafeteria job, it is still difficult to get it. Cafeteria with Canadian customers will not hire immigrants, particularly those with Asian face. . . . Immigrants have different pronunciation and look different. From the perspective of manager, [Asian] immigrants are expected to have communication problems. So, it is not easy to find a job.

Confronted by such challenges, Miyoung has alternatively pursued a more feasible career path. That is, she acquired a certificate to teach Korean from a local college and then became a Korean language teacher at a local school board. Miyoung is very unique, in that she not only earned new educational credential from the host society but also actively utilized her ethnic identity to find a job in the local area where there was high demand for foreign language teachers. Miyoung's education and employment in the host society have further empowered her to become more assertive and autonomous in her transnational spousal relationship. Miyoung recounts:

> While I was not independent [before migration], I have become independent [after migration]. I also have become much more assertive than before. When I lived in Korea, I always had to walk on eggshells around my husband. I even couldn't say what I wanted to say. However, here, if I want something, I openly tell my husband. I never would have become so frank, if I had kept living in Korea.

On the other hand, the educational patterns of wild geese mothers who would like to find jobs after returning to Korea are more diverse. Women who already had good careers prior to migration but wanted to have better jobs after return to Korea often choose majors that are closely related to their prior education and/or careers and try to strengthen their educational credentials by achieving a higher degree in North America such as master's or doctoral degrees.

A former wild geese mother named Mina held a doctoral degree in English and worked as an adjunct lecturer at several universities prior to migration. Because foreign experiences are highly valued in her specialty area, she migrated to the United States with her child and completed another degree program. After returning to Korea, Mina got a faculty position with a better job prospect and greater stability, which has substantially promoted both her social and domestic status.

In contrast, wild geese mothers who did not work prior to migration tend to choose more practical educational programs that can help them overcome their weaknesses in the Korean job market as ones who underwent long career disruption.

A wild geese mother named Sujin was a full-time homemaker in Korea. After migration to the United States, she was initially studying English at a local ESL institute and has recently started additional educational program, called TESOL (Teachers of English to Speakers of Other Languages), at a local college. Sujin has made such a decision, because she strongly would like to find a job after returning to Korea based on her practical education during her migration period. Sujin explains:

> I came here with a five-year plan. One day, I felt that I would be a useless person when I just returned to Korea after attending the ESL only for five years. Even

though I am a little too old [to get a job in Korea], I believe that I can earn some money when I return to Korea with the [TESOL] certificate. My final goal is to find a job at a private English institute [in Korea].

Postsecondary education in the host societies definitely has merits with respect to wild geese mothers' domestic status. Regardless of whether they plan to stay in the host countries or return to home country, wild geese mothers who are pursuing postsecondary education in the host countries are not particularly discouraged by their current economic dependence on their husbands. As mentioned earlier, these women believe that their economic dependence is only temporary and that they can eventually make significant economic contribution to the family after completing the programs. While previous studies have emphasized migrant women's *current* economic contribution to the family as their critical resource to renegotiate the patriarchal gender relations,[75] my study further demonstrates that migrant women's economic potential and expected contribution to the *future* family economy also can empower these women and help them overcome their current economic dependence on their husbands.

Former wild geese mothers' educational choices and their following job trajectories after family reunification also support many family theorists' argument that women's education and employment are key resources to promote their gender status.[76] Out of the sixteen former wild geese mothers who migrated to North America,[77] four women were full-time homemakers during their stay, seven were international students, two found professional jobs such as registered nurse and professor after having completed postgraduate education, and three did not pursue any further education in the host societies but worked as cook, entrepreneur, and businesswoman.

After having returned to Korea, all four homemakers continue to be homemakers. Among the two mothers who held professional jobs in the United States, the nurse found a job in the hospital, but has recently quit it because she has to take care of her husband who has developed a serious health issue, and the professor has found a faculty job in a prestigious Korean university. Three mothers who worked in the host countries without any further education have continued to work after returning to Korea, but in different fields: one has become an environmental activist, and two others have opened small new businesses. Among the seven international students, four women who attended the ESL programs have become full-time homemakers, whereas the other three who completed higher educational programs have found gainful jobs after returning to Korea: one has become a professional artist based on her college major; another has become an assistant director of a private English institute thanks to her TESOL certificate and her experience as a mother who successfully sent her child to a prestigious American university; and the last has obtained an university faculty position thanks to her new degree abroad. Stories of former wild geese mothers are further discussed in chapter 6 to demonstrate how migrant women's additional education in the host country empowers them both socially and domestically after family reunification.

Above findings cannot be generalized due to the small size of my sample. Yet, these trajectories indicate that migrant women with further educational credentials and/or employment in the host societies have a greater chance of finding new employment even after their return to home countries, whereas the others tend to be confined within domesticity as full-time homemakers.

In sum, additional education in the destination countries is empowering as it enhances wild geese mothers' employability in both home and host countries. For wild geese mothers who have continued to work, additional education provides a good chance to upgrade their qualifications and find better jobs. For wild geese mothers who have experienced career disruptions, additional education offers a new opportunity to return to the official job market and resume their new career. Therefore, wild geese mothers' education increases their potential contribution to the family economy and helps improve their domestic status.

CONCLUSION

This chapter explores how transnational spousal separation unexpectedly puts wild geese couples' existing patriarchal gender relations into renegotiation. Wild geese mothers have been liberated from their former subordination to the traditional gender patriarchy that normalizes women's lower status and sacrifice for the families. Through migration, wild geese mothers also have accumulated autonomous decision-making and problem-solving experiences as a sole resident mother who takes care of their children and overcomes many predicaments independently in the foreign country. This not only enhances wild geese mothers' overall self-esteem, confidence, and a sense of independence but also endows them with greater leverage to contest unequal spousal power relations.

Yet, the outcomes of transnational spousal separation and the patterns of wild geese mothers' gender empowerment tend to be quite divergent based on the way they utilize their new resources of the host societies, such as legal status, employment, and additional education.

This chapter highlights the significance of official legal status as migrant women's critical resources. In my study, wild geese mothers, as active agents of transnational migration and strategic decision-makers, choose diverse legal statuses when they enter North America. Wild geese mothers' legal statuses have not been constant but changed flexibly throughout their migration, as these women try to maximize their migration benefits while coping with increasingly restrictive immigration and citizenship policies of the host countries. While each visa renders unique challenges and opportunities to the wild geese mothers in North America, wild geese mothers who hold temporary worker visa, permanent residency, and citizenship status are likely to enjoy greater leverage and higher status in their transnational households than those with international student, visitor, and dependent visas. This demonstrates that migrant women's degree of gender empowerment is quite diverse by the type of their visas and particularly by the different levels of temporality and (in)stability attached to each visa category.

Here, I would like to put a special emphasis on the importance of legal status, because it can serve either as an obstacle to or as a steppingstone for migrant women to gain access to other important resources of the host societies that are integral for their empowerment. Nonetheless, I do not argue that one legal status is always better than the other. The level of wild geese mothers' empowerment tends to be widely varied within the same legal status group based on the way they utilize other important economic and social resources such as employment and additional education. Likewise, the same legal status can lead to different outcomes in different destination countries, as implied by the different life paths of wild geese mothers with the same legal statues (e.g., the international student status) between the United States and Canada. This corroborates that macro-level structural conditions such as the nation-state and its immigration and settlement policies play an important role in shaping individual migrant women's lives, as noted by the studies of Bloemraad,[78] Menjívar,[79] and Portes and Rumbaut.[80]

This chapter sheds light on the important but often overlooked legal hardships of Asian documented immigrants with respect to their prolonged stay in North American while holding temporary visas. Building on the Menjívar's study which explores how Latino immigrants' lengthy *in-between status* (i.e., moving back and forth between *temporary legality* and *nonlegality*) negatively shapes their lives in the United States,[81] I further suggest that even if wild geese mothers are documented immigrants, when their *temporary legality* is prolonged, it also negatively shapes their family relations as well as their everyday lives in the host society, because of many uncertainties and challenges associated with the temporary legitimate legal status.

In addition to legal status, this chapter also provides the readers with more nuanced explanations of the impact of employment on migrant women's gender status. I agree that migrant women's economic contribution to the family is critical for them to reconfigure the patriarchal gender relations.[82] For Korean wild geese mothers in my study, their paid employment in the host countries, whether it is official or unofficial, is certainly helpful to challenge male dominance in their families during transnational spousal separation, as it relieves their families' imminent economic hardships.

Yet, I further suggest the critical differences between official and informal employment as resources for migrant women's empowerment. Official employment not only enables wild geese mothers to contribute to their family economy but also gives them a legal power to sponsor their families' application for the permanent settlement in the host countries, whereas unofficial employment lacks such a legal power. Moreover, the positive impact of official employment tends to last even after family reunification, whereas that of informal employment tends to be confined to the period of transnational family separation. Former wild geese mothers who have official employment in the host countries tend to continue working even after having returned to Korea and maintain their enhanced gender status thanks to their continued economic power and social status attached to their new jobs in Korea. On the other hand, those have informal employment in the host countries tend to regard them as temporary means to supplement their family income and readily return to the full-time homemaker positions after having returned to Korea, which in turn makes it more difficult for this group of women to maintain much of enhanced sense of social power and autonomy after family reunification.

Despite the paramount importance of migrant women's employment and income as resources for their empowerment, I also note that wild geese mothers' domestic status is not always weakened by their increased economic dependence on their husbands. In case of wild geese mothers who used to be full-time homemakers in Korea, the level of their economic dependence on their husbands has not changed through migration. Rather, these women have strengthened their economic leverage by playing the role of remittance manager and by reframing their mothering as a fruitful economic activity for their transnational family.

Compared to their homemaker counterparts, wild geese mothers who used to have jobs prior to migration tend to be sensitive not only to their loss of income and social status attached to their former employment but also to their increased economic dependence on husbands. Nonetheless, they are still likely to evaluate their transnational gender status more positively, when the following conditions are met: their economic dependence on husbands is expected to be only temporary and/or spousal confrontations on the division of household labor are substantially decreased.

Finally, I emphasize migrant women's additional education in the host countries as a critical resource to promote their social and domestic statuses of both present and future. Education empowers wild geese mothers to overcome spousal power imbalance incurred by their current economic dependence on their husbands thanks to their potentials for a future economic contribution to the family. In this respect, this chapter contributes to extending the knowledge of transnational migration studies, which have mainly focused on the positive impacts of migrant women's current economic contribution to the family.

In addition, my examination of the former wild geese mothers' diverse job trajectories after their family reunification in Korea corroborates education's long-lasting positive impacts on migrant women's empowerment. Even if migrant women are full-time homemakers and/or have long career disruption, education offers them a new opportunity to find a gainful job, resume their social life, and reconstruct their domestic relations both in the host and home countries.

NOTES

1. Glenn, "Split Household," 39; Hondagneu-Sotelo, *Gendered Transitions*, 62–67; Kyle, *Transnational Peasants*, 107–109; Pribilsky, "Aprendemos a Convivir," 322–329.
2. Glenn, "Split Household," 39.
3. Hondagneu-Sotelo, *Gendered Transitions*, 148–185.
4. Ibid., 104–105; Pribilsky, "Aprendemos a Convivir," 318–320.
5. Hondagneu-Sotelo, *Gendered Transitions*, 113–115.
6. Parreñas, "Transnational Fathering," 1063–1064.
7. Kyle, *Transnational Peasants*, 107.
8. Hondagneu-Sotelo, *Gendered Transitions*, 68–69; Pribilsky, "Aprendemos a Convivir," 327.
9. Hondagneu-Sotelo, *Gendered Transitions*, 59; Kyle, *Transnational Peasants*, 107–108; Pribilsky, "Aprendemos a Convivir," 320–321.
10. Hondagneu-Sotelo, *Gendered Transitions*, 69–70; Kyle, *Transnational Peasants*, 107–108.
11. Pribilsky, "Aprendemos a Convivir," 327–329.
12. Hondagneu-Sotelo and Avila, "I'm Here," 559–560; Rhacel Salazar Parreñas, "Migrant Filipina Domestic Workers and the International Division of Reproduction," *Gender & Society* 14, no. 4 (2000): 572; Parreñas, "Long Distance Intimacy," 327, 331–332. See McKay, "Sending Dollars Shows Feeling," 187 for exception.
13. Asuncion Fresnoza-Flot, "Migration Status and Transnational Mothering: The Case of Filipino Migrants in France," *Global Networks* 9, no. 2 (2009): 257; Hondagneu-Sotelo and Avila, "I'm Here," 559–560; Parreñas, "Migrant Filipina Domestic Workers," 572–573; Parreñas, "Long Distance Intimacy," 324–325, 331–332; Leah Schmalzbauer, "Searching for Wages and Mothering from Afar: The Case of Honduran Transnational Families," *Journal of Marriage and Family* 66, no. 5 (2004): 1323–1324.
14. Alice M. M. M. T. Aye and Bernard Guerin, "Astronaut Families: A Review of Their Characteristics, Impact on Families and Implications for Practice in New Zealand," *New Zealand Journal of Psychology* 30, no. 1 (2001): 9–16; Chang and Darlington, "Astronaut Wives," 61–77; Chee, "Migrating for the Children," 137–156; Elsie Ho and Richard Bedford, "Asian Transnational Families in New Zealand: Dynamics and Challenges," *International Migration* 46, no. 4 (2008): 41–62; Waters, "Flexible Families," 117–134.
15. Mei Lin Eyou, Vivienne Adair, and Robyn Dixon, "Cultural Identity and Psychological Adjustment of Adolescent Chinese Immigrants in New Zealand,"

Journal of Adolescence 23 (2000): 531–543; Elsie Ho, "Chinese or New Zealanders? Differential Paths of Adaptation of Hong Kong Chinese Adolescent Immigrants in New Zealand," *New Zealand Population Review* 21, nos. 1 & 2 (1995): 27–49; Marjorie Faulstich Orellana et al., "Transnational Childhoods: The Participation of Children in Process of Family Migration," *Social Problems* 48, no. 4 (2001): 572–591; Rogelia Pe-Pua et al., "Astronaut Families and Parachute Children: Hong Kong Immigrants in Australia," in *The Last Half Century of Chinese Overseas*, ed. Elizabeth Sinn (Hong Kong: University of Hong Kong Press, 1998), 279–298.

16. Huang and Yeoh, "Study Mothers," 379–400.

17. Chang and Darlington, "Astronaut Wives," 68; Huang and Yeoh, "Study Mothers," 392; Waters, "Flexible Families," 120–121.

18. Huang and Yeoh, "Study Mothers," 387–388, 393–394; Minjeong Kim, "'Forced' into Unpaid Carework: International Students' Wives in the United States," in *Global Dimensions of Gender and Carework*, ed. Mary K. Zimmerman, Jacquelyn S. Litt, and Christine E. Bose (Stanford, CA: Stanford University Press, 2006), 162–175; Guida Man, "From Hong Kong to Canada: Immigration and the Changing Family Lives of Middle-Class Women from Hong Kong," in *Family Patterns, Gender Relations*, ed. Bonnie J. Fox (New York: Oxford University Press, 2001), 420–440; Brenda S. A. Yeoh and Louisa-May Khoo, "Home, Work and Community: Skilled International Migration and Expatriate Women in Singapore," *International Migration* 36, no. 2 (1998): 168.

19. Chang and Darlington, "Astronaut Wives," 65, 69; Huang and Yeoh, "Study Mothers," 392; Waters, "Flexible Families," 121–122.

20. Huang and Yeoh, "Study Mothers," 392.

21. Chang and Darlington, "Astronaut Wives," 68–69; Waters, "Flexible Families," 126–127.

22. Dreby, "Honor and Virtue," 32–59; Lee, "Closer or Estranged," 509–510; Montes, "Role of Emotions," 486.

23. Suzanne M. Bianchi et al., "Is Anyone Doing the Housework? Trends in the Gender Division of Household Labor," *Social Forces* 79, no. 1 (2000): 191–228; Scott South and Glenna Spitze, "Housework in Marital and Nonmarital Households," *American Sociological Review* 59 (1994): 327–347; Candace West and Don H. Zimmerman, "Doing Gender," *Gender & Society* 1, no. 2 (1987): 143–144.

24. Chang and Darlington, "Astronaut Wives," 73; Chee, "Migrating for the Children," 147; Huang and Yeoh, "Study Mothers," 382; Waters, "Flexible Families," 120–121.

25. Glenn, "Split Household," 35–46; Hondagneu-Sotelo, *Gendered Transitions*; Kyle, *Transnational Peasants*; Pribilsky, "Aprendemos a Convivir," 313–334.

26. Glenn, "Split Household," 35–46.

27. See chapter 3 for the further discussion of spousal conflicts over the leadership of transnational households.

28. See chapter 6 for the cases of intensified spousal confrontations over the leadership of the households after family reunification.

29. Cecilia Menjívar, "Family Reorganization in a Context of Legal Uncertainty: Guatemalan and Salvadoran Immigrants in the United States," *International Journal of Sociology of the Family* 32, no. 2 (2006): 231–238.

30. Ibid., 232–234.

31. Ibid., 235–236.

32. Joanna Dreby, *Everyday Illegal: When Policies Undermine Immigrant Families* (Oakland: University of California Press, 2015), 57–75.

33. Ibid.

34. Menjívar also notes that multiple legal categories stratify immigrants' incorporation to the host society, as they are treated differently before the immigration laws. See Cecilia Menjívar, "Liminal Legality: Salvadoran and Guatemalan Immigrants' Lives in the United States," *American Journal of Sociology* 111, no. 4 (January 2006): 1006.

35. Seonmi Kim, "A Qualitative Study on the Life Experience and Identity Maintenance of the Full-Time Housewives of the Korean Wild Geese Family in U.S.A.," *Journal of Korean Home Management Association* 11, no. 4 (2007): 171–189 (in Korean); Seonmi Kim, "A Qualitative Study on the Wild Goose Mother's Everyday Life, Family Relationship and Social Networking," *Korean Family Resource Management Association* 13, no. 1 (2009): 41–59 (in Korean); Lee, "Kirogi Mother," 250–264.

36. Menjívar, "Liminal Legality," 1008–1009 and 1016–1031.

37. Ibid., 1000–1001.

38. Department of Homeland Security, "Curricular Practical Training (CPT)," accessed February 6, 2015, http://www.uscis.gov/working-united-states/students-and -exchange-visitors/students-and-employment.

39. More rigid immigration regulations over time are also noted by Dreby, *Everyday Illegal*, 3–5; Menjívar, "Family Reorganization," 224–226; Menjívar, "Liminal Legality," 1006.

40. Department of Homeland Security, "Optional Practical Training (OPT)," accessed February 10, 2015, http://www.ice.gov/doclib/sevis/pdf/opt_policy_gui dance_042010.pdf.

41. Ibid.

42. I-20 is a supporting document of F1 international students issued by their academic or language programs.

43. Study permit in Canada corresponds to a F1 international student visa in the United States.

44. Terry Arendell, "Conceiving and Investigating Motherhood: The Decade's Scholarship," *Journal of Marriage and the Family* 62, no. 4 (2000): 1192–1207; Angela Hattery, *Women, Work and Family: Balancing and Weaving* (Thousand Oaks, CA: Sage, 2001); Sharon Hays, *The Cultural Contradictions of Motherhood* (New Haven, CT: Yale University Press, 1996).

45. Government of Canada, "Student Work Permit–Work on Campus," accessed July 14, 2014, http://www.cic.gc.ca/english/study/work-oncampus.asp.

46. Ibid.

47. For the most updated information, see Government of Canada, "Work or Live in Canada after You Graduate," modified March 17, 2021, https://www.canada.ca/en/ immigration-refugees-citizenship/services/study-canada/work/after-graduation.html.

48. Interestingly, Dreby notes the opposite of my study. In her study, documented Mexican migrant women who married to undocumented men do not enjoy greater equality in their division of household labor. Rather, these documented women take greater responsibilities and burdens than their undocumented husbands. See Dreby, *Everyday Illegal*, 76–80.

49. Growing distinctions between U.S. citizens and permanent residents and the advantages of the U.S. citizenship is also noted by Susan Coutin, "Denationalization, Inclusion, and Exclusion: Negotiating the Boundaries of Belonging," *Indiana Journal of Global Legal Studies* 7 (2000): 592.

50. For further scholarly discussions on the *mixed-status families,* see Dreby, *Everyday Illegal*, 57–75 and Michael Fix and Wendy Zimmermann, "All Under One Roof: Mixed-Status Families in an Era of Reform," *International Migration Review* 35, no. 2 (2001): 397–419.

51. Linda Bosniak, "Citizenship Denationalized," *Indiana Journal of Global Legal Studies* 7 (2000): 489.

52. Kim England, "Mothers, Wives, Workers: The Everyday Lives of Working Mothers," in *Who Will Mind the Baby: Geographies of Child Care and Working Mothers*, ed. Kim England (New York: Routledge, 1996), 109–122; Barbara Ehrenreich and Arlie Russell Hochschild, "Introduction," in *Global Woman: Nannies, Maids, and Sex Workers in the New Economy*, ed. Barbara Ehrenreich and Arlie Russell Hochschild (New York: Metropolitan Books, 2003), 1–13; Moon, "Immigration and Mothering," 840–860; Parreñas, "Migrant Filipina Domestic Workers," 560–580.

53. Ibid.

54. Parreñas, "Migrant Filipina Domestic Workers," 560–580.

55. Hondagneu-Sotelo, *Gendered Transitions*, 121–127; Nazli Kibria, "Migration and Vietnamese American Women: Remaking Ethnicity," in *Women of Color in U.S. Society*, ed. Maxine Zinn and Bonnie Dill (Philadelphia, PA: Temple University Press, 1994), 247–264; In-Sook Lim, "Korean Immigrant Women's Challenge to Gender Inequality at Home: The Interplay of Economic Resources, Gender, and Family," *Gender & Society* 11, no. 1 (1997): 31–51; Pyong Gap Min, "Changes in Korean Immigrants' Gender Role and Social Status, and Their Marital Conflicts," *Sociological Forum* 16, no. 2 (2001): 301–320; Paul Ong and Tania Azores, "The Migration and Incorporation of Filipino Nurses," in *The New Asian Immigration in Los Angeles and Global Restructuring*, ed. Paul Ong, Edna Bonacich, and Lucie Cheng (Philadelphia, PA: Temple University Press, 1994), 164–195; Patricia R. Pessar, "The Linkage between the Household and Workplace in the Experience of Dominican Immigrant Women in the United States," *International Migration Review* 18 (1984): 1188–1211; Kristine M. Zentgraf, "Immigration and Women's Empowerment: Salvadorans in Los Angeles," *Gender & Society* 16, no. 5 (2002): 625–646.

56. For Hong Kong and Taiwanese *astronaut families,* see Johanna L. Waters, "Transnational Family Strategies and Education in the Contemporary Chinese Diaspora," *Global Networks* 5, no. 4 (2005): 359–377; Chang and Darlington, "Astronaut Wives," 61–77; and Chee, "Migrating for the Children," 137–156. For *parachute kids* in Canada and Australia, see Pe-Pua et al., "Astronaut Families and

Parachute Children," 279–298. For Chinese *study mothers* in Singapore, see Huang and Yeoh, "Study Mothers," 379–400.

57. Kim, "Wild Geese Family," 171–189 (in Korean); Lee and Koo, "Wild Geese Fathers," 533–553.

58. Kyle, *Transnational Peasants,* 107.

59. Pribilsky, "Aprendemos a Convivir," 313–334.

60. Pierrette Hondagneu-Sotelo, "Overcoming Patriarchal Constraints: The Reconstruction of Gender Relations among Mexican Immigrant Women and Men," *Gender & Society* 6, no. 3 (1992): 393–415; Kyle, *Transnational Peasants*; Pribilsky, "Aprendemos a Convivir," 313–334.

61. Chang and Darlington, "Astronaut Wives," 61–77; Chee, "Migrating for the Children," 137–156; Huang and Yeoh, "Study Mothers," 379–400.

62. For the detailed policy for the Korean public-school teachers' leave of absence, see Korean National Law Information Center, "Korean Educational Public Official Law" (Article 7.44 and 7.45) (in Korean), accessed May 28, 2020, http://www.law.go .kr/법령/교육공무원법.

63. South and Spitze, "Housework," 327.

64. Moon, "Immigration and Mothering," 840–860 also finds the similar entitlement among Korean immigrant women who retreated to full-time motherhood after several years of working as professionals.

65. Se Hwa Lee, "The Bifurcated Statuses of the Wives of Korean International Students," in *Koreans in North America: Twenty-First Century Experiences*, ed. Pyong Gap Min (Lanham, MD: Lexington Books, 2013), 135–156.

66. See chapter 5 for the in-depth discussion of the remittances sent by wild geese fathers.

67. Pierre Bourdieu, *Outline of a Theory of Practice* (New York: Cambridge University Press, 1977), 72–95.

68. Huang and Yeoh, "Study Mothers," 379–400; Kim, "Kirogi Fathers," 141–158 (in Korean); Man, "Hong Kong to Canada," 420–440; Waters, "Flexible Families," 117–134; Yeoh and Khoo, "Home, Work and Community," 159–184.

69. See Takeyuki Tsuda, *Strangers in the Ethnic Homeland: Japanese Brazilian Return Migration in Transnational Perspective* (New York: Columbia University Press, 2003), 383–384.

70. Patricia Hill Collins, *Black Feminist Thought: Knowledge, Consciousness, and the Politics of Empowerment,* 2nd ed. (New York: Routledge, 2000); Dreby, "Honor and Virtue," 32–59; Yen Le Espiritu, *Asian American Women and Men: Labor, Laws, and Love,* 2nd ed (Thousand Oaks, CA: Sage Publications, 2008); Fresnoza-Flot, "Migration Status," 252–270; Kamini Maraj Grahame, "'For the Family': Asian Immigrant Women's Triple Day," *Journal of Sociology & Social Welfare* 30, no. 1 (2003): 65–90; Hondagneu-Sotelo and Avila, "I'm Here," 548–571; Parreñas, "Migrant Filipina Domestic Workers," 560–580; Parreñas, "Long Distance Intimacy," 317–336; Patricia R. Pessar, "On the Homefront and in the Workplace: Integrating Women into Feminist Discourse," *Anthropological Quarterly* 68, no. 1 (1995): 37–47.

71. Impact of wild geese mothers' paid employment on the changing quality of spousal relationship is discussed in detail in chapter 4.

72. Hondagneu-Sotelo, "Overcoming Patriarchal Constraints," 393–415; Hondagneu-Sotelo, *Gendered Transitions*.

73. Hondagneu-Sotelo, "Overcoming Patriarchal Constraints," 393–415; Hondagneu-Sotelo, *Gendered Transitions*; Nazli Kibria, *Family Tightrope: The Changing Lives of Vietnamese Americans* (Princeton, NJ: Princeton University Press, 1993); Kibria, "Migration and Vietnamese," 247–264; Lim, "Korean Immigrant Women's Challenge," 31–51; Min, "Korean Immigrants' Gender Role," 301–320; Pessar, "Dominican Immigrant Women," 1188–1211; Patricia R. Pessar, "The Role of Gender in Dominican Settlement in the United States," in *Women and Change in Latin America*, ed. June Nash and Helen Safa (South Hadley, MA: Bergin and Garvey, 1986), 273–294.

74. Huang and Yeoh, "Study Mothers," 379–400; Waters, "Flexible Families," 117–134.

75. Hondagneu-Sotelo, "Overcoming Patriarchal Constraints," 393–415; Hondagneu-Sotelo, *Gendered Transitions*; Kibria, *Family Tightrope*; Kibria, "Migration and Vietnamese," 247–264; Lim, "Korean Immigrant Women's Challenge," 31–51; Min, "Korean Immigrants' Gender Role," 301–320; Pessar, "Dominican Immigrant Women," 1188–1211; Pessar, "Role of Gender," 273–294.

76. Bianchi et al., "Is Anyone Doing," 191–228; Scott Coltrane, "Research on Household Labor: Modeling and Measuring the Social Embeddedness of Routine Family Work," *Journal of Marriage and the Family* 62 (2000): 1208–1233; Paula England, "Marriage, the Costs of Children, and Gender Inequality," in *Ties that Bind: Perspectives on Marriage and Cohabitation,* ed. Linda Waite, Christine Bachrach, Michelle Hindin, Elizabeth Thomson, and Arland Thornton (New York: Aldine de Gruyter, 2000), 320–342.

77. Among the seventeen former wild geese families in North America, I exclude one gender role reversed family from the discussion of former wild geese mothers' job trajectories after family reunification Korea. Unlike sixteen former wild geese mothers, this mother kept remaining in Korea with her job and sending remittances to her husband and children abroad.

78. Irene Bloemraad, "Becoming a Citizen in the United States and Canada: Structured Mobilization and Immigrant Political Incorporation," *Social Forces* 85, no. 2 (2006): 667–695.

79. Menjívar, "Liminal Legality," 999–1033; Cecilia Menjívar, "Transnational Parenting and Immigration Law: Central Americans in the United States," *Journal of Ethnic and Migration Studies* 38, no. 2 (2012): 301–322.

80. Alejandro Portes and Rubén G. Rumbaut, *Immigrant America: A Portrait,* 3rd ed. (Berkeley: University of California Press, 2006).

81. Menjívar, "Liminal Legality," 999–1033.

82. Hondagneu-Sotelo, "Overcoming Patriarchal Constraints," 393–415; Hondagneu-Sotelo, *Gendered Transitions*; Kibria, *Family Tightrope*; Kibria, "Migration and Vietnamese," 247–264; Lim, "Korean Immigrant Women's Challenge," 31–51; Min, "Korean Immigrants' Gender Role," 301–320; Pessar, "Dominican Immigrant Women," 1188–1211; Pessar, "Role of Gender," 273–294.

Chapter 2

Changing Housework Patterns through Migration

It is noteworthy that the division of household labor is one of the good indicators of spousal power distribution. Wild geese parents in my study did not equally share household labor including childrearing when they lived together in Korea. Yet, such patterns have been challenged and re-negotiated through their transnational spousal separation. In this chapter, I analyze the changing housework patterns of wild geese parents on the basis of three theories of household labor: (1) the time availability perspective, (2) the relative resources perspective, and (3) the gender perspective. I also pay particular attention to the impact of transnational separation as a turning point which contests the patriarchal housework patterns of married couples.

THREE APPROACHES TO GENDER INEQUALITY IN HOUSEWORK

There are three major theoretical perspectives in gender and family scholarship that explain gender disparity in housework: (1) the time availability perspective, (2) the relative resources perspective, and (3) the gender perspective. First, the time availability perspective argues that wives' and husbands' time for housework is rationally allocated, and wives perform more housework than their husbands because women tend to spend less time in the labor market and accordingly have more time available to complete the household tasks than men.[1] This perspective reflects that women are more likely than men to have part-time jobs and work fewer hours even if they have full-time jobs.[2]

Second, the relative resources perspective views housework patterns as a manifestation of power relations between couples, and wives perform more

87

housework than their husbands because they have fewer relative resources or power.[3] This model emphasizes women's education and income (from paid employment) as critical sources for their empowerment. Therefore, compared to women who are unemployed and economically dependent on their husbands, women who work longer hours and make a greater financial contribution to their household economy are expected to achieve more egalitarian division of household labor.[4]

Both time availability and relative resources perspectives well explain the reasons why wild geese mothers who used to be full-time homemakers in Korea did the vast majority of housework: they not only had more time than their husbands to perform housework, they were also economically dependent on their husbands. Yet, these two perspectives do not provide good explanations for why wild geese mothers, who had full-time paid employment, earned as much as (or more than) their husbands and were as busy as (or busier than) their husbands still performed a lion's share of housework. This indicates that time availability and economic resources are not the only factors of the gendered housework arrangements.

Third, the gender perspective suggests that housework should be understood as a "symbolic enactment of gender relations"[5] rather than time availability or relative resources.[6] This perspective is developed based on West and Zimmerman's "doing gender" theory, which does not define gender as what we *have* but what we *do*.[7] Because housework is a means for couples to demonstrate and accomplish their gender in their everyday interactions with others, its patterns are highly influenced by social, cultural, and institutional norms; and when women and men violate the culturally approved gender standards, they are asked to be accountable for their deviant behaviors.[8]

There are plenty of research findings that support the gender perspective. For example, South and Spitze's study on the housework by marital status shows that gender gap in housework time is the greatest in marital households where wives and husbands live together.[9] Moreover, married men's contribution to housework tends to be confined to male-typed tasks, such as outdoor chores and automobile maintenance, whereas divorced and widowed men perform much more female-typed housework, such as preparing meals, washing dishes, cleaning house, washing and ironing, and shopping, than married men.[10]

Similarly, in the study about the effects of men's transitions in marital statuses on their housework performance, Gupta notes that men spend less time on housework when they enter "coresidential unions" through marriage and cohabitation, while women reduce their housework time when they leave "coresidential unions" through separation or widowhood.[11] These two studies demonstrate that men and women are doing gender not only through the different amount of housework they perform but also through the different types of housework they do.

In addition, conducting a longitudinal analysis of married couples' housework patterns, Brines shows that the more husbands are economically dependent on their wives, the less housework they do.[12] This finding confronts the relative resources perspective that stresses wives' economic dependency as a powerful predictor of women's greater share of housework. Alternatively, Brines explains that married couples with economically dependent husbands rather resort to traditional housework arrangement (i.e., only wives do housework while husbands avoid it) as a "means of reclaiming gender accountability in the eyes of self, partner, and others."[13] In sum, all these findings support that men and women are doing gender via their routine performance of housework, particularly when they live together. In this chapter, I analyze how wild geese parents' patterns of housework have changed through transnational spousal separation.

GENDERED HOUSEWORK PATTERNS BEFORE SEPARATION

Before transnational spousal separation, wild geese parents did not equitably share household labor including childrearing. For about three-fourths of wild geese parents in the study, it was women who performed almost all of the housework and childcare regardless of women's employment status, while their husbands were exempted from such responsibilities as the ones who had to be served by their wives. This patriarchal arrangement was often mentioned in the narratives of many wild geese parents. For example, a wild geese mother named Jaehee defined herself as "one who raises and feeds children." A wild geese father named Hyungdon proudly said, "When we lived together [in Korea], my wife was awfully good to me. She even washed my feet whenever I came home from work." Another wild geese father named Sangho asserted, "I did not even lift my finger [at home]." A third wild geese father named Dongyup stated, "My wife took care of me [when we lived together in Korea] . . . from my socks to tie."

While about one-fourth of wild geese parents shared the household labor with their spouses, it was still almost always women who performed more housework than their husbands. Of the sixty-four wild geese parents in my study, no one reported that men did more housework than their wives prior to transnational family separation. Instead, wild geese fathers generally meant more work to their wives. At best, these men were seen as helpers rather than equal contributors to housework. Hence, wild geese fathers' offerings of sharing housework or even *substitute offerings*[14] in another area were still praised as something that their wives should be very grateful for. For example, according to a wild geese mother named Eunji, she had a lot of additional housework in Korea because of her husband. She had to clean up her husband's mess, cooked gourmet food for him, cleaned his toilet, and washed his smelly clothes because of his heavy smoking and drinking. Even though she did more than 90 percent of housework, Eunji still claimed that her husband was attentive and that she even felt grateful to him, because when she did not want to cook, he caught her mood and suggested going out for dinner.

Accordingly, wild geese fathers' share of household labor, if they ever shared, was usually 10 percent to 20 percent and did not exceed more than 30 percent at best. Fathers often contended that their standard of cleanness was much lower than their wives' and they were likely to wait until their wives asked to share housework.[15] Fathers' household tasks were often confined to the male-typed jobs such as repairing, carrying heavy stuffs, and doing out-door chores,[16] which were not a part of routine daily housework. Even if they sometimes shared the female-type housework, fathers still tended to perform more enjoyable and noticeable tasks on an irregular basis,[17] such as playing with kids only on some weekends while their wives were cleaning, vacuuming, mopping, or doing the dishes. Fathers often had leverage to choose the types of housework they liked to perform based on their own preferences. In contrast, wild geese mothers, as primary homemakers, had to perform the much greater share of housework. Their tasks were also typically regular, dirtier, devalued, and less favorable.[18] In particular, meal preparation and doing laundry were the two typical female-type tasks that were rarely shared by wild geese fathers.

Interestingly, wild geese mothers' paid employment was not sufficient to lead to an egalitarian division of household labor between wild geese couples when they lived together in Korea. Working wild geese mothers still performed the *second shift* without much support from their husbands, as Hochschild observed more than three decades ago in American dual-income households.[19] Many wild geese fathers with full-time working wives often argued that they had busier work schedule than their wives and/or they earned greater income than their wives. Such arguments were wild geese fathers' effective gender strategies for justifying their smaller share of housework, as suggested by the time availability perspective and the relative resources perspective.

A wild geese father named Changsung is a businessman who works for a global corporation. When he was living with his family in Korea before trans-national family separation, his wife also had a professional career as a highly ranked public official in Korean government. Nonetheless, Changsung still asserted his busier and unpredictable work schedule in a private company, combined with his higher income than hers, as the legitimate reasons for his not sharing housework with his full-time working wife:

Changsung: When my wife was in Korea, because I was busier and earned more than her, I told her that "You do all the [house]work," and I was just working [outside] . . .

Sehwa: It is very interesting. Can you explain a little more about it?

Changsung: When I told her, "You have to do more [house]work because you earn less than me," then my wife responded to me "Ok, but let's see later." [Although she earned less than me], she would have stable income from her public official pension after her retirement [laugh] . . . In addition, [unlike me] she also went to her office on time and left on time. Because she came home exactly on time, my wife could manage it [without my help].

Oftentimes, husband's busier work schedule was also accepted by their wives as the legitimate reason for the unequal distribution of household labor between spouses, particularly if wild geese mothers were full-time homemakers or worked part-time in Korea. For example, Dambi, a wild geese mother who used to work part-time as a private tutor prior to migration, says that she did all the housework in Korea because her husband was a public official and was very busy:

My husband was so busy [in Korea]. He rarely helped me with managing our household. For example, I repaired the electricity [typical men's housework], did all the housework, and managed bank accounts. In short, my husband just went to work, and I did all the rest.

Moreover, even though some wild geese mothers earned much more than their husbands in Korea, their higher income did not help these women reduce their amount of housework. These highly achieving women still performed the majority of housework, whereas their husbands were still avoiding housework.[20] Three women's stories are followed.

Bora, a wild geese mother who used to work in Korea as a teacher and tutor, earned more money prior to migration than her husband who was studying for a long time until he finally became a professor. Nonetheless, she still had to perform all the housework alone without her husband's help. According to Bora, her husband always told her, "Complete the housework first and then do other works in your spare time. If you cannot adequately perform [your] housework, don't have other jobs." Encountered by her husband's such patriarchal attitudes, Bora did not challenge him. Rather, she felt guilty and ashamed if house was not neat and clean, as if she neglected her duty as a good housewife.

Another wild geese mother named Sowon was a banker and earned much more money than her husband who was a small business owner. During her marriage in Korea, Sowon not only made a living with her own salary but also paid for her husband's university tuition and financially supported her husband to launch new businesses several times. Nonetheless, Sowon neither nagged her husband with financial issues nor asked her husband to share housework. Sowon said that she did not want to hurt her husband's pride as a man because he had already had a hard time outside due to his series of unsuccessful business.

Third wild geese mother named Seyoung had a very successful career as a professor and directly mentioned protecting her husband's masculinity as the primary reason for her unequal distribution of household labor before transnational spousal separation. Both Seyoung and her husband were doctoral degree holders. She got her degree earlier than her husband, though. After graduation, she was the first one to get an academic job and received numerous awards as a professor, whereas her husband got a researcher position, although he aspired to be a professor. Accordingly, even though Seyoung's husband was quickly promoted to the position of senior engineer in his company and earned four to five times higher income than her, they both still felt that he achieved much less than her because of the disparity in their jobs' prestige, which continued to remain as a serious source of their spousal tension throughout the marriage. Accordingly, as a tactic to protect her husband's masculinity and maintain their marital relationship peaceful and intact, Seyoung minimized her academic accomplishment in front of her husband and performed all the housework alone rather than asking for equal sharing:

> [When we lived together] I could not tell him that I received an award. Because he did not know my field, I minimized [the value of] it, saying "This is nothing special," although it was a very renowned award. I did so to protect his self-esteem. At that time, I did the dishes more, because, if I made him do the dishes, he would have been so pitiful. I only asked him to help me with something that I could not do, such as carrying heavy stuffs like a pack of water bottles and big trash bags. I could not ask him to prepare meals or do the dishes, because he might have thought that "My wife made me do these because I was not so successful." Because my husband had not achieved as much as he wanted, I could not demand him to share the household labor. I wanted to protect his masculinity. I wanted to respect his territory so that he could be more successful.

These three stories certainly evidence that it was neither relative income nor available time that resulted in the unequal division of household labor between these couples whose wives had greater income or higher social status than their husbands. It is gender that provides a better explanation of such a patriarchal housework pattern of these couples. Wild geese mothers who earned greater income than their husbands tried to show their conformity to the patriarchal social norms of ideal wifehood by doing most of housework alone, whereas wild geese fathers who earned lesser than their wives tried to reassert their threatened masculinity and symbolic authority as the head of the household by avoiding housework. This is also similar to the patterns observed among the American dual-earner couples in Hochschild's study, in that "the more severely a man's identity is financially threatened—by his wife's higher salary, for example—the less he can afford to threaten it further by doing 'woman's work at home.'"[21]

Of course, such an unequal division of household labor was not maintained without spousal confrontations. Some wild geese mothers, particularly those who had successful professional careers with very busy work schedules, were quite upset with such an unfair situation and attempted to challenge it. Unfortunately, their trials often led to serious spousal conflicts and confrontations rather than an improved division of labor.[22] Chaerim, a successful businesswoman who worked in a global company prior to migration, well describes how she had a hard time with her husband in Korea:

Actually, I was very discontented in Korea. I had to work [outside], take care of a child, and do all the housework, whereas my husband only worked [outside]. So, we fought a lot. "Why do I have to do all, while you just work [outside]?" I could have been more successful if I had only worked [outside]. However, because of my child, I had to leave my office on time while reading my supervisor's face. I also did not work on weekends because of my child. I gave up so many things [about my career], but my husband worked as hard as he wanted. I was very discontented with it.

Some wild geese parents, both mothers and fathers, further admit that they cursed and even threw stuffs at each other during their quarrels. A few also report that they had thought of divorce because of the endless spousal conflicts on the division of domestic responsibilities.

Finally, after years of spousal struggles, many working mothers in my study adopted an alternative gender strategy to reduce their domestic workload, which was getting help from other women, particularly from their own mothers and paid help rather than continuously fighting with husbands who were reluctant or refused to share. Middle-class women's reliance on other women to relieve their burden of domestic duties is not unique to Korean wild geese mothers. It is rather commonly observed across generations and cultures.[23] In summary, many wild geese mothers managed a quite patriarchal life in Korea, performing multiple roles for their families, often sacrificing their careers and interests, and being subordinate to their husbands.[24]

CHANGING HOUSEWORK PATTERNS AFTER SEPARATION: WILD GEESE MOTHERS

Significant changes in the gendered patterns of household labor have emerged after transnational spousal separation on both ends, that is, wild geese mothers and fathers. On the one hand, wild geese mothers no longer find reasons for *doing gender* by performing a lot of housework in the absence of their husbands, needless to say that they do not have to (and cannot) take care of their husbands. Like women who left "coresidential unions" through separation or widowhood in Gupta's study,[25] most wild geese mothers in my study perform much less amount of housework after migration. Yet, they no longer feel guilty about reduced housework because they have left "coresidential unions" through transnational spousal separation and have been released from the patriarchal social pressure to perform good wifehood. Rather, they are greatly satisfied with their decreased load of household labor.

A wild geese mother named Sohee used to be a full-time homemaker in Korea. Prior to migration, Sohee felt that she was like a *maid* of her husband. However, after migration, Sohee feels much more comfortable and freer, because she no longer has to perform housework perfectly to meet her husband's high expectation. Sohee is particularly happy because she does not have to iron scores of her businessman husband's dress shirts every weekend and wait for his approval.

Similarly, another wild geese mother named Bora used to work full-time in Korea. Prior to migration, Bora performed all the housework without her husband's support. After migration, Bora feels that she is now *liberated* from the pressure forcing her to maintain her house in a very neat and clean condition. Bora no longer feels ashamed even if she does not wash dishes after every meal, as she is not living with her husband who used to keep a close eye on her performance as a good homemaker.

In addition to wild geese mothers who used to be full-time homemakers in Korea, wild geese mothers who used to have professional jobs and suffered from serious spousal conflicts on the division of housework in Korea also feel much more relaxed after migration as they no longer face such disputes. The following stories of three wild geese mothers provide good examples.

A wild geese mother named Jiyoung had a job as a programmer in Korea. After transnational spousal separation, Jiyoung feels that she has become happier not just because of her lessened housework time for cleaning and cooking. She is even more satisfied because she no longer has any conflict with her husband over the division of household labor. Jiyoung adds:

One important benefit of living apart [from husband] is that I no longer have a quarrel with my husband [about sharing housework]. Rather, we try to share something good on the phone. I no longer have argument with him on such topics as "who should do cleaning." I like the fact that we don't confront each other on the division of daily household duties.

Another wild geese mother named Minhee worked as a journalist in Korea. Similar to Jiyoung, Minhee expresses great satisfaction with her reduced burden of housework and greater freedom after transnational spousal separation, even if she still continues fulfilling the role of a mother:

The upside [of transnational spousal separation] is that I no longer have to spend a lot of time for cooking. I can just prepare the food that my kids like and enjoy more free time in the evening. When I lived with my husband, I had to spare my time for him, because he was like a child, and I had to take care of this *big* child [my husband]. However, now, when I go outside for dinner or shopping, I am very comfortable because there is no longer my husband who does not like eating outside . . . I also have much fewer laundry now [after spousal separation], because I have less socks, outers, underwear, and pants.

Lastly, a wild geese mother named Dambi had a hard time handling her dual jobs as a private tutor and a homemaker in Korea. In the interview, Dambi explains how her life after transnational spousal separation has become much more de-stressed:

Frankly speaking, I did not have my own life before. I lived very busily for my husband and children. But now, I have less works as my children have become more independent and my husband is in Korea. While I did not have much time to take care of myself, I am now more relaxed and able to enjoy more time for myself. While I used to live like a superwoman, I now feel that it is not always the right path. Now, I have more room to take a rest, as I take many burdens off my shoulders.

In sum, after transnational spousal separation, the amount of housework that wild geese mothers perform has substantially decreased, which makes these women feel happier and even liberated. Such a reduction in wild geese mothers' housework load has been achieved despite their increased free time to perform housework and their greater economic dependence on their husbands, as many of them have to quit their prior jobs in Korea due to migration. Instead, wild geese mothers perform less housework after migration, because they no longer need to *do gender* in the absence of their husbands. Above all, transnational migration plays a significant role in liberating many wild geese mothers from the constant surveillance of the patriarchal home country, which forces women to endure an unfair share of housework.

CHANGING HOUSEWORK PATTERNS AFTER
SEPARATION: WILD GEESE FATHERS

To begin with, a majority of wild geese fathers in my study (60 percent) have considerably increased their amount of housework right after transnational spousal separation, similar to men who left "coresidential unions" through separation or widowhood in Gupta's study.[26] Certainly, these fathers no longer have reasons for doing gender or demonstrating their male dominance by avoiding housework in the absence of their wives. Above all, their wives are not living with them to do their chores. Nonetheless, these wild geese fathers still present a great variation in the ways they handle the increased housework responsibilities.

First, a few wild geese fathers with egalitarian gender norms gladly perform their increased housework, even including female-type housework, such as cooking, doing the dishes, and doing laundry, which many wild geese fathers are quite reluctant to perform.[27] For example, a wild geese father named Hojun was a very home-bound man. Even when he lived with his wife in Korea, house cleaning and dishwashing were his responsibility. He also enjoyed cooking some simple Korean food, even though his wife was a main chef of the house. After transnational spousal separation, he happily prepares all his meals by himself and is very proud that his overall homemaking skills have improved:

> It seems that I [now] spend about an hour [per day] for housework. If I include the time to prepare for breakfast, it may be around 1.5 hour [per day]. This includes the time for preparing a meal, doing the dishes, and cleaning up. And, while not doing on weekdays, I on weekends vacuum, run the washing machine, hang the clothes [to dry], fold them, and put them into the drawers. [. . .] I always eat both my breakfast and dinner at home except when I have to dine out with my colleagues at work. This saves my money and it is more nutritious [than eating outside]. [. . .] As I live alone, my [homemaking] skills have improved. In fact, [when living together with wife] I was good at making miso soup, kimchi stew, and steamed egg, while my wife cooked the rest of the food. Now, I not only can make various kinds of pickled vegetables. I have also tried making kimchi[28] since I lived alone.

Second, in contrast to a few wild geese fathers mentioned above, most wild geese fathers in my study find it difficult to manage the increased burden of domestic duties. Among them, some fathers even have much harder time than others, particularly because they used to be cared for by their wives from head to toe and had very little experiences of dealing with basic daily tasks. For example, an entrepreneur named Jaeman, who used to enjoy a comfortable life as his full-time homemaker wife did all the domestic work for him, provides a good description of how hard time he has been undergoing after family separation as he has to adapt himself to a new environment and handle all the daily issues by himself:

> My wife used to do everything for me, even including washing my underwear by hands [before putting it in washer]. [. . .] However, as I have to handle all the [daily] household tasks by myself [after family separation], it has become extremely difficult and challenging to me. I now skip my breakfast and have lunch at my work. Then, the next mission is how and where to have dinner. I also have to clean the house, buy new bedding for each new season, and choose my daily outfit, even though they were not my jobs before. I am also gradually learning how to do grocery shopping. There has been such a big change in my life, since I have performed many household tasks that I never did before.

Moreover, even if other wild geese fathers manage to do housework, many of them still find it especially challenging to perform the two female-type housework tasks: cooking and doing laundry. Therefore, they attempt to handle these two tasks by outsourcing them to the market economy. For example, a wild geese father named Dongyup, who has hard time in cooking and washing/ironing his clothes, tries to solve his most challenging problems by eating outside or ordering fully prepared meals online and using paid laundry services:

> I don't have time to do housework on weekdays. Instead, I do such work [housework] on weekends, such as doing laundry, cleaning, and preparing meals. On weekends, I eat a half of my meals outside and cook the other half of my meals at home. I like cooking kimchi soup and ramen. [. . .] I also go to grocery shopping on weekends. I go to the laundry shop on weekends to dry clean my dress shirts. I wash other regular clothes by myself using washing machine [at home]. [. . .] I order some food via internet. I buy kimchi via internet. When I order food online that I want to eat such as soup or stew, it is delivered by the next morning. Then, I just open and heat it to eat.

So far, I have discussed how a majority of wild geese fathers (60 percent) in my study have strived to handle the increased burden of housework after transnational spousal separation. Yet, my study also reveals that the absence of wives does not always increase wild geese fathers' instant involvement with housework: the other 40 percent of wild geese fathers in my study try to avoid any major changes in their gendered patterns of housework and to maintain their existing patriarchal lifestyle, at least at the beginning of their transnational spousal separation. Specifically, 30 percent of wild geese fathers in the study primarily rely on their own mothers and/or mothers-in-law (and sometimes sisters) as their new caretakers, whereas the remaining 10 percent of wild geese fathers get help from the female housekeepers whom their wives pre-arranged prior to the transnational spousal separation.

It is interesting to discuss how and why these 40 percent of wild geese fathers refuse to assume the increased housework. First, they may be still expected to continue *doing gender* despite their wives' absence. Given that wild geese fathers remain alone in their home country after sending their wives abroad, these left-behind men may be under the stricter surveillance of the Korean society on their manhood, because their life without wives may be deemed to violate the culturally approved gender standards. Consequently, these left-behind wild geese fathers may be highly pressured by their own families, friends, and/or colleagues into displaying the "compensatory traditional behavior" by avoiding housework, just like the economically dependent husbands in Brines's study.[29]

Second, some wild geese fathers may have greater resources than others to avoid doing housework. In Hondagneu-Sotelo's study,[30] working-class Mexican bachelors lived alone in the male-only immigrant communities after migration to the United States, and thus they had to learn how to perform housework. In contrast, wild geese fathers in my study remain in their home country where their patriarchal resources are available. Thus, some fathers may be able to absorb the initial shock of transnational spousal separation and avoid the sudden increase in their housework, (1) if they have female family members (e.g., mothers, mothers-in-law, or sisters) who are healthy enough and willing to take care of them, or (2) if they have enough money to hire domestic help (while sending a huge amount of remittances to their families abroad), or (3) if they have both female family members and enough money.

Now, let me explain how 30 percent of wild geese fathers in my study get help from their mothers and/or mothers-in-law. As both wild geese mothers and fathers commonly pointed out in their interviews, the reactions of wild geese parents' mothers to their transnational family separation tend to be quite patriarchal, in that their mothers (and their mothers-in-law) are eager to become these left-behind wild geese fathers' substitute caretakers and do the housework so that these fathers do not have to burden themselves with housework even in the absence of their wives. Wild geese fathers' mothers tend to feel enormous pity for their left-behind sons, and some of them are even upset with their daughters-in-law who are leaving their sons behind. Wild geese mothers' mothers often feel guilty and sorry for their sons-in-law as if their emigrating daughters neglect their marital duties for their own sake. This implies that the patriarchal gender ideology, which defines housework as exclusively women's domain,[31] is still deeply embedded in the Korean society, particularly among the older generations.

Because both mothers and mothers-in-law of these wild geese parents try to take care of these left-behind men as much as possible, some fathers have moved-in to their parents' or parents-in-law's houses after their wives and children emigrated. Or, they have been residing (or have relocated) very close to their mothers, sisters, or mothers-in-law so that these women regularly visit and take care of these left-behind men.

Next, about 10 percent of wild geese fathers in my study strive to continue their patriarchal lifestyle after transnational spousal separation with the assistance of female housekeepers whom their wives pre-arranged prior to their emigration. For example, a former wild geese mother named Minkyung claims, "My husband did not have any hard time [while I was gone], because at that time a housekeeping lady came twice a week to take care of him." Another former wild geese mother named Sunmi also arranged paid help to exempt her husband from doing housework during her absence:

My husband originally never helped me with housework [when we lived together in Korea]. [While I was gone], he didn't do any housework either. He just accumulated the unwashed dishes even for three to four days until the housekeeping lady came and cleaned them up.

By arranging paid domestic workers for their husbands to continuously maintain a patriarchal lifestyle, these wild geese mothers try to continue fulfilling (at least partially) their roles as good wives from distance and protect themselves from harsh criticism of neglecting their families. All in all, female family members and paid help are deemed to be successful gender strategies for both wild geese fathers and mothers to avert doubts about their gender accountability.

Nonetheless, it is important to note that living with their parents or parents-in-law does not exempt wild geese fathers from all the new challenges after transnational spousal separation. A following story of wild geese father named Kangsan provides a good example.

Kangsan, a journalist, moved into the house of his parents-in-law right after sending his wife and children abroad. Thus, domestic chores are not his challenges. Nonetheless, Kangsan still deeply feels the absence of his wife, as he encounters a new challenge after spousal separation: Getting a pitiful and critical look from his colleagues. As a journalist who has lots of social interactions with many people, Kangsan puts a great emphasis on his neat and trendy appearance. However, his mother-in-law cannot go for shopping with him, although she is an excellent substitute caretaker for his wife in other aspects. More often than not, his colleagues give him a pitiful gaze at his shabbier look, as if it were the evidence of his deviance from an intact marriage, which Kangsan finds it very difficult to endure. Kangsan expresses his frustration:

> My quality of life was substantially lowered [after transnational spousal separation]. I used to be totally dependent on my wife when buying some daily necessities, such as business outfit. When we went out together for shopping, she advised me which clothing was better for me. However, I no longer have such a person. While I need to buy new clothes for a new season, I don't have anyone to go shopping with. Buying clothes has become one of the most challenging things to me, because I don't know what is necessary for me and what provides good fit to me. It is such a hard job to me. My colleagues at work often tease me and say, "It is so noticeable that you live alone." Do they really notice from my appearance that I am no longer cared for by my wife? I try not to disclose [the absence of my wife], but it is so obvious.

Besides, living with parents or parents-in-law often poses additional issues: Wild geese fathers who live with either their parents or parents-in-law may feel growing emotional burdens. Some feel sorry to continuously rely on their aging mothers. Others feel uncomfortable to live with their parents, because they have lived independent lives for a long time after marriage. Consequently, some of these fathers have finally moved out of their parents' houses to live alone.

Likewise, getting help from the paid domestic workers is not a viable solution either, particularly when their transnational spousal separation is lengthier, because wild geese fathers are confronted by the increasing economic burdens of maintaining two middle-class transnational households. Thus, among the wild geese fathers who were dependent on paid help in the beginning of transnational spousal separation, some have stopped using expensive housekeeping services and have a hard time to adjust to their new independent life. The following story of a former wild geese father named Joonsoo offers a good example.

Joonsoo is a professor at a prestigious university in Korea and has recently reunited with his family after nine years of transnational family separation. For the first three years of separation, Joonsoo lived in his spacious house alone and relied on paid help. However, for the following six years, Joonsoo moved to a small studio and performed all housework by himself without getting any paid help, because of budget constraints. Joonsoo gives a detailed description of his struggles and challenges with housework, including his unsuccessful efforts to eat healthy and keep his house clean:

When I used to live with my wife [before transnational spousal separation], because she was a committed woman, I did not have to care about the domestic work. So, after she left, I didn't know what to do. If I had been trained, I could have done housework [by myself]. However, I was not. So, I was compelled to use a housekeeping lady. However, over time, I felt it was very expensive. So, I moved to a small studio nearby [and stopped using housekeeping service]. However, after living in a small studio, I had a very hard time doing laundry and cleaning. And the most serious problem was what to eat. I even did not know how to cook miso soup or soft tofu soup. [. . .] After I learned how to cook tofu, I ate only tofu for a year. [. . .] In my house, some flies were always flying around, because there was always leftover food in the sink. Even if I ate just a fruit [at home], once I peeled off its skin I should have thrown it away [to the trash can] but I did not, which made some pest swarming in my house.

Overall, while their paths are quite different, most wild geese fathers in my study have eventually assumed a greater amount of housework after lengthy transnational spousal separation. Although a few men perform their house-work without much difficulty, many other wild geese fathers have hard time in handling increased domestic duties in their everyday lives.

Interestingly, wild geese fathers' new challenges have some positive impacts on their transnational spousal relationships. As they struggle with housework, wild geese fathers happen to recognize the overlooked sacrifices of their wives who endured the unfair share of domestic responsibilities. Thus, they start increasingly expressing their gratitude and affection to their wives abroad. They are also more willing to share domestic duties with their wives, whenever they visit their families abroad. Of note, how wild geese fathers' increased amount of housework, combined with their expression of gratitude for their wives, affect their transnational spousal relationship is discussed in-depth in chapter 3.

CONCLUSION

This chapter explores how wild geese parents' housework patterns have reconstructed through transnational spousal separation. Prior to their transna-tional spousal separation, wild geese parents did not equally share domestic duties. Even wild geese mothers who earned higher income than their hus-bands also performed a vast majority of housework. However, after trans-national spousal separation, wild geese parents' housework patterns have significantly changed. Wild geese mothers have substantially reduced their housework as they no longer have to show their love and subordination to their husbands by doing more housework. Likewise, a majority of wild geese fathers have incredibly increased their housework after transnational spousal separation, as they can no longer demonstrate their self-esteem and masculinity by avoiding housework. This finding empirically supports the gender perspective, because it is gender rather than available time or relative resources that have shaped the patterns of housework between wild geese couples.

In addition, this chapter shows that transnational spousal separation plays a critical role in liberating many wild geese mothers from the patriarchal surveillance of the home country on their ideal wifehood so that these women are able to reduce the amount of housework without feeling guilty. That is, not only by leaving "coresidential unions" but also by leaving the home country, wild geese mothers are freed from pressure of doing gender as they no longer encounter questions on their gender accountability from family members, friends, and/or the Korean society.

On the other hand, the impact of transnational spousal separation is more complicated for wild geese fathers. Even if wild geese fathers have left the coresidential unions through transnational spousal separation, they still remain in their home country. Because of their apparent deviance from the living arrangement of so-called ideal marriage (i.e., married couples living together in the same household), these fathers tend to get many questions from the society on the intactness of their marriage. They are also exposed to the stricter surveillance on their ideal manhood. Therefore, to reclaim their gender accountability, some wild geese fathers, who have greater patriarchal resources (such as female family members) and/or economic resources (such as paid help), continue doing gender and maintaining traditional housework patterns. This indicates that changes in the patriarchal housework patterns are more difficult to happen to wild geese fathers who remain in home country than their wives who have left the country.

Nonetheless, as transnational separation is lengthier, even if some wild geese fathers used to stick to the patriarchal housework arrangement in the beginning, they also have eventually increased their involvement with domestic duties. This demonstrates that the effect of leaving "coresidential unions" is strong enough to reconfigure the patriarchal housework patterns of married couples in the transnational context and that this effect is stronger when the spousal separation is lengthier.

Finally, this chapter extends the existing theories of household labor, which have been developed mainly based on the experiences of married couples residing in the same country, to the transnational context. The analysis of wild geese parents' changing housework patterns through transnational spousal separation helps further test and elaborate those theories of household labor to better explain the experiences of diverse groups of people in various household types.

NOTES

1. Shelly Coverman, "Explaining Husbands' Participation in Domestic Labor," *Sociological Quarterly* 26 (1985): 81–97.

2. Bureau of Labor Statistics, "American Time Use Survey – 2019 Results" (Washington, DC), accessed November 25, 2020, https://www.bls.gov/news.release/atus.nr0.htm.

3. Julie Brines, "Economic Dependency, Gender, and the Division of Labor at Home," *American Journal of Sociology* 100 (1994): 655–657.

4. Ibid., 673–676.

5. South and Spitze, "Housework," 327.

6. Bianchi et al., "Is Anyone Doing," 194.

7. West and Zimmerman, "Doing Gender," 125.

8. Ibid., 135–137.

9. South and Spitze, "Housework," 340–341.

10. Ibid., 342–343.

11. Sanjiv Gupta, "The Effects of Transitions in Marital Status on Men's Performance of Housework," *Journal of Marriage and Family* 61 (1999): 706–708.

12. Brines, "Economic Dependency," 676–682.

13. Ibid., 665.

14. See Hochschild, *Second Shift*, 210–212 for men's diverse gender strategies of not sharing housework with their wives. According to Hochschild, "substitute offerings" mean that men's support to their wives in alternative realms rather than actually sharing housework.

15. Similar patterns were observed in American families. See Hochschild, *Second Shift*, 210–211.

16. Gender differentials in the types of household labor performed by married couples were also commonly observed in American households. See South and Spitze, "Housework," 342–343.

17. Similar patterns were observed in American families. See Bianchi et al., "Is Anyone Doing," 195.

18. This is also commonly observed in American households. See South and Spitze, "Housework," 342–343; Bianchi et al., "Is Anyone Doing," 195.

19. Hochschild defines women's paid work at the office or factory as the "first shift," and their unpaid work at home as the "second shift." See Hochschild, *Second Shift*, 4.

20. Economically dependent husbands' resistance to sharing housework with their wives with higher income is also observed in other studies. The more men were economically dependent on their wives, the less they were willing to share housework with their wives. See Brines, "Economic Dependency," 677–682; Hochschild, *Second Shift*, 231–232.

21. Hochschild, *Second Shift*, 221.

22. For discussion on economically active Korean immigrant women's challenge to unequal gender status at home and following marital conflicts, see Min, "Korean

Immigrants' Gender Role," 311–314; Lim, "Korean Immigrant Women's Challenge," 37–42.

23. For other cases, see Evelyn Nakano Glenn, "From Servitude to Service Work: The Historical Continuities of Women's Paid and Unpaid Reproductive Labor," *Signs: Journal of Women in Culture and Society* 18, no. 1 (1992): 30; Hochschild, *Second Shift*, 207–208; Parreñas, "Migrant Filipina Domestic Workers," 569–571.

24. Similar pattern is also documented in Asian immigrant women. See Grahame, "For the Family," 80.

25. Gupta, "Effects of Transitions," 706–708.

26. Ibid.

27. Lee, "I am Still Close," 12; See Gupta, "Effects of Transitions," 707 and South and Spitze, "Housework," 342–343 for men's increased share in gender-typed housework.

28. Kimchi is very popular traditional Korean fermented vegetable dish. While many Koreans eat kimchi everyday as their side dish, it is generally difficult to make it so that many full-time housewives buy it rather than make it.

29. Brines, "Economic Dependency," 666.

30. Hondagneu-Sotelo, *Gendered Transitions*, 104–106.

31. England, "Mothers, Wives, Workers," 109–122; Ehrenreich and Hochschild, "Introduction," 1–13; Moon, "Immigration and Mothering," 840–860; Parreñas, "Migrant Filipina Domestic Workers," 560–580.

Chapter 3

Transnational Spousal Relationships

Wild geese parents are child-centered.[1] That is, they tend to prioritize their parenting duties over their spousal relationship and readily sacrifice their marital relations for the sake of their children's education.[2] It is known that such child-centeredness can have a deleterious effect on the quality of the spousal relationship, especially if the spousal separation lasts long. For example, a study of Chinese *study mothers* who live apart transnationally from husbands for children's education shows that some mothers engage in sex work at massage and foot reflexology centers in the host countries to earn additional income for their children's education abroad, that some husbands in China have extramarital affairs, and that these couples often end in divorce.[3] Likewise, Korean wild geese parents may not be free from such marital issues during their lengthy transnational separation. Even if such drastic events as marital affairs or divorce do not occur to every couple, it seems evident that transnational spousal separation has some adverse effects on the quality of their spousal relationship over time.[4]

Then, does marital quality always deteriorate as spouses stay separate longer? Previous studies on wild geese families have mainly focused on the negative experiences due to transnational separation,[5] and they have neglected the fact that many wild geese couples make tremendous efforts to overcome the challenges throughout their separation and maintain their emotional connection.

Of the sixty-four wild geese parents in my study, most have maintained an intact marriage by the time of interview, while seven are undergoing marital crises, including divorce, divorce proceedings, separation, remarriage, and spousal death. Wild geese parents, on average, have been separated transnationally for about four years with a wide range from six months to thirteen years. Interestingly, however, the length of transnational spousal separation is not much longer for the seven parents who are undergoing marital crises than the rest, as it is 4.5 years for these seven parents (mostly two to five years, eight months for the divorced parent, and thirteen years for a separated parent). In other words, the length of separation may not necessarily undermine the quality of spousal relationships. Rather, many wild geese parents in my study have managed to overcome various challenges throughout the separation and have maintained intimate spousal relationships until they successfully reunite after a long transnational separation, or at the time of the interview.

In this chapter, I explore how the spousal relationships between wild geese parents have changed during their transnational separation. Specifically, I examine how transnational spousal separation triggers a reconfiguration of the spousal relationship, as it removes some sources of the existing spousal conflict and creates new sources. Then, I discuss how wild geese parents' emotional and sexual relationships with their spouses have changed during their transnational separation. With regards to the spousal problems that arise during the separation, I pay close attention to how some wild geese parents address such issues more successfully than others. Lastly, some changes in the spousal relationship that have occurred after family reunification are also explored. In doing so, I seek to better illuminate some of the consequences, as well as the full processes, of transnational spousal separation for the spousal relationships.

CHANGING MEANING OF MARRIAGE

Most studies of wild geese families have focused primarily on the motivations[6] for becoming transnationally split families and the changes and challenges[7] in wild geese parents' everyday lives after their separation. While a small number of studies have discussed changes in wild geese parents' spousal relationships over time,[8] they fail to provide an in-depth analysis of the reasons why the quality of the transnational spousal relationships has deteriorated. In addition, the sexuality of these transnational couples has been largely overlooked. Only a few studies have briefly mentioned, without further explanation, that sexual relations are an important issue for wild geese fathers but not for wild geese mothers.[9]

My analysis of the changing spousal relationships between Korean wild geese parents is geared toward answering these questions: How does the transnational separation trigger changes in the conjugal relationships and how does spousal intimacy change? Theories in the areas of migration and family studies provide a useful framework for the analysis. Scholarship on migration has emphasized transnational spousal separation as a critical event that triggers significant changes that otherwise would have been unimaginable and has tried to explain how such changes affect the conjugal relations.[10] Some studies have found that women's migration elevates their bargaining power in family matters and increases men's share of housework, resulting in more egalitarian conjugal relations during the lengthy spousal separation[11] and after the reunification of the transnational couples in the host countries.[12] Other studies have suggested the opposite findings: Migrant women's status is lowered because of their increased economic dependence on their husbands, combined with their failure to address the continuous challenges and uncertainties they encounter in the host society as *transient sojourners*.[13] These different findings in migration scholarship indicate that even if transnational spousal separation triggers significant changes in the spousal relations, such changes can be quite heterogeneous depending on various other factors.

Previous studies on wild geese families uniformly have focused on the negative effects of the lengthy spousal separation on intimacy between wild geese couples.[14] However, my study challenges such a simplistic description. I argue that transnational spousal separation can have varying effects, depending on the ways in which wild geese parents define marriage, conjugal roles, and the success of marriage. In this regard, theories in the field of family studies are quite useful to understand the varying effects of transnational spousal separation on the conjugal relations of migrant couples.

In particular, Cherlin's discussion of the changing meaning of marriage helps understand why the patterns of wild geese parents' transnational spousal relationships are much more heterogeneous than how they are commonly characterized by the mass media and scholars. According to Cherlin, American marriage has changed from (1) *institutional marriage* before industrialization to (2) *companionate marriage* in the twentieth century and to (3) *individualized marriage* in the contemporary era.[15] In institutional marriage, the marital relationship is built on economic needs and familial obligations. Thus, the success of marriage is defined by the partners' successful fulfillment of their marital roles rather than by their romantic intimacy. In companionate marriage, marital success is determined by the emotional ties between spouses, that is, "companionship, friendship, romantic love, and sex life,"[16] as well as by each spouse's fulfillment of distinctive gender roles. In the contemporary era of individualized marriage, marital success is mainly evaluated by the degree to which the each spouse feels happy and fulfilled as an individual within marriage.

WILD GEESE PARENTS' DEFINITION
OF SUCCESSFUL MARRIAGE

Then, what does successful marriage mean to wild geese parents? None of them pursue marital satisfaction primarily through their individual fulfillment. Instead, they are highly satisfied with their marriage when they fulfill their marital roles and maintain close emotional ties with their spouses, which fits Cherlin's definition of companionate marriage. That is, emotional ties and marital roles are the two pivotal elements of the high-quality spousal relationships between wild geese parents, as they do for American couples in Cherlin's study.[17]

However, my study modifies Cherlin's framework of companionate marriage, as I analytically separate sexual intimacy from emotional intimacy. Whereas American couples in Cherlin's study emphasize romantic love or sex life as an integral part of their successful companionate marriage,[18] most wild geese parents (both women and men) in my study do not consider spousal sexual intimacy to be a critical factor of their marital success. Rather, many wild geese parents still maintain intimate emotional connections with their spouses even if they do not have frequent and regular sexual intercourse during the lengthy transnational separation.

Moreover, wild geese parents tend to believe that their marriage is intact and successful if the spouses successfully fulfill their traditional gender roles as parents (the wife as a caretaker and the husband as a breadwinner) and if their children achieve successful educational outcomes (i.e., children improve in English proficiency and/or enter prestigious universities in North America or Korea).[19] Many parents resonate such definitions of successful marriage in their comments:

> When you make a decision of living apart, you admit that it [sex life] is not so critical. We have a child. For me, it is more important that we devotedly fulfill our roles as mother and father. (Chaerim, second-year wild geese mother)

> In the third year [of transnational separation], I once became doubtful of my spousal relationship. I was wondering whether we had to keep living this way, meeting just once a year. However, considering how much my children would have suffered if they returned [to Korea prematurely], I felt pathetic for them. So, we decided to endure couple more years. After my son entered a prestigious university, I have concluded that we made a great decision. [Sangho, thirteenth-year wild geese father]

At the same time, serious spousal conflicts arise between wild geese parents when spouses do not seem to adequately fulfill their expected gender roles, that is, when wild geese children show unsatisfactory educational outcomes or when husbands fail to send enough remittances:

> I am lucky because my wife is such a good person and we rarely fought. Nonetheless, I was still upset and fought [with her] whenever I found that my children's [academic] record was not good. I tended to evaluate the [marital]

success based on children's record. So, I nagged [her] a lot, which I regret. (Joonsoo, former wild geese father who reunited with his wife after nine years of transnational separation)

[After sending families abroad] I opened a new business and underwent some rise and fall [financially]. Whenever the remittances were delayed just couple days, my wife nagged me. She did not know the situation here. She might have a hard time because of [economic] difficulty, but I was annoyed because she did not understand my hardships. (Jaeman, fifth-year wild geese father)

Contrarily, when asked questions about their marital satisfaction primarily based on their own sake (rather than based on their entire family), many wild geese parents express mixed feelings. Both wild geese mothers and fathers admit that they have greatly sacrificed their spousal relationship for their children's future. Some also note that they seem to have weaker emotional ties with their spouses after separation. Half of the wild geese parents feel that they have been gradually estranged from their spouses through the lengthy spousal separation, whereas the other half believe that they have successfully maintained a companionate marriage by keeping or even enhancing their emotional intimacy (and often sexual intimacy as well) with their spouses.

QUALITY OF SPOUSAL RELATIONSHIPS BEFORE SEPARATION

Marital relationships prior to transnational spousal separation are greatly varied among wild geese parents. At one extreme, some had a strong emotional bond with their spouses and a happy marriage. In these families, wild geese fathers tended to be home-oriented men, and couples spent a lot of time together, actively expressed their affection to their spouses, and talked a lot about diverse issues, from everyday lives of their family and children to more serious topics such as planning for retirement and elderly life. Some wild geese parents described their spousal relationship as friend-like. Moreover, others reported that they were so close to each other that they could not live without their spouses.

At the other extreme, some wild geese parents had conflictual spousal relationships. The sources of spousal conflicts before transnational separation included the unequal division of household labor and child-rearing responsibilities between spouses, wives' heavy burden of traditional obligations as wives and filial daughters-in-law, husbands' inappropriate behaviors (such as heavy drinking, smoking, and staying out all night), and husbands' domineering demeanor in their interactions with their wives. A former wild geese mother named Sunmi explains how she had a conflictual marriage prior to her migration because of her husband's misbehaviors:

> Not to mention the large number of mistakes my husband had made from the beginning of our marriage, he liked stuffs like smoking, drinking, singing, and dancing. When I once counted on a calendar, he came home at dawn twenty-five days in a month. He believed he was always right and acted as he pleased. Thus, we could not help but confront each other in every aspect. At that time, I gave up and treated him like a man who was living in my neighborhood. If I had not had a religion, I never would have lived with him.

Such marital tension and conflict were more common and serious between dual-career couples than between single-career couples (i.e., working husband and homemaker wife). Professional wild geese mothers in my study had jobs as good as their husbands' and made equal or similar contributions to their family economy. Nevertheless, as described in chapter 2, these women still had to perform the majority of housework and child-rearing duties, even if some of them earned more than their husbands, because of the patriarchal gender ideology that relegated housework and nurturing exclusively to women.[20] When these women challenged such an unfair situation, it often resulted in serious spousal conflicts and confrontations.

Some of the wild geese parents in my sample admitted that they cursed their spouses and threw items at each other during their quarrels, and a few even considered divorce because of the endless conflict regarding the division of domestic responsibilities. A former wild geese father named Jaehoon says, "We had many fights before she went abroad. Because we fought too many times, we even considered divorce couple of times." Interestingly, such a serious marital crisis also made it easier for some wild geese parents to make their decision on transnational separation. A wild geese mother named Bora is a good example. Bora says:

> We had a hard time back then because of our persistent conflicts. It was a [marital] crisis, right before I came to Canada. That's why we could relatively easily make a decision [of our transnational spousal separation]. It was about the fifteenth year of our marriage.

Between these two extremes, there were some parents who were gradually entering a stage of ennui after many years of marriage. Some had come to feel estranged from their spouses over time so that they no longer expressed their affection or had frequent sexual relations. These wild geese parents also stopped having meaningful conversations and spending time with their spouses. For example, a wild geese father named Seunghyun describes his pre-migration relationship with his wife as "friends-enemies who lived together so long time that each felt bothersome." Thus, these wild geese parents' marriage shifted from companionate marriage that emphasized the emotional and sexual ties between spouses to institutional marriage which was primarily maintained by the performance of each spouse's marital roles.

Surprisingly, despite such great variations, the quality of spousal relationships before the separation was not a critical determinant of spousal relationships after the separation. That is, neither a conflictual relationship nor an intimate relationship necessarily remained the same after the transnational spousal separation. Rather, other important factors influenced the quality of transnational spousal relationships between wild geese parents: (1) the spousal separation itself, which reminded them of the overlooked value of each other and removed some prior sources of spousal conflict, (2) the maintenance of emotional intimacy through the expression of gratitude and affection to spouses, and (3) the maintenance of sexual intimacy.

CHANGES THROUGH TRANSNATIONAL SPOUSAL SEPARATION

For most wild geese couples in my study, the decision-making process on transnational separation was generally peaceful and based on mutual agreement rather than conflict. To the eyes of wild geese parents who were highly child-centered,[21] their children's (potential) benefits from education abroad absolutely outweighed the possible sacrifice of their own spousal relationships due to lengthy transnational spousal separation.

Interestingly, spousal separation has played some positive roles and has contributed to enhancing the quality of the conjugal relationship between many wild geese parents, as it unexpectedly provides them with a valuable opportunity to reflect on their marital relationship and recognize the overlooked value of their spouses. For example, a wild geese mother named Damso, who used to be an extremely busy high school teacher in Korea, had a conflictual spousal relationship prior to her migration:

> My class began in the very early morning and oftentimes it ended at 9:00 pm or 9:30 pm. Then, when I got home, it was 10:30 pm. I was as busy as typical male businessmen working for big corporations. I was always nervous and extremely tired and had many troubles with my husband.

However, after migration, Damso has developed a better spousal relationship:

[After migration] I have become much more relaxed, as I no longer have a title of teacher. [. . .] We also increasingly feel sympathy for each other because of our similarly lonely situations. So, my husband and I have fought much less now, while we used to fight a lot [when we lived together]. We have a better relationship now [laugh].

Similarly, Changsung, first-year wild geese father who used to have lots of conflict with his wife before separation, also has recognized the overlooked value of his wife through transnational separation and makes a greater effort to restore his spousal relationship:

[At the time of transnational separation] We had been married for about ten years and felt bored about each other. We also fought a lot. She complained that I drank a lot, came home late, and just slept all day long on weekends while not caring about children, even if all the [Korean] businessmen were doing like me. We had many troubles on it. However, since we lived part, my wife seems to re-appreciate the value of her husband, and I also have come to think that I should have been nicer to her. Through our separation, although we both never intended, we have recognized the value of each other and have come to make more efforts to better understand each other. If we had kept lived together, I might have fought even more with her.

In addition, transnational spousal separation promotes marital quality as it removes the existing sources of spousal conflicts. In particular, it is noteworthy that spousal disputes on the unfair division of domestic responsibilities have substantially decreased through transnational separation.[22] Wild geese mothers have enjoyed a greater level of freedom as they find much smaller amount of housework in the absence of their husbands. Wild geese fathers have increasingly felt grateful to their wives who used to perform most housework, which many of these fathers found overwhelming. In short, significant changes in the amount of housework performed by each spouse greatly help many wild geese parents to positively re-shape their spousal relationships.

Interestingly, the positive impact of spousal separation is even more noticeable among the dual-career couples who used to have serious spousal conflicts over the division of domestic obligations, because they no longer have to argue about such issues with their spouses. The following story of wild geese father named Sungjae provides a good example.

When Sungjae lived together with his wife in Korea, both of them had prestigious professional careers and yet his wife took care of their child almost exclusively. Sungjae always refused to share domestic duties with his wife, saying, "I am so busy" or "I have an important meeting today." As a result, Sungjae had a very conflictual relationship with his wife:

[When we lived together in Korea] I fought with my wife every day, really. We badly cursed each other due to the [division of] childcare in particular. We fought to the extent that I thought I had mental illness.

However, after living apart, Sungjae and his wife have time to cool down and have profound conversations to learn about each other's position. In addition, having performed the housework that he did not previously do, Sungjae has finally understood how difficult it was for his working wife to manage both work and family without his support. Thus, he has become, for the first time, willing to share household labor with his wife. Sungjae says:

Managing my everyday life, I have realized how much I did not help my wife. As I live alone, there is more housework to do than I expected. I have to water the plants. I have to do housework that my wife used to do, such as vacuuming the floor and cleaning the bathroom. I now realize that women's life in Korea is not so easy. They have to take care of children. They have to clean the house. So, I now want to help my wife do housework.

Like Sungjae, many wild geese fathers have recognized and appreciated their wives' sacrifices as the primary homemaker and caregiver, regardless of their wives' employment status, and are more willing to share domestic duties with their wives, which opens up the possibility for many wild geese parents to greatly improve their spousal relationship.

Moreover, through transnational spousal separation, many wild geese fathers' domineering demeanor over their wives, which used to be another important source of spousal conflict, have gradually disappeared. This positive change is closely related to the fact that many wild geese mothers have assumed more expanded roles after migration and challenged the taken-for-granted male supremacy in their transnational households. Wild geese mothers, after migration, are supposed to dedicate themselves to their domestic responsibility, which is performing *intensive mothering*[23] to achieve their children's successful educational outcomes. Nonetheless, as noted earlier in chapter 1, some wild geese mothers actively seek paid employment in the host countries in order to overcome the imminent budget constraints they encounter after migration. These women further do not mind taking the low-paid under-the-table job that are not commensurate with their high level of education and careers in Korea. Wild geese mothers' such share of the economic provider role with their husbands often positively influences their spousal relationship, because many wild geese fathers greatly appreciate their wives' unexpected economic contribution and change their patriarchal perspectives of their wives from economic dependents to equal partners.

In addition, many wild geese mothers also very independently handle their everyday challenges and make important decisions about their children's education by themselves not only because their husbands are absent but also because their husbands are not familiar with the institutions and culture of the host societies, as discussed earlier in chapter 1. Wild geese mothers' experiences as independent decision-makers have greatly increased their confidence, self-esteem, and autonomy to the level that they longer tolerate their husbands' authoritative and disrespectful attitudes toward them. Therefore, these women proactively ask their husbands to provide more emotional support for them and to explicitly express appreciation and sympathy for their hardships in the foreign country.

One wild geese couple, for which I interviewed both wife and husband, demonstrates very well how wild geese fathers' role has gradually adjusted from the leader or decision-maker to the emotional (and economic) supporter of the family over the long period of transnational spousal separation. Prior to separation, Kangsan, the husband, used to look down on his wife as someone confined to the domestic sphere. However, after migration to the United States, Kangsan's wife has successfully raised their children by herself and sent the older son to a prestigious university in the United States, while she has also contributed to the family economy through her full-time employment in a Korean immigrant-owned office. Her achievement has dramatically changed Kangsan's perspective on his wife from a disrespectful scullery maid to a respected partner:

> [Through the transnational separation,] I came to respect her, in my case. My wife independently raised my children well. She got along pretty well with [Korean] immigrants there, mostly in the Catholic Church community. She lived excellently there. I have come to think that she is a really amazing person. I want to give her a chance to keep working [when she returns to Korea]. Beforehand, she just lived like a scullery maid. . . . However, I now think of her as my partner. In my family community, she is my partner, and we no longer have a superior-subordinate relationship.

Mira, Kangsan's wife, expresses a similar sentiment. Mira says that her husband shows profound trust and respect toward her during the wild geese period, which makes her very happy and fulfilled and has greatly improved their relationship. In short, transnational spousal separation has removed some of the existing sources of spousal conflict and expanded the roles of both wild geese mother and father beyond the traditional gendered boundaries. These changes in turn have helped improve the spousal relationships between wild geese parents, because they have improved a mutual understanding of each other and because wild geese fathers show respect for their wives' improved domestic and social status.

Nevertheless, it is important to note that wild geese mothers' empowerment does not always improve the quality of their transnational spousal relationships. If wild geese fathers resist accepting their wives' enhanced authority and try to reinforce male dominance, it may intensify their conflict over the leadership within their family and thus make their transnational marital relationship much worse than before separation. The story of Yuna, a wild geese mother who has been separated from her husband for ten years, highlights this point. During the lengthy transnational spousal separation, Yuna greatly enjoys her enhanced decision-making power as an emerging leader of her family. However, in this process, Yuna has to cope with continuous conflicts with her husband:

> Being a wild geese family is not so good for spousal relationships. It needs both spouses' training. I had to humor him rather than getting into an argument. I also needed to be patient. Sometimes, I exploded and shouted at him, "Why do you try to shackle my freedom?"

Moreover, such spousal tension can even elevate after family reunification, if wild geese couples have failed to successfully rearrange their changed roles during their separation. While wild geese mothers do not want to relinquish their enhanced status, their husbands want to recover their supremacy as the head of the household and the primary decision-maker. Stories of former wild geese families that show the elevated spousal conflict after family reunification are discussed in chapter 6.

MAINTENANCE OF EMOTIONAL INTIMACY

Another important condition of intimate transnational spousal relationships is having an active verbal exchange of compassion and gratitude for their spouses' efforts, hardships, and sacrifices for the family, as Hochschild has noted earlier.[24] In my study, wild geese parents' expression of gratitude for their spouses' economic support is particularly important for maintaining a good transnational spousal relationship. Many wild geese mothers explicitly express their thankfulness and sympathy to their husbands who maintain frugal lives alone in Korea and suffer from the high stress of sending substantial remittances as the family's sole economic provider. Likewise, wild geese fathers feel that their hardships and sacrifices are rewarded when their wives and children explicitly appreciate their economic support, because sending remittances is their way of expressing love and devotion toward their families abroad.[25] Some wild geese fathers also express their deep gratitude to their wives who find employment in the host societies and share the heavy burden of economic provider.

Because of such importance of economic provision in the transnational context, when wild geese mothers are not satisfied with the amount of remittances or when wild geese fathers have an impression that their economic contribution is invisible to or taken for granted by their families abroad, wild geese couples have serious confrontations and their transnational marital relationships are deteriorated. A wild geese father named Inho exemplifies this point in his account:

> Now [after transnational spousal separation], we have conflicts because of economic issues, I mean because [my wife believes] I do not sufficiently support children. While I do my best from here [to send remittances], she asks, "Is this all?" I understand her in some way, but when she kept asking me to send more money even if I was in the difficult situation, we fought a lot. [. . .] If I were an entrepreneur, I could have sent more money [as she requested]. But, because I am a public official receiving a fixed pay, I have to handle the situation [wife's request of sending more money] by getting additional loan and paying interests. When I send her [more] money, she just says, "Thank you! I will use it well." Then, I am getting sad, because she doesn't appreciate how I managed to send that money. She doesn't consider there are many extra costs that I have to handle [in Korea] within my limited salary. For example, if I send tuition, it involves increasing interests because I have to get a tuition loan. My overdraft is increasing.

After migration, many wild geese parents also increasingly express their various emotions to their spouses, which is helpful to strengthen their emotional intimacy. In particular, wild geese fathers' growing emotional expression is noteworthy. Many wild geese fathers in my study tended to focus on their careers and overlook the importance of their families when they were living together in Korea. However, after remaining alone in Korea, a majority of wild geese fathers that I interviewed have felt deep loneliness and greatly missed their families abroad, like Mexican guest worker fathers in the Schmalzbauer's study.[26] These fathers tend to feel particularly lonely when they are sick, when they have to spend holidays and weekends by themselves, and when other people, including friends, colleagues, and even their own families, cast pitiful and critical looks on them.

A former wild geese father named Jaehoon has recently reunited with his family after three years of transnational separation. He provides a detailed description of his emotional hardships during his wild geese period, which is divided into two phases: (1) the first phase when he lived with his parents and (2) the second phase when he lived alone:

> The disadvantage [of becoming a wild geese father] is feeling solitary and lonely. It was extremely difficult time. Absolutely. When I lived with my

parents [in the first phase of the wild geese period], it was a little better, because I could control my emotions. When I started to feel depression, I could control it because I had other families who took care of me. I did not fall into the extreme [emotional] conditions. After I lived alone [in the later phase of the wild geese period], I was also OK during weekdays because I went to work early, came home late, and then just slept at home. However, on weekends, when I spent time alone on Sunday, extreme loneliness strongly hit me. It was the most difficult time for me, because I could not control my emotions at times. Once a feeling of loneliness surged on me, it surged on me without any limits.

While Jaehoon was supported by his own family during the first phase of his wild geese period, family members at times can be the main source of stress for some wild geese fathers like Sangho:

For me, it is particularly difficult to endure others' extremely negative perspectives [on my family]. My mother absolutely hates it [that I have become a wild geese father]. My younger sisters [hate it] as well. They keep questioning why I have become a wild geese father, citing other children who got a good job even if they went to a college in Korea. They ask "Why do you live so miserable, living apart from your family? Sangho, you are an idiot!"

A few wild geese fathers have even suffered from severe depression and panic disorders after transnational spousal separation, which is discussed in detail in chapter 5.[27]

Such unexpected emotional turmoil after transnational family separation provides many wild geese fathers with a valuable opportunity to deeply reflect on the overlooked importance of their families and to start more openly expressing to their wives their various emotions, ranging from love, gratitude, respect, and trust to loneliness and frustration. This would not have happened under normal circumstances, as Montes has noted in her study of Guatemalan migrant men.[28] Wild geese fathers start to tell their wives how much they love them and how happy they are when they meet their families abroad and spend time together. They also express their gratitude and respect to their wives for taking care of their children alone in foreign countries while overcoming many challenges. A substantial number of wild geese fathers even cry (with their wives noticing it) when they are talking on the phone or when they return to Korea alone after having visited their families abroad. Such an open expression of wild geese fathers' emotions has made many wild geese mothers feel increasingly sympathetic and closer to their husbands despite their physical distance and lengthy separation. The following accounts of two wild geese mothers well demonstrate this point:

Whenever we have a conversation, my husband tells me it is so difficult for him to be there [in Korea] alone. My life here is rather OK. It is the most difficult thing for me to see my husband struggling. [. . .] When we used to be together, we often fought. However, we no longer do that. We try to share good stories and console each other. I also recognize how much I am grateful to my husband. When I express how thankful I am to him, he is extremely pleased. So, I always say, "I love you, thank you." Likewise, my husband is also thankful to me because he has learned how important person I am to him since I no longer lived right next him. [. . .] I also feel pathetic about him, because of his sacrifices [for family]. While I live happily here, my husband has a hard time there, and I really feel sorry to see him struggle. (Hana, first-year wild geese mother)

When I first left Korea, I was very surprised to see my husband cry a lot in the airport, because he was not the type of person who is affectionate. Rather he is very cool-headed. I was very surprised to see he shed tears like a waterfall. Since then, whenever I made a phone call, he cried. I did not know he could be like that. While he says he gets better, I am worrying more [about him]. As we are getting older, I am more sympathetic to him. I don't know if he knows that. But, as I see he is getting older, I think how difficult he is by himself. While it is not easy for me to be here [America] alone, but I have a child with me. In contrast, he is all alone [there], which makes me really worry. [. . .] As we live apart, I am increasingly sympathetic to him, and understand him better. I also want to be good to him whenever he visits. He may have the same idea. (Sujin, sixth-year wild geese mother)

Surprisingly, not only wild geese mothers who used to have affectionate spousal relationships but also those who were estranged from their husbands prior to separation still feel great sympathy and pity for their husbands who used to be once strong, rational, and cold but are now emotionally vulnerable and craving their wives' (and children's) attention and love.

Yuri is a second-year wild geese mother who has been married for fourteen years at the time of the interview. Yuri's story demonstrates how the exchange of gratitude can significantly improve the emotional ties between transnational couples, regardless of their prior spousal relationship. According to Yuri, she had a very dry relationship with her husband in Korea and did not have much conversation with him:

My [spousal] relationship [in Korea] was not bad, but after ten years of marriage, you just live habitually. You cannot see much difference between living with this guy and that guy. In fact, I did not have much to talk about [with my husband]. I asked him on the phone, "Did you have dinner? When will you come home? Don't drink too much," and our conversation just ended. After we returned home from work, we both were tired. So, he watched TV while I was taking care of my son, helping with his homework and checking his school materials.

However, through the transnational separation, the quality of Yuri's spousal relationship has greatly improved, because both spouses exchange their gratitude toward each other and increase the sharing of their emotions through frequent transnational communication. Prior to migration, Yuri, a professional wife who made an equal economic contribution to the family but did most of the household labor alone, never felt grateful to her husband. However, after her migration, Yuri starts living solely on the remittances sent by her husband and expressing thankfulness to him, who agreed to her living abroad despite the expected increase in his burden as the sole breadwinner. Furthermore, Yuri's husband, who did not show much interest in family matters when they lived together in Korea, starts paying much greater attention to the life of his wife and child in the new society, wanting to talk longer and share more with her even minor daily events and issues, and explicitly expressing his gratitude for Yuri's hardships as a de facto single mother coping with all new challenges alone.

A majority of wild geese parents in my study maintain active daily transnational communication with their spouses, utilizing various advanced technologies, such as smart phones, emails, and Skype, which enormously helps them maintain (sometimes even enhance) emotional intimacy despite their physical separation. This is well-illustrated by the accounts of the following two wild geese fathers:

I think that my current spousal relationship is similar to or slightly better than before. . . . It is the effects of advanced communication technology. Therefore, I don't feel that I live apart [from my wife]. I always have phone calls with her. I sometimes have a video chat with her. (Kanghyuk, fifth-year wild geese father)

I don't find much difference in my communication pattern with her [after transnational spousal separation]. Because internet phone is free, I frequently talk with her about thirty minutes to an hour and catch up with her daily events. I also find that the [communication] environment has changed compared to the past. When she [first] went abroad, I talked with her using Skype on the computer. But, now I can talk with her while seeing her face on my phone. I can also instantly communicate with her via phone chatting. Because I always communicate with her, even if we physically live apart, I don't feel that we are really living apart. (Kyusik, man who has become a wild geese father twice)

In contrast, a few wild geese parents who do not frequently communicate with each other tend to find that their emotional intimacy is weakened, particularly when their separation is lengthier. Moreover, even if wild geese couples regularly communicate, their emotional ties can be still damaged if they exclusively talk about the *necessary* topics (such as remittances) without sharing their emotions and various aspects of their lives. Sharing their trivial daily events and feelings may be seen as *unnecessary* for wild geese parents to continue their transnational lives. Nonetheless, it turns out to be essential for wild geese couples to keep emotionally connected during their lengthy spousal separation.

A former wild geese father named Woosung explains how his communication with his wife, which was heavily concentrated on remittances and financial issues, has deteriorated the spousal relationship during the eleven years of transnational separation to the extent that he now feels his wife as a "stranger":

> Whenever we talked on the phone, the only one topic [that my wife told me] was "Honey, send me money." We mainly had conversations about money. From her side, financial issues were always the top priority. [. . .] Simply put, [for about eleven years of transnational separation] my spousal relationship has been deteriorated, not to mention my sexual relations [with her]. We gradually had fewer conversations. Even if we had conversation, as I have said, the topic was really limited. Whenever I got the international call [from my wife], I deeply sighed, because I already knew what she was going to tell me. Money! Therefore, after living apart, my spousal relationship has substantially changed, just like a [Korean] proverb, conjugal relations can easily change from lovers to strangers.

In addition, some wild geese fathers tend to hide their current economic hardships and concerns about the future from their families abroad, whereas wild geese mothers tend to show only their children's positive aspects to their husbands in order not to worry or disappoint them. Even though both spouses may mean well, their practice of such censorship of information do not help maintain good transnational spousal relationships in the long run.[29]

In sum, when wild geese parents recognize the overlooked value of their spouses through transnational spousal separation[30] and openly express their gratitude and affection to each other, the quality of their transnational spousal relationship improves as their emotional ties strengthen, even if they did not maintain intimate relationships prior to the spousal separation. Yet, it is important to note that such deepening emotional ties between wild geese parents during their transnational spousal separation are far from romantic love or sexual intimacy between (young) lovers. Rather, it is much closer to the feelings of trust and loyalty toward long-time companions or partners who have overcome challenges together over a long period of marriage. The following section discusses sexual intimacy between wild geese parents through transnational spousal separation.

MAINTENANCE OF SEXUAL INTIMACY

According to wild geese parents' definition of successful marriage, having frequent sexual relations is not as important as maintaining deep emotional connections. In particular, as middle-aged couples with a long period of marriage, many wild geese parents already ceased to have an active sexual life with their spouses even prior to their transnational spousal separation. Nonetheless, these facts do not necessarily mean that sexual intimacy is not meaningful at all to wild geese parents.

Rather, sexuality still matters to many wild geese mothers and fathers but in different ways. Notably, a much greater number of wild geese fathers than wild geese mothers relate their transnational marital satisfaction to sexual intimacy with their spouses and express a higher level of dissatisfaction with a decreased frequency of sexual relations. Specifically, one-quarter of wild geese fathers whom I interviewed express their dissatisfaction with a decreased sexual intimacy with their spouses, as depicted by the accounts of the following three fathers:

I have some problems on it [sex life]. In my case, I do not want to violate the law[31] [having affairs with another woman] to get what I want. However, it is difficult to practice abstinence if your [spousal] separation is longer. If one to two more years pass, people may turn their eyes to the other side [other women]. (Taehoo, second-year wild geese father)

The downside [of becoming wild geese family] is that my relationship with my wife gets worse. My wife [abroad] is always suspicious of what I am doing in Korea. She also worries what if I meet another woman. [. . .] Because I am a man, I occasionally find myself becoming closer to another woman by mistake. So, I try to avoid having such chances. However, I think it is not sustainable. (Sangmin, first-year wild geese father)

I happen to find that I may be physically and physiologically able to fall into temptation [of having extramarital relations], because my wife is absent. I think a lot about that possibility [love affairs]. I also sometimes happen to think what if my wife meets another man. When I jokingly asked my wife, "Did you meet Michael? [an imaginary man]," my wife responded to me, "How fortunate you are! While I am not [in Korea], you can have many affairs." (Jihwan, first-year wild geese father)

Contrarily, more than one-third of wild geese mothers whom I interviewed express their anxiety about their husbands' discontent with the reduced number of sexual relations with them and/or their husbands' potential love affairs with other women.

There are several reasons for these gendered differences. First, wild geese parents typically have patriarchal perspectives on men's and women's sexuality. Many of them view men's sexuality as their instinct and right and women's sexuality as their marital obligation in relation to men. Many wild geese fathers also explicitly relate their manhood to their active sexual life. Some wild geese fathers further insist that their wild geese life is built upon a huge sacrifice of their sexuality. In contrast, wild geese mothers neither relate their womanhood to active sexual life nor admit that their wild geese life is maintained at the expense of their spousal sexual relations.

Second, wild geese mothers' emphasis on their lack of sexual desire should be understood partly as their strategy to survive in the conservative Korean immigrant community.[32] During interviews, many wild geese mothers strongly asserted that they didn't have any sexual desire as if the lack of libido was an integral component of their virtuous womanhood. It is also possible that some wild geese mothers may have weak sexual desire or have lost it over time.

Yet, given that sexual reputations of wild geese mothers are closely monitored by the Korean immigrant community,[33] whose members implicitly assume that wild geese mothers may be easily engaged in affairs with Korean immigrant men because of the absence of their legitimate sexual partners (i.e., their husbands), it is more accurate to understand wild geese mothers' emphasis on their asexuality as their survival strategy in the Korean immigrant community. Above all, whether wild geese mothers are actually indifferent to sexual relations or just pretend to be asexual, women's sexuality is indeed something of a taboo that most wild geese mothers cannot dare to pursue while they are living separately from their husbands.

Third, such a double standard (i.e., sexual desire is tabooed for women and expected for men) also applies to wild geese parents' marital satisfaction. On the one hand, wild geese mothers contend that their marriage will remain intact as long as both spouses successfully perform their marital roles (i.e., the wife as a caretaker and the husband as a breadwinner) even if they don't have active sexual relations with their husbands. These women, instead, express great sorrow for their husbands who, they believe, find it difficult to quench their manly sexual desire during the transnational spousal separation. Thus, even if wild geese mothers allegedly do not find much joy in sexual intercourse, some of them admit that they still have frequent sexual relations with their husbands whenever they meet them, saying that they do so to make up for their unfulfilled marital obligations as good wives. A third-year wild geese mother named Minhee makes an interesting remark on this issue:

I know if my husband keeps accumulating his sexual desire, he will be unsatisfied with our relationship. Thus, whenever he comes, I try to have sex with him two or three times a week. He must have a hard time [in Korea] because of his [forced] celibacy. Because of that, I do have sex with him, even if I am not that type of woman who likes sex. If I don't take care of his sexuality, it would be very hard for my husband. Guess why a husband flies such a long distance to meet his wife. He never just wants to see his wife's face.

On the other hand, wild geese fathers tend to view active sexual relations as the evidence of a strong spousal relationship. Accordingly, wild geese fathers feel as if they were downgraded into a family ATM machine when they do not have enough intercourse during the face-to-face encounters with their wives. Likewise, a few wild geese fathers confidently say that they are closer to their wives, because they have increased the frequency of sexual relations with their wives during the wild geese period than they used to have when they were living together in Korea. Hojun, a wild geese father who has been in the fourth year of transnational spousal separation at the time of the interview, provides a good example:

[After becoming a wild geese couple] We have phone sex. We also share each other's masturbation, not to mention we have a lot of intercourse when I go there. We see each other's bodies beautifully. We also share each other's shower scenes, even though it is via video chatting. As we share such things, we keep maintaining [spousal] intimacy. I don't think that we have been estranged. Rather, I highly appreciate her body and mind.

Last, the double standard also applies to wild geese parents' attitudes toward an infidelity issue during transnational spousal separation. Both wild geese mothers and fathers highly emphasize monogamy as an integral part of their companionate marriage. Nonetheless, they present different levels of approval for their own and their spouses' infidelity. None of the wild geese mothers state that they have ever had extramarital relationships during the transnational spousal separation. Instead, they talk about the Korean immigrant community's gossip about some bad wild geese mothers who betrayed their husbands and got divorced.

On the contrary, many wild geese fathers openly tell me during the interview that they have frequently thought of meeting another woman to relieve their (physical) loneliness. Some men even admit that they have had extramarital relationships during their transnational spousal separation. A wild geese father named Youngtae even contends that his extramarital relationships during spousal separation can't ever be considered infidelity. Rather, he justifies his extramarital relationships as an indispensable way of maintaining his marriage in the transnational setting. Youngtac asserts:

> Are there any other countries than Korea where men can so easily satisfy their sexual desire? Because selling sex is so prevalent in Korea, there is a law that sex shops can be opened anywhere as long as they are two hundred meters away from schools. That means men's [extramarital] relations are already all excused.[34]

With respect to their spouses' infidelity, many wild geese parents strongly believe that their spouses have never had any extramarital sexual relationships. Nonetheless, many wild geese mothers still mention that they are willing to maintain their transnational marriage even if they find their husbands having extramarital relationships. For example, Sujin, a sixth-year wild geese mother who has been married for eighteen years, told her husband on the phone, "If you have a sexual relationship with another woman, never tell me about it. . . . Hide it from me completely." Sujin also told herself, "Even if I sense any clue of his infidelity, I will not pry into it." Similarly, according to a wild geese father named Dongkun, his wife even told him, "It is OK [for you] to meet another woman, but just terminate the relationship when I come back [to Korea]."

Then, is wild geese mothers' such high level of tolerance of their husbands' liaisons only the result of the patriarchal gender ideology that defines men's and women's sexuality differently? I disagree. I rather argue that wild geese mothers' high tolerance of their husbands' infidelity is also deeply related to their structural and economic marginality in their transnational households. Note that other migrant women in different social class and ethnicity also have presented a similar attitude toward extramarital affairs of their husbands.[35]

It is also noteworthy that wild geese families' transnational living arrangement is established and maintained by the strict transnational gender role division between spouses. Because many wild geese mothers happen to increase their economic dependence on their husbands during spousal separation, and because wile geese mothers have decided to pursue their children's education at the price of their marital quality, these women do not want to be divorced even if they know about their husbands' infidelity. Rather, wild geese mothers want to maintain their transnational marriage, as long as their husbands send sufficient remittances, and thus they can continue educating their children in the host countries.

Nonetheless, if they know about their husbands' extramarital relationships, wild geese mothers will certainly lose their trust and loyalty to their husbands. A former wild geese mother named Minji, who has been reunited with her husband after seven years of transnational separation, explains how her husband's infidelity has made her lose her trust in her husband and deteriorated their marital quality:

> [During transnational separation] I had never thought that my husband was having an affair. As I did not live that way, I perfectly believed my husband. I never had any suspicion on him. However, after my return, I couldn't believe . . . [sob]. He was changed. . . . He lived so lewdly to the extent that I even couldn't imagine. I never knew about it [husband's infidelity] until I returned [to Korea]. . . . He just lived as he wanted without any control. I was so disappointed. I really really hated it. I cannot explain it [husband's infidelity] in too detail, because it makes me so miserable. . . . Now, I have come to lose my trust in him. Because I was so emotionally upset and traumatized, it has been so difficult to overcome it.

Wild geese mothers also no longer feel much gratitude to their husbands or sympathy for their husbands' hardships or loneliness, if they know about their husband's affairs. This means that wild geese fathers' infidelity has transformed their marriage, if not divorced, from companionate marriage, which is built upon both strong emotional ties and successful fulfillment of marital roles, to institutional marriage, which is maintained primarily by each spouse's marital function. In this process, wild geese mothers' notion of their husbands is also transformed from "companion" or "soul mate" to "father" who is not expected to do anything more than to economically support his children's education abroad.

CONCLUSION

In this chapter, I have explored the changes in the quality of spousal relationships between wild geese parents through transnational spousal separation. First, I have shown how the effects of transnational separation on the spousal relationships can be quite heterogeneous and depend on the complex interactions among various factors. On the one hand, transnational spousal separation triggers many positive changes in wild geese parents' marital relationships, as it removes some of the existing sources of spousal conflicts, such as the unequal division of household labor and husbands' domineering manners. Their spousal relationships also tend to improve when wild geese parents recognize the overlooked value of their spouses and actively express gratitude, respect, compassion, love, and loyalty in response to their spouses' efforts, hardships, and sacrifices for the family through their frequent and regular transnational spousal communications. Having active sexual relations during face-to-face encounters is also helpful, although sexual intimacy is not as important as emotional connections.

On the other hand, the quality of wild geese parents' spousal relationship tend to be lowered if they have serious confrontations over the leadership of their transnational households, if they do not regularly communicate with their spouses, if they do not sufficiently share their emotions, if they practice censorship over the information to be shared, and/or if they fail to perform their expected marital roles (i.e., if fathers provide insufficient remittances or if the children have disappointing educational outcomes).

Second, the marital quality of wild geese couples is re-evaluated in terms of their emotional and sexual intimacy. Both Korean society and overseas Korean immigrant communities tend to have a rigid understanding of marriage. That is, so-called normal marriage can be (and should be) accomplished only if married couples live together in the same households. Accordingly, wild geese parents in the transnational context, as deviants from the so-called conventional marital norms, often have been negatively described by the media as well as by researchers as having problematic spousal relationships and/or as being so obsessed with children's education that they give up their marital relationships. However, I have found that, despite the long distance and lengthy separation, the transnational spousal relationships between wild geese parents are much closer and stronger than what is commonly assumed.

Wild geese parents believe that their marital success and satisfaction are determined not only by each spouse's satisfactory fulfillment of their roles (i.e., the husband as a breadwinner and the wife as a caretaker) but also by the strong emotional ties (e.g., gratitude, compassion, trust, and loyalty) between spouses. Wild geese parents generally define their spouses as companions and partners who pursue the same goals in life and overcome many challenges together over a long period of marriage, rather than as romantic lovers. Accordingly, sexual intimacy is not deemed to be an integral part of their companionate marriage. Nonetheless, wild geese parents' (particularly, fathers') marital satisfaction is positively related to their active sexual life with spouses.

Finally, spousal relationships between wild geese parents are further discussed for theoretical implications. Based on Cherlin's three definitions of marriage (i.e., institutional marriage, companionate marriage, and individualized marriage),[36] wild geese parents' spousal relationship is found to be similar to companionate marriage. Individualized marriage does not fit wild geese parents very well, because wild geese parents readily sacrifice their individual fulfillment (such as mothers' careers, spousal relationships, middle-class lifestyle, and post-retirement plans) for the sake of their children's education (and bright future from it). Also, wild geese parents' spousal relationship unfolds a lot more than what is defined as institutional marriage, because, despite their physical distance and lengthy separation, emotional connections, and sexual intimacy are still essential for wild geese parents to overcome many challenges and keep their strong spousal bond. In addition to borrowing Cherlin's framework, I propose taking emotional intimacy and sexual intimacy as analytically separate terms, because emotional connections and sexual relationships do not always work together between wild geese parents and because many wild geese parents state that they value emotional intimacy more than sexual intimacy.

NOTES

This chapter is a revised version of an article originally published as Se Hwa Lee, "Closer or Estranged: Transnational Spousal Relationship between Korean Wild Geese Parents," in *Companion to Korean American Studies*, ed. Rachael Joo and Shelley Lee (Boston, MA: Brill, 2018), chapter 20. Reprinted with permission from Brill.

1. Cho, "Korean Families," 148–171 (in Korean); Lee, "Kirogi Mother," 250–264; Lee, "Only If," 71–94.

2. In my study, the "family" is primarily a unit defined by heterosexual and patriarchal relations. Such heterosexual assumption of migration in this study might be criticized as marginalizing lesbian and gay relations as well as single-parent households. For the further critique about the privileging of a patriarchal nuclear family, see Martin F. Manalansan, IV, "Queer Intersections: Sexuality and Gender in Migration Studies," *International Migration Review* 40 (2006): 224–249. On wild geese parents' relationships, see Cho, "Korean Families," 148–171 (in Korean); Choi, "Geese Families," 37–65 (in Korean); Lee, "Kirogi Mother," 250–264; Lee, "Only If," 71–94; Lee and Koo, "Wild Geese Fathers," 533–553.

3. Huang and Yeoh, "Study Mothers," 379–400.

4. Kim, "Wild Goose Mother," 41–59 (in Korean); Yang Hee Kim and On Jeong Chang, "Issue of Families That Run Separate Households for a Long Time: The So-called 'Wild Geese Family,'" *Korea Association of Family Relations* 9, no. 2 (2004): 1–23 (in Korean); Lee and Koo, "Wild Geese Fathers," 533–553.

5. Ibid.

6. On motivations, see Cho, "Korean Families," 148–171 (in Korean); Kim, "'Downed' and Stuck," 271–311; Kim, Choi, and Lee, "Geese Mothers," 145–146 (in Korean); Lee, "Kirogi Mother," 250–264; Lee and Koo, "Wild Geese Fathers," 533–553; Jung Mi Nam, "The Changing Role of English in Korea: From English as a Tool for Advancement to English for Survival," *Pan-Pacific Association of Applied Linguistics* 9, no. 2 (2005): 227–240; Park and Abelmann, "Class and Cosmopolitan

Striving," 645–672; and Rosa Jinyoung Shim, "Englishized Korean: Structure, Status, and Attitudes," *World Englisher* 13, no. 2 (1994): 225–244.

7. On life changes and challenges after separation, see Choi, "Geese Families," 37–65 (in Korean); Kim, "Wild Geese Family," 171–189 (in Korean); Kim, "Wild Goose Mother," 41–59 (in Korean); Kim and Chang, "Issue of Families," 1–23 (in Korean); Kim, Choi, and Lee, "Geese Mothers," 145–146 (in Korean); Lee, "Kiroghee Fathers," 24–26 (in Korean); Lee, "Kirogi Mother," 250–264; and Lee and Koo, "Wild Geese Fathers," 533–553.

8. Kim, "Wild Goose Mother," 41–59 (in Korean); Kim and Chang, "Issue of Families," 1–23 (in Korean); Lee and Koo, "Wild Geese Fathers," 533–553.

9. On fathers, see Choi, "Geese Families," 37–65 (in Korean); and Kim and Chang, "Issue of Families," 1–23 (in Korean). On mothers, see Cho, "Korean Families," 148–171 (in Korean); and Choi, "Geese Families," 37–65 (in Korean).

10. Hondagneu-Sotelo, "Overcoming Patriarchal Constraints," 393–415.

11. Glenn, "Split Household," 35–46; Parreñas, "Transnational Fathering," 1063–1064.

12. Hondagneu-Sotelo, *Gendered Transitions*; Hondagneu-Sotelo, "Overcoming Patriarchal Constraints," 393–415.

13. For Hong Kong and Taiwanese *astronaut families*, see Waters, "Transnational Family Strategies," 359–377; Chang and Darlington, "Astronaut Wives," 61–77; and Chee, "Migrating for the Children," 137–156. For *parachute kids* in Canada and Australia, see Pe-Pua et al., "Astronaut Families and Parachute Children," 279–298. For Chinese *study mothers* in Singapore, see Huang and Yeoh, "Study Mothers," 379–400.

14. Kim, "Wild Goose Mother," 41–59 (in Korean); Kim and Chang, "Issue of Families," 1–23 (in Korean); Lee and Koo, "Wild Geese Fathers," 533–553.

15. Andrew Cherlin, *The Marriage-Go-Round: The State of Marriage and the Family in America Today* (New York: Knopf, 2009), 36–115.

16. Ibid., 68.

17. Ibid., 63–86.

18. Ibid.

19. Lee, "Only If," 71–94.

20. England, "Mothers, Wives, Workers," 109–122; Hochschild, *Second Shift*; Moon, "Immigration and Mothering," 840–860; Parreñas, "Long Distance Intimacy."

21. Cho, "Korean Families," 148–171 (in Korean); Lee, "Kirogi Mother," 250–264; Lee, "Only If," 71–94.

22. Chapter 2 provides an in-depth discussion on the wild geese parents' changing patterns of housework through migration.

23. Arendell, "Conceiving and Investigating Motherhood," 1192–1207; Hattery, *Women, Work and Family*; Hays, *Cultural Contradictions of Motherhood*.

24. Hochschild, *Second Shift*, 79–99.

25. Economic support as a means of expressing transnational fathers' love to their children is also noted from other studies. See Heather A. Horst, "The Blessings and Burdens of Communication: Cell Phones in Jamaican Transnational Fields," *Global Networks* 6, no. 2 (2006): 143–159; Majella Kilkey, Ania Plomien, and Diane

Perrons, "Migrant Men's Fathering Narratives, Practices and Projects in National and Transnational Spaces: Recent Polish Male Migrants to London," *International Migration* 52, no. 1 (2014): 178–191; McKay, "Sending Dollars Shows Feeling," 175–194; Schmalzbauer, "Family Divided," 329–346.

26. Schmalzbauer, "Temporary and Transnational," 211–226.

27. Men's emotional distress caused by transnational family separation is also found among Latino transnational fathers. See Dreby, "Honor and Virtue," 32–59; Leah Schmalzbauer, *Striving and Surviving: A Daily Life Analysis of Honduran Transnational Families* (New York: Routledge, 2005), 68–69; Schmalzbauer, "Temporary and Transnational," 211–226.

28. Montes, "Role of Emotions," 469–490.

29. Regarding migrant families' censorship of information, see Madianou and Miller, "Mobile Phone Parenting," 457–470; Schmalzbauer, "Family Divided," 329–346; Ayşem R. Şenyürekli and Daniel F. Detznera, "Communication Dynamics of the Transnational Family," *Marriage & Family Review* 45, nos. 6–8 (2009): 807–824; and Kristine M. Zentgraf and Norma Stoltz Chinchilla, "Transnational Family Separation: A Framework for Analysis," *Journal of Ethnic and Migration Studies* 38, no. 2 (2012): 345–366.

30. On recognizing overlooked value of families, see Dreby, "Honor and Virtue," 32–59.

31. "Law" here means adultery law in Korea, which was still effective in Korea at the time of interview. Adultery law was finally sentenced to unconstitutional in 2015.

32. For more in-depth discussion on wild geese mothers' social life in the Korean immigrant community, see chapter 4.

33. Lee, "Only If," 88.

34. In contrast to Youngtae's account, selling sex is illegal in Korea. See Korean National Law Information Center, "Act on the Punishment of Arrangement of Commercial Sex Acts" (in Korean), accessed May 28, 2020, https://www.law.go.k r/법령/성매매알선등행위의처벌에관한법률.

35. Ecuadorian women also have presented a tolerant attitude toward the infidelity of their working-class husbands who migrated abroad alone to earn money. See Pribilsky, "Aprendemos a Convivir," 313–334.

36. Cherlin, *The Marriage-Go-Round*, 36–115.

Chapter 4

Mothering and Socializing in Korean Immigrant Community

In Korean tradition, as noted in Introduction, children's education is highly valued as a family's important means of achieving upward social mobility.[1] Furthermore, the rapidly changing economic and social contexts of the contemporary Korean society have led Korean parents to put high emphasis on English fluency as one of the most crucial social capital and cultural symbols for their children to survive in the increasingly competitive global job market.[2] Accordingly, middle-class Korean parents heavily invest in their children's education (including the acquisition of English proficiency), and organize their family lives around their children's schooling and extracurricular activities. At the same time, middle-class Korean women's motherhood is increasingly evaluated by their children's academic attainments and admission to prestigious universities, and many middle-class Korean mothers achieve a sense of fulfillment by performing the role of a competent *educational manager*[3] for their children.

In Introduction, I have suggested that wild geese mothers' primary goal of migration is to enhance their children's English proficiency and/or to help their children enter a prestigious university either in Korea or the host country. Fulfilling their children's educational goals through mothering is critical for wild geese mothers, because it is deeply related not only to the future upward social mobility of their children but also to their current bargaining power and relative gender status within their transnational households. Interestingly, however, soon after migration, many wild geese mothers have realized that they cannot easily achieve their educational goals, because they are newly migrated foreigners and lack important educational information and resources in the host society.

In this chapter, I seek to explain how Korean wild geese mothers try to overcome their unexpected challenges in the host societies and achieve high educational aspirations for their children. Among the various resources that wild geese mothers can utilize, I pay particular attention to their social networks within the Korean immigrant community, given that ethnic immigrant communities are known to be one of the most important social structures for new immigrants.[4] Specifically, I first describe how wild geese mothers performed the roles of the educational manager for their children in Korea. Then, I examine the kinds of challenges wild geese mothers have encountered after migration and the reasons why the Korean immigrant community has emerged as their primary (and sometimes the only) source of support. Finally, I analyze the advantages and disadvantages of the Korean immigrant community to these women. On the one hand, I focus on the ways in which wild geese mothers' needs are met through Korean social networks, such as the Korean Parents Association (KPA) and Korean immigrant churches. On the other hand, I investigate the costs that wild geese mothers have to pay for their access to the valuable information and resources from their ethnic community. This chapter explores the ambivalent impacts of Korean immigrant communities on wild geese mothers and offers a more nuanced explanation of the complex interplay between the immigrant social networks and middle-class Asian migrant women's mothering and fulfillment.

INTENSIVE MOTHERING AND ETHNIC COMMUNITY

Previous studies have often viewed the transnational migration of middle-class Asian mothers as something mandated by the patriarchal Asian culture and have focused on their hardships in the host society.[5] However, in this chapter, I provide an alternative perspective: Korean wild geese mothers' migration is a voluntary and strategic decision to actively perform *intensive mothering*,[6] which is a global phenomenon of middle-class mothers across racial/ethnic backgrounds and nationalities, as Pierrette Hondagneu-Sotelo and E. Avila have argued.[7]

The ideology of *intensive mothering* frames mothering as an exclusive, child-centered, and time-consuming practice[8] and dictates that Korean wild geese mothers devote themselves to taking care of their children and sacrifice their own lives and interests. Furthermore, combined with the Confucian Korean culture that values success through education,[9] the intensive mothering ideology pressures wild geese mothers to become so-called *tiger mothers*[10] who can and should do whatever is needed for their children's education. Thus, even prior to migration, wild geese mothers actively played the role of an ambitious educational manager for their children and tended to equate their own success with their children's educational achievement. In short, wild geese mothers "live vicariously through their children, viewing them as extensions of themselves," like Asian American parents in Yi's study.[11]

The ideology of intensive mothering further normalizes the strict and transnational division of traditional gender roles between wild geese couples (i.e., husbands remain alone in Korea to serve the role of breadwinners and wives willingly cross national borders as caregivers).[12] In addition to their motivations for transnational migration, the intensive mothering ideology also explains why wild geese mothers are so desperate to continue playing the role of competent educational managers for their children after migration. Wild geese mothers migrate abroad to better achieve their children's educational goals, even if it entails the significant sacrifice of their spousal relationships and the loss of income and social status as successful career women in Korea, and even if they do not find many chances to recover their lowered social status and self-esteem in the host societies. Therefore, many of them tend to associate their satisfaction and self-realization mainly with their children's outstanding educational attainment (i.e., enhanced English proficiency and entrance to a prestigious university). Likewise, wild geese fathers who remain alone in Korea believe that their children's extraordinary academic achievement compensates for their sacrifice and proves their wives' good performance in their expected role as ideal mothers. In sum, many wild geese mothers are highly motivated to fulfill their role of effective educational managers for their children throughout migration.

Min Zhou's concept of *ethnic community*[13] provides a good foundation for understanding why maintaining membership in the Korean immigrant community is so critical for most wild geese mothers to effectively perform their roles of mothers and educational managers, while coping with adversities in the host society. In her comparative study of Chinese, Korean, and Latino immigrant communities in Los Angeles, Zhou shows that the Korean ethnic community is quite vibrant with the significant presence of middle-class immigrants and diverse official ethnic organizations, such as commercial, religious, and education-related groups.[14] Thanks to the ethnic community's educational resources and the social capital available for Korean Americans, Zhou argues that Korean immigrant children in Los Angeles Koreatown can achieve more satisfactory educational outcomes than their Latino counterparts, who lack such supports from their own ethnic community.[15] It is also noted that the Korean immigrant community is quite exclusive and allows only its co-ethnic members to gain access to its abundant educational resources and information.[16]

While Zhou claims that new Korean immigrants can benefit from their ethnic community's resources based on their co-ethnicity, I extend her argument, by demonstrating that the ethnic community's support is unevenly distributed, even among the same ethnic immigrants depending on the existing community's acceptance of the newcomers. That is, the first task of newly migrated wild geese mothers who seek assistance from the Korean immigrant community is to be accepted as legitimate members. Maintaining their membership and not losing the support from the community are the next tasks for their survival.

In the following sections, I discuss (1) how wild geese mothers performed intensive mothering in Korea prior to migration, (2) what challenges they encounter in the host societies and why they find it difficult to keep their role as an effective educational manager after migration, (3) how they turn to the Korean immigrant community (e.g., the KPA and Korean churches) as the main source of support for their successful performance of intensive mothering and achievement of their educational goals as well as their survival in the host societies, and (4) how they struggle to maintain their membership within the Korean immigrant community and gain access to its resources and information while the Korean immigrant community also places constraints on wild geese mothers' mothering capabilities and gender roles.

WILD GEESE MOTHERS' INTENSIVE MOTHERING IN KOREA

When they lived in Korea, wild geese mothers were very enthusiastic about their children's education and actively performed *intensive mothering*[17] for their children. Some of them even introduced themselves to me as highly disciplinary *tiger moms*[18] who could (and should) do whatever was needed for their children's education. This section discusses two main aspects of wild geese mothers' mothering practices in Korea, prior to their migration: daily childcare and educational management.

Providing Daily Physical and Emotional Care in Korea

While their husbands tended to be exempt from childrearing responsibilities, which was often justified by their busy work schedule, wild geese mothers were expected to provide daily care for their children regardless of their employment status. In my study, about a half of wild geese mothers were full-time homemakers prior to migration, while the other half were working mothers. All full-time homemakers maintained quite child-centered lives in Korea as the intensive mothering ideology dictates. They provided their children with physical and emotional care and organized their daily lives primarily based on their children' educational schedules.[19] For example, Eunji, a wild geese mother who used to be a full-time homemaker prior to migration, defines herself as a "ride mom" who was always busy with giving rides to her daughter to various academic and extracurricular activities.

> My daughter went to good schools in Korea, starting from kindergarten. She went to a private elementary school from Ilsan to Seoul.[20] I was very enthusiastic about her education. I strongly wanted to educate her in a good school, although she did not ask for it. She also attended an English kindergarten when she was five years old. At that time [in Korea], ten years ago, it was not so common to send a five-year-old child to an English kindergarten [which was very expensive]. I was a kind of enthusiastic mom. [. . .] Because she went to a [elementary] school far away from home, it took very long time for me to give her a ride. Further, because she was a member of the school orchestra, I had to give her a ride to the Saturday practice session as well. I was a ride mom. [While she went to school in Seoul], she also took classes from private academic institutions [after school] in Ilsan. [To give her a ride], I came back and forth [between Seoul and Ilsan]. I just followed her all day long.

In contrast to full-time homemakers, a majority of working mothers confess that they did not perform their mothering role adequately in Korea. Compared to homemaker mothers, working mothers were too busy with their work to spend much time with their children or to pay enough attention to building an intimate relationship with their children. For example, a wild geese mother named Mira says that the only work she was doing as a mother in Korea was sending her children to private academic institutions after school because she was busy with her teaching job.

The two other wild geese mothers in my study did not even provide daily care for their children due to their career, which was deemed to be a serious violation of the norm of intensive mothering. According to Chaerim, a wild geese mother who used to be a businesswoman in Korea, her daughter spent weekdays in the house of her mother-in-law who lived nearby. Chaerim stayed together with her daughter only during the weekends. She did not cook much for her daughter either, because she spent the weekends in playing outside with her daughter and dining out. In case of Sowon, a banker, her own mother lived together with her and provided daily care for her two sons, such as giving snacks, taking them to doctor's appointments, providing voluntary services at school, and attending the PTA meetings.

Although working mothers could not aggressively perform the idealized role of devoted mothers compared to their full-time homemaker counterparts, they still tried to balance between their work and family. Furthermore, as the intensive mothering ideology mandates, these working mothers sacrificed their career development when it was necessary for their children.[21] For instance, a wild geese mother named Bora used to be a very successful teacher at a private academy, but, as her children grew up, she quit her high-paying job and became a private tutor who taught students at her own house. While she could not earn as much as she had earned before, she was still pleased because she could spend more time with her children thanks to her more flexible work schedule. A wild geese mother named Sukhee is another example. Sukhee was a busy high school teacher in Korea but taught her own children at home as if she were their private tutor, and eventually retired when she decided to accompany her children abroad.

As implied by these examples, it is important to point that gender inequality is deeply embedded in the script of intensive mothering. Like middle-class mothers in the United States,[22] wild geese mothers in my study felt guilty for pursuing their own careers and dividing their commitments between work and family. Furthermore, it was always wild geese mothers who were in charge of arranging alternative child caretakers. Thus, many wild geese mothers who were working in Korea tried to relive the burden of childcare by sharing it with other women, not with their husbands.

To make things more difficult, many wild geese mothers had a strong negative attitude toward paid child caretakers, which is quite different from their Chinese counterparts.[23] Consequently, even if they could afford to hire nannies or babysitters, wild geese mothers tended to share their childcare responsibilities with their own mothers and/or mothers-in-law, often having to read their mothers-in-law's countenance.

A story of Chaerim, a wild geese mother who used to be a businesswoman prior to migration, shows how wild geese mothers with employment were not seen as good mothers as full-time homemakers, despite their successful coordination of necessary care for their children. In Korea, Chaerim often dropped by her mother-in-law's house on the way home to see her daughter on weekdays. In contrast, her husband always went home directly from work so that he could rest more. While Chaerim did not go to her office during weekends in order to spend more time with her daughter, her husband often did a lot of work during weekends for his company. While Chaerim sacrificed her promotion opportunities to be a better mother, her husband kept pursuing his career-oriented life regardless of her struggles. Despite Chaerim's greater commitment to their daughter, it was not her husband but she who felt sorry for her daughter as if she were a bad mother, which was one of the main reasons that motivated Chaerim to migrate abroad:

> When I lived in Korea, I did not spend much time with my child. I thought that I could spend a more time with her if we went to Canada. I also thought that I could better serve the role of mother. I thought that it [migration] was a really great idea.

Chaerim's case is also commonly observed in the middle-class families in the United States,[24] in that professional mothers are juggling between work and family whereas their professional husbands are freed of such work-family conflicts and often indifferent to their wives' suffering. This reflects pervasive patriarchal gender ideology that defines childcare as primarily women's responsibility.[25] Even though some wild geese mothers confronted such unfair situations, it often led to more serious spousal conflict rather than more equal share of childrearing responsibilities with their husbands.

Performing the Role of an Educational Manager in Korea

While full-time homemakers and working mothers showed a wide gap in the amount of time spent with their children and their provision of daily physical care for children, it is evident that both groups of mothers actively performed the role of a competent educational manager for their children prior to migration. As middle-class parents, wild geese mothers commonly hoped that their children would get good grades at school and be admitted to prestigious universities. In turn, the quality of their mothering role was gauged by their children's academic performance.

To achieve their ambitious educational goals, most wild geese mothers in my study heavily invested in their children's education: not only in formal schooling but also in private supplementary education, so-called *shadow education*.[26] For example, Jina, who used to be a full-time homemaker with a son attending an elementary school, spent $2,000 monthly just for her son's private education in Korea, such as English tutoring, math tutoring, history camp, science camp, clarinet lessons, and swimming lessons. Damso, a wild geese mother who used to be a high school teacher, spent $80,000 annually (more than a half of the family income, which was $150,000, combining her and her husband's income) on her two children's education (including their expensive tuition for a private international school in Korea) until she migrated to the United States two years prior to the interview.

Furthermore, in order to achieve their high educational goals (i.e., children's entrance to prestigious universities), wild geese mothers kept a close eye on their children's academic records even when they were very young, and then carefully selected and organized their children's educational programs to improve their academic performance. In particular, under the Korean education system, the scores on the standardized exams were critical for their children's admission to prestigious universities.[27] Therefore, wild geese mothers often enrolled their children in private academic institutions (i.e., cram schools) to prepare for such high-stakes tests. Many wild geese mothers also arranged additional one-to-one tutoring for their children in the subject areas where their children needed further improvement for their university admission.

For example, according to Damso, her two children already had more advanced English proficiency than other typical Korean students, because they were immersed in the English-speaking environment of their private international school in Korea. Nonetheless, she still thought that her children's English fell behind compared to their classmates who were native English speakers. To improve their English fluency, Damso arranged private English lessons for her children. Furthermore, to support her son's activity at the (English) debate club of the school, she organized another private English tutoring team with other club mates' mothers who also wanted to improve their children's English fluency. Similar to Damso, the majority of wild geese mothers in my study highly relied on private supplementary education to maintain or improve their children's academic performances in the formal education system.

As much as wild geese mothers valued their children's academic excellence, they also put great emphasis on their children's extracurricular education in arts, music, and sports. Therefore, they provided their children with diverse educational opportunities in music (e.g., taking lessons for piano, violin, cello, clarinet, and drum, and attending a youth orchestra), arts (e.g., painting and ballet), and sports (e.g., martial arts such as Taekwondo and Kendo, swimming, tennis, skating, skiing, and ice hockey). Wild geese mothers strongly believed that their children would greatly benefit from such extensive enrichment programs, as they could cultivate confidence, creativity, and cultural sophistication balanced with their high intelligence. In this respect, Korean wild geese mothers were very similar to American middle-class parents who "engage in concerted cultivation by attempting to foster children's talents through organized leisure activities and extensive reasoning" in the Lareau's study.[28]

To better perform the role of an educational manager for their children, wild geese mothers were also actively involved in various activities and events of their children's schools and interacted with their children's teachers. They regularly attended school events such as PTA meetings, arranged individual consultation sessions with their children's teachers, and provided various voluntary services such as serving children's school lunch and guiding students at crosswalks in front of the school. Some mothers further served as the members of the school board, members of a committee for school operation, and members of a parent committee (including parent representative of the school and parent representative of the Girl Scouts).

Wild geese mothers also worked hard to build and maintain extensive social networks with other school mothers who were also enthusiastic about their children's education. Through their own exclusive social networks, these mothers shared important educational information of, for example, fast-changing Korean college admission system, good private cram schools and good private tutors. If necessary, they also organized study groups and invited famous teachers from private academic institutions. Of course, behind their great educational enthusiasm about their children's education were harsh competition and jealousy among mothers, which further encouraged wild geese mothers to invest more in their children's education.

With such tremendous efforts described above, wild geese mothers quite successfully performed their expected role of educational managers for their children in Korea. However, there were some side effects of their intensive mothering and high educational zeal. A substantial number of wild geese mothers in my study confess that they did not have good relationships with their children in Korea. As over-solicitous mothers, wild geese mothers continuously nagged and pushed their children to study harder and to get better scores. They were commanders, and their children were followers. Rather than having conversations with their children, wild geese mothers often gave directions and orders to their children about what to do. They often compared their children with other children because of a furtive competitive spirit to win over other school mothers. They also forced their children to do many after-school activities regardless of their children's willingness. As a result, there were lots of tensions and confrontations between mothers and their children prior to migration.

Jiyoung, a wild geese mother with an eleven-year-old daughter and a six-year-old son, well-articulates how her excessive educational pressure on her daughter ruined their relationship:

When my first child was young, although I did not think about sending her to IVY leagues yet, I wanted her to do everything that other children did. If others played the piano, my daughter had to play the piano. If a neighborhood child knew how to multiply, my children had to know how to multiply. In the same vein, when she went to a preschool, I taught her phonics, and we fought a lot. I also fought a lot with her when I taught her playing the piano. But, the outcome [of my pressure] was just a bad relationship with her. Although she did not play the piano so well nor did she have much talent in it, I pressured her too much.

Sunmi, a former wild geese mother with a 25-year-old daughter and a 23-year-old son, also expresses the similar sentiment for being too pushy in Korea:

At that time, I obsessed about my children. I never should have done so. I did not have to do it like that. At that time, I excessively pressured my children on their study, sports, and instruments. I always stayed together with them. Luckily, my son was OK with it [my pushy mothering]. However, for my daughter, it was like hell.

So far, I have discussed wild geese mothers' mothering practices in Korea prior to their migration, focusing on their daily physical and emotional care and educational management roles for their children. Full-time homemakers devoted themselves to taking care of their children, as intensive mothering ideology dictates. In contrast, working mothers could not spend much time with their children, nor did they provide much daily physical care for children. Nonetheless, with a strong desire to pursue the idealized norm of intensive mothering, working mothers struggled to balance between their work and family obligations and arrange necessary care for their children and often sacrificed their work and career for their children's education. In addition, both full-time homemakers and working mothers actively performed the role of a competent educational manager for their children: (1) they carefully selected and organized their children's academic and extracurricular activities and (2) they actively engaged with their children's school, teachers, and other school parents. Finally, a ruined relationship with their children is addressed as a side-effect of these mothers' enthusiastic (sometimes pushy) intensive mothering for their children's education.

CHALLENGES TO PERFORMING INTENSIVE MOTHERING IN HOST SOCIETIES

In this section, I explore wild geese mothers' mothering practices in the host societies after migration. Particular attention is paid to the changes and differences in their mothering practices and capabilities between when they were living in Korea (prior to migration) and when they are living in the host societies (after migration).

Providing Daily Physical and Emotional Care after Migration

After migration, a majority of wild geese mothers in my study have become either international students or full-time homemakers regardless of their prior careers in Korea so that they can better perform full-time motherhood and better conform to the ideology of intensive mothering. While half of wild geese mothers worked prior to migration, many of them no longer work after migration. Even though substantial numbers of wild geese mothers spend their time in studying to legitimately maintain their full-time international student status, most of these mothers attend private ESL (English as Second Language) institutes and complete their school-related works while their children are at school. Even though some wild geese mothers have paid employment after migration, their jobs are mostly part-time ones with a flexible schedule and do not seriously hinder them from performing their mothering roles.[29] Accordingly, after migration, most wild geese mothers spend much more time with their children, provide more physical and emotional care for their children, and better conform to the ideology of intensive mothering than they did prior to migration.

Hyomin, a wild geese mother with three adolescent children, well describes her busy day in Canada as a full-time mother, giving rides to her three children at three different times every morning:

> In Korea, I did not have to wash my face [in the morning], but just gave them [children] breakfast and said bye-bye at the door. However, in here, because I have to give them a ride, I first wash myself and prepare [three] lunch boxes from six o'clock. Then, I start to carry my kids one by one [by car] as their band practice sessions begin at 7 o'clock. I am extremely busy [every morning]. [. . .] When I was in Korea, I could deal with my children's matters with money and online banking. But here, I have to do mothering with my body.

Hyomin also expresses satisfaction with her new life as a ride mom after migration:

> In Korea, my children spent a much longer time outside. We did not have much time together face-to-face. We just lived separately in the same space. However, in here, I have to give them a ride. I have to ride them everywhere they go. So, we have a lot of conversation in the car. We also have some fun together [in the car]. I feel that I am closer to them, as our time together has increased.

Curiously, spending more time with their children is not always a positive experience for wild geese mothers. Among the wild geese mothers who used to work prior to migration, some feel uncomfortable spending so much time with their children in a small apartment (e.g., one- or two-bedroom apartment) or find it tiresome to prepare their children's meals three times a day (including a lunch box). Some wild geese mothers who are attending degree programs after migration feel annoyed that they cannot find much time to study for themselves because of their increased burden as a sole caretaker. Some wild geese mothers have some conflicts with their children in the beginning of migration, as they adjust to each other. A few mothers have increased tension with their children (particularly with adolescent sons) as they no longer live with their father who used to mediate disputes between mothers and children. Nonetheless, in general, wild geese mothers' relationships with their children have greatly improved over time as they spend more time together and overcome challenges together in the host societies.

The improvement in the mother-child relationship is partly due to the changes in wild geese mothers' educational enthusiasm, as substantial numbers of wild geese mothers have transformed from pushy tiger moms to more relaxed ones. One possible reason is the different educational system of North America that less emphasizes students' cramming for standardized exams. Another reason may be wild geese mothers' unexpected downgrade in their capabilities from competent educational experts to marginalized migrant mothers who are neither fluent in English nor familiar with the educational system of the host society.

Ironically, instead of feeling anxious and concerned about not knowing what is best for their children, many wild geese mothers rather have felt comfortable and relaxed after migration, because they no longer have any comparison group to compete with and because they are also liberated from the competitive Korean educational atmosphere. As they pressure their children less into studying and allow them more to do what they like, many wild geese mothers acknowledge that they have become closer to and built stronger emotional bonds with their children after migration than in Korea. Jina, a wild geese mother with a son who is attending elementary school in the United States, explains how her relationship with her son has improved through migration:

> I used to compete a lot with other mothers in Korea. I even once fought with my child's friend's mother [because of severe competition] when he was a first grader. However, [after migration] I don't have anyone to compare with my child and thus have become much more relaxed. So, I don't shout at my child anymore. And my child rather shows better [academic] performance with mom's decreased pressure. And my relationship with the child has significantly improved. [. . .] He is so happy now.

Performing the Role of an Educational Manager after Migration

If wild geese mothers migrated for the purpose of having a better relationship with their children, the outcome would have been more satisfactory for them. However, their goal of migration is not to improve their relationship with their children but to accomplish their children's educational goals (i.e., enhancing their children's English fluency and/or helping their children enter prestigious universities either in the host country or Korea). After migration, many ambitious wild geese mothers are greatly embarrassed and even frustrated because they find it much more difficult to perform their role as competent educational managers for their children. In particular, most wild geese mothers are no longer able to obtain important educational information and resources that they took for granted in Korea.

In this section, I discuss the structural disadvantages that wild geese mothers are faced with as newly migrated foreigners in the host society, including (1) language and cultural barriers and (2) their isolation from mainstream social networks. I also analyze how those challenges make it difficult for wild geese mothers to perform their expected role of competent educational managers for their children after migration.

First of all, wild geese mothers are daunted by the language barriers they encounter in North America. Those who could barely speak English prior to migration tend to feel that they have become deaf, neither speaking nor listening to English. Accordingly, they are quite reluctant to visit their children's schools when they are asked to attend various school events such as open houses, parent-teacher conferences, or school counseling. Others who speak better English still feel it difficult to communicate with teachers and parents in their children's schools. For example, Heeyoung is a wild geese mother who was able to speak some English prior to migration. Nonetheless, after migration, she feels greatly humiliated when Americans do not understand what she says, and thus she is further discouraged from speaking with anyone in English. Another wild geese mother, Jina, narrates how the lack of confidence in her language proficiency prevents her from interacting with American teachers and parents in her child's school:

> Although it is never difficult for me to speak English when I go grocery shopping or in my ESL class, I cannot talk comfortably with my son's teachers or his friends' moms. I feel really timid. So, I rather close my mouth in order not to cause any harm to my kid.

Furthermore, a story of Sukhee, a wild geese mother with a twelfth grade girl, shows that even if some wild geese mothers gradually have overcome their language barriers, they are still frustrated by the fact that their cultural background and knowledge based on the Korean society are of no use in the host countries. When Sukhee and her daughter came to the United States three years prior to the interview, Sukhee's daughter was supposed to write a response paper to a video clip on public health as her school assignment. Because her performance in that course was not so great due to the language barrier, Sukhee's daughter wanted to make it up by producing stronger homework. Thus, she watched the video clip several times (she had to do so because she could not understand the content at once), researched online for related information, and then summarized the video to demonstrate her thorough understanding of the content. Watching her daughter studying hard, Sukhee was so proud and expected a good grade for the assignment.

However, in contrast to their expectations, Sukhee's daughter was charged with plagiarism and given a failing grade for the course, because she missed citations in the paper. This happened when Sukhee and her daughter had just migrated from Korea, where the formal education system was so centered on standardized exams that students did not have much experience of writing essays or response papers, and thus did not have a clear understanding of plagiarism in the American context. Although Sukhee met teachers and counselors at school to resolve the situation, she failed to defend her daughter against an F grade in the course. Sukhee greatly reproached herself because she thought that she failed to defend her daughter due to the language barrier. Sukhee believed that her daughter could have taken a lighter punishment than the failing grade, if she, as a mother, had better explained her daughter's good will, the language and cultural barriers she faced, and her likely ignorance of stricter American standards for plagiarism to school authorities.

The language and cultural barriers are not easy to overcome. Even though three years have passed since the plagiarism case, Sukhee still feels nervous and incompetent whenever she meets her daughters' American teachers. Sukhee further expresses her frustration as a *perpetual foreigner* or *unassimilable alien*[30] who comes from a different culture and thus will never become a part of the dominant society:

> Because I don't know the American cultural background so well, I am always mindful whether my behavior is culturally acceptable or not. After migration, I have realized how my cultural background and knowledge [based on Korean society] is deeply entrenched in me. In [South] Korea, everything was so natural, and I did not have to be conscious of what I was doing. It was like breathing air. However, in America, I feel that I am walking on eggshells every moment. [. . .] I know nothing here. There is nothing that I know by itself. I have to think carefully at all times.

If wild geese mothers, like Sukhee, keep struggling to deal with everyday challenges they encounter as parents due to their lack of (confidence in) English fluency and cultural competence, they end up having lower self-esteem, tolerating unfair disadvantages, and giving up further communication and interaction with their children's school administration and teachers, which in turn prevents wild geese mothers from effectively performing their expected role of competent educational managers for their children in the host society.

Interestingly, despite the language and cultural barriers that I have described above, many wild geese mothers often hope that their children and they themselves can closely interact with people in the dominant society and be immersed with the mainstream middle-class community. Such hopes are particularly strong at the beginning of their migration. Local churches can be considered good venues for the realization of such hopes. Based on the concrete foundation of sharing the same religion, members in local churches are generally more favorable to and more eager to accept wild geese mothers than people outside of church communities, although wild geese mothers cannot immediately reciprocate their friendship and assistance.[31]

Hana, a wild geese mother who has tried hard to socialize with mainstream Americans through her American Catholic church, well describes the positive role of religious institutions in incorporating new migrant women in the host society:

> When I first came [to America], my goal was to learn English. So, I intentionally went to the American Catholic church near my house. I attended the service every day and became close to old ladies who also came every day. [. . .] Then, one of the old ladies invited me to her bible study group in a Catholic church in another town. There, I met women of diverse ages from those who were younger than me to older ladies. [. . .] I felt comfortable among them because we shared the same religious belief. They were so nice to me. [. . .] Through my bible study group, I could join another prayer gathering composed of younger women. In that way, I could easily become a part of [American] religious community here.

However, attending local churches is not such a common path for most wild geese mothers to socialize with mainstream society. Only a few wild geese mothers, who have strong Christian beliefs and are highly motivated to learn English, choose to regularly attend local church services and/or bible study groups.

Rather, wild geese mothers' more common pattern of socializing with the dominant groups of citizens is engaging with parents whom they have met at their children's schools. Wild geese mothers of older children often meet their local friends through their children's extracurricular activities, such as football, ice hockey, and youth orchestra, whereas wild geese mothers of younger children make their local friends by arranging playdates with classmates or hosting their children's birthday parties.

Nonetheless, most wild geese mothers in my study admit that it is very hard for them to maintain their membership in mainstream social networks. There are several reasons for the exclusion of these women from mainstream social networks. First, upon arrival, wild geese mothers soon find that middle-class (often white) mothers in the locality have known one another for a long time and have already built strong social networks among themselves. These mothers do not have much incentive to become friends with wild geese mothers who have just migrated and seem to be seeking help rather than making contributions to their communities.

Accordingly, except for only a few wild geese mothers who are fluent in English, very sociable and able to make tremendous efforts toward new friends, most wild geese mothers have not become a part of pre-established social networks among the middle-class mothers in their communities. The story of Jina, whose son is attending a private elementary school in the United States, well portrays such difficulties:

> My child currently goes to a private school and all his classmates have known one another since kindergarten. So, all their parents know one another and have a very strong in-network among themselves. So, I could not become one of them. Of course, they did not block me. They were very nice to me. Nonetheless, I still feel that I cannot be one of them. One day my child asked me, "Mom, why am I not an American?" I felt really sorry for him. I could not help him. This is beyond my ability.

Second, wild geese mothers' unique situation as a sole mother residing in the host country without their husbands make them feel uneasy when they interact with mainstream middle-class mothers. In particular, by exposing themselves to the North American middle-class family culture that requires not only mothers but also fathers to actively participate in their children's school and extracurricular activities,[32] many wild geese mothers realize that the absence of their husbands may look unusual to their North American counterparts. Because many wild geese mothers feel awkward due to their unique situation as a de facto single parent, they tend to withdraw from married couple-based parental social groups, even if they have not experienced any explicit attempt at exclusion by the parents at their children's schools.

Third, wild geese mothers' sense of lowered social status after migration also hinders their active interaction with mainstream middle-class mothers in private spheres. Most wild geese mothers in my study enjoyed comfortable lifestyles corresponding to their upper-middle-class *habitus*[33] in Korea. For example, they owned and lived in spacious premium condominiums in Seoul;[34] enjoyed high-end cultural experiences, such as watching musicals, going to art galleries, and learning foreign languages; maintained their wellness by regularly going to fitness centers; and had a vibrant social life through their children's schools, including gourmet brunches with other mothers at luxurious restaurants.

After migration, however, many of them have suffered from imminent economic pressures, as they have to maintain two costly transnational split households. Accordingly, many wild geese mothers rent small, shabby apartments in affluent residential areas. Even though it is a necessary strategy for them to provide their children with free public education in a good school district while saving on living and educational costs, many wild geese mothers are quite depressed because of their lowered quality of living. They are also afraid that their children may become dispirited if their middle-class local friends happen to witness their living situation. Thus, some of the wealthier wild geese mothers even purchase and move to a townhouse or single-family house for them (and their children) to better socialize with middle-class families of the host society. However, most wild geese mothers lack such financial resources and tend to close their doors to their children's local friends and their mothers.

Finally, wild geese mothers' newly obtained status as racial/ethnic minority women in the host society also significantly discourages them from actively engaging with mainstream middle-class mothers. In particular, because they have migrated from a country of racial and ethnic homogeneity,[35] many wild geese mothers keenly sense their racial and ethnic difference from the majority of mothers (mostly white) at their children's schools.

A story of former wild geese mother named Minkyung illustrates how wild geese mothers' sense of *otherness*[36] as Asian and minority women, combined with their foreigner status, prevents them from both actively engaging with their children's school mothers and holding any leadership positions in their children's schools in the host society, even if they used to hold such positions in Korea prior to migration. Prior to migration, Minkyung was a mother who actively engaged with her daughter's school community and socialized with other school mothers. She even served as the parent representative of her daughter's school. She was also quite confident in her English because she had spoken English for her work at international company until she became a full-time homemaker in Korea.

After migration to the United States, Minkyung tried to continue her intensive mothering: She attended PTA meetings, went to open houses, and met her daughter's teachers. Nonetheless, Minkyung admits that she could not actively interact with American mothers as she used to do in Korea, because of her newly obtained status as a racial/ethnic minority mother who is new to the host country. Minkying explains, "All of them [except me] were [white] American mothers. . . . And I felt awkward [when I was interacting with them] because I was different from them." Therefore, during wild geese period, Minkyung alternatively turned to the Korean immigrant networks for her successful mothering.

As discussed so far, most wild geese mothers in my study have not been so successful in socializing with the larger mainstream society after migration despite their strong needs and desire for it, because of their marginality due to language barriers, cultural differences, the single-mother status, a sense of lowered social status, and *otherness* as minority women from Asia.

Accordingly, most wild geese mothers have not made any North American friends. Nor do they actively participate in the social groups in the host communities such as American Parent Teacher Association (PTA).

Only some wild geese mothers have managed to make a close local (i.e., American or Canadian) friend or two, but this small social network is not usually extended to the bigger social networks. Rather, if their close local friends relocate to another city, wild geese mothers lose their connections with existing friends and then no longer make new American or Canadian friends, as represented by the stories of following two wild geese mothers:

> I was lucky because I could meet a good Canadian neighbor in my apartment [community]. We do many things together. Um . . . more accurately say, she helps me a lot. Our kids are also friends of the same age. Because I don't speak English well, she helps me in many ways. She also suggests joining my child in her child's running club. . . . We also go grocery shopping together. (Younghwa, a wild geese mother who has one close Canadian friend)

> I met an Italian [American] friend [through my child's school]. She and I met almost five days a week, shopping together, and going to museum in Manhattan. We had similar interests, although she was seven years older than me. In some ways, I felt like I was dating with her, because we were so close and understood each other. We both had one child in the same grade. So, when our children were at school, we had lots of fun. Thanks to her, I started to find fun in my life in America. So, when she left [and moved to another city] after two years, I was really sad. [. . .] After that, I started to make many Korean friends. (Minhee, a wild geese mother who made one close American friend)

In sum, while wild geese mothers tend to develop improved relationships with their children after migration, many of them find it difficult to serve the role of competent educational manager for their children due to various unexpected obstacles and challenges they encounter as minority migrant women in the host countries.

KOREAN IMMIGRANT NETWORKS AS AN ALTERNATIVE SOURCE OF SUPPORT

This section explores how Korean immigrant communities serve wild geese mothers as their primary source of support and help them perform intensive mothering and achieve their educational goal. After migration, as discussed above, many wild geese mothers are confronted by social isolation from mainstream parents' social networks and do not find enough resources and information that are essential for their children's educational success. Accordingly, many wild geese mothers alternatively resort to Korean immigrant communities to achieve their goal of migration and continue their role of effective educational managers for their children.

Same ethnic immigrant communities are known to be the primary social infrastructure to meet immigrant women's diverse needs.[37] Zhou[38] further argues that "total strangers among co-ethnics in their own ethnic community [. . .] are able to reconnect and rebuild networks with relative ease through the involvement in ethnic institutions because of their shared cultural and language skills." Likewise, I have found that Korean immigrant networks not only provide wild geese mothers with useful educational information but also satisfy their desire to socialize, relieve their loneliness, and find support. To further compensate for their lowered social status after migration, some wild geese mothers assume leadership positions in various Korean immigrant social groups.

Interestingly, wild geese mother's socializing patterns after migration are not monolithic. Some wild geese mothers have their own families, relatives, or friends who have already resided in their destination countries. In this case, wild geese mothers can greatly benefit from their pre-established personal network both before and after migration. For instance, they can more accurately estimate their expected living and educational costs in the host society and prepare their financial resources accordingly. These mothers also can choose better schools and educational programs for their children without making much trial and error, based on the educational information provided through their personal networks. Some wild geese mothers can save their living expenses by sharing their residential areas with families and friends in the host countries. A few mothers further find paid employment in co-ethnic enclave through their family networks.[39]

Other wild geese mothers are supported by their (and/or their husbands') social and professional networks that they have established in the host society before they become transnational families. As I have described in chapter 1, some women initially migrated to the United States with their husbands as legal dependents, and then became wild geese mothers later by remaining in the United States after their husbands' return to Korea. Since they have lived in the United States before becoming a transnational family, they have more time to become familiar with the dominant society and to construct their social network, including their husbands' professional networks. Hence, even if they encounter new challenges as wild geese mothers after remaining in the host society alone, they tend to handle those challenges with relative ease thanks to useful information and support through their pre-established social networks and resources.

Unfortunately, the majority of wild geese mothers in my study does not have such pre-established kinship or social ties and thus are highly motivated to construct new social networks after migration, mainly through Korean immigrant communities. Furthermore, some wild geese mothers who have families and friends in the host countries undergo conflicts with them after migration. Consequently, wider Korean immigrant communities are still needed by almost all wild geese mothers as the locus of socializing and the source of support.

There are two most common routes through which wild geese mothers construct their new ethnic social networks: (1) KPA in their children's schools and (2) Korean immigrant churches. In the followings sections, I discuss how these two Korean immigrant networks affect the ways in which wild geese mothers overcome challenges in the host societies, achieve their educational goals, and enhance their gender and social statuses.

Korean Immigrant Parents at KPA:
Source of Education Information

To gain access to the most updated education information in the host societies, wild geese mothers want to socialize with American or Canadian middle-class mothers through their children's schools. However, it turns out to be a mission impossible for most wild geese mothers because of various issues discussed above, such as language barriers, cultural differences, unique family situation as a sole parent, the sense of lowered social class status, and *otherness* as racial/ethnic minority women. Some of them also feel uncomfortable to attend the PTA conferences or meet their children's American teachers for college counseling.

As an alternative, wild geese mothers try hard to strengthen their mothering capability by obtaining information and resources through their social networks with Korean immigrant parents whom they meet in their children's schools. In particular, many wild geese mothers whom I interviewed in the United States regard it as mandatory to socialize with Korean immigrant mothers through the KPA so as to obtain necessary educational information and resources in the host society.[40] A wild geese mother named Sukhee provides a detailed explanation of how she benefits from the KPA networks.

> I mostly socialize with school mothers. Because there are many Koreans here, we have the KPA. It makes an effort [to help Korean mothers]. It introduces Korean traditional culture [to Americans] through Lunar New Year's Event. In addition, it asks school administration to hold college admissions briefing sessions for Korean American mothers. [. . .] I met many Korean mothers through

the high school KPA meeting on October. Because we were mothers in the similar situations, we made our own regular gathering. Since then, we have met once a week. I absolutely love it! [Through the KPA] I can get educational information and satisfy my socializing desire.

As Sukhee has described above, for newly migrated wild geese mothers, Korean immigrant mothers whom they meet through their children's schools are one of the most useful venues for building up their first social networks, obtaining helpful educational information, and having their children settled in the new educational environment. Moreover, a few wild geese mothers who have stayed for a longer period in the United States also achieve a sense of fulfillment as they serve as the president or a board member of the KPA and play the role of opinion leaders and/or a source of educational knowledge for other Korean immigrant mothers in their school community.

Korean Immigrant Churches:
Sources of Emotional and Practical Support

Whereas the KPA is primarily the source of educational information, the Korean ethnic churches satisfy wild geese mothers' more diverse needs and thus are vital for their survival in the host societies. First of all, wild geese mothers are emotionally supported by the Korean immigrant church community, which shares the same culture and language. Below account by Damso, a wild geese mother in a New Jersey Koreatown, stands out:

My Korean friends support my emotional side. When I wake up in the morning, I have just a short conversation with my husband on the phone, because both of us are busy. My children are not so young anymore. So, I don't have anyone home to talk to. But, with the Korean mothers, I exchange the Kakao Talk [a mobile application for free text message, very popular among Koreans] messages all day long. There is nothing special in our conversation. We just share funny video clips or humors or anything. That is it. Nevertheless, I sometimes think like this: Without them, who will know if I am sick and pass out alone in this apartment?

Such emotional support and the sense of belonging it engenders make Korean churches the greatest social asset[41] for many wild geese mothers who want to overcome their frustrating experiences of being downgraded into incompetent mothers who cannot effectively perform their expected role of educational managers for their children after migration.

To many wild geese mothers, the Korean church community means more than just a religious organization. It serves as a haven where wild geese mothers can find comfort and rely on others, particularly when they are frustrated within the dominant society. Wild geese mothers assume leadership positions within the Korean church community, such as deaconess, cell group leaders, bible study group leaders, and/or Sunday school teachers, so that they can recover their lowered confidence and self-esteem after migration.

Some wild geese mothers who have lived in the host country for a longer period of time feel a sense of achievement when they help newly migrated women adjust to the new environment. This experience contrasts with George's study of Indian immigrant families in the United States,[42] which has noted that the benefits of the immigrant church are often limited to men. According to George, the Indian immigrant church helps Indian American men regain their lowered social status after migration by providing them with an opportunity to participate in the public area of church, while it forces their wives not to challenge the hegemonic male status in their religious organizations.[43] However, the experiences of Korean wild geese mothers in my study demonstrate that immigrant churches can also empower immigrant women to enhance their social status, by offering leadership positions that they cannot otherwise have attained in the broader host society.

Second, in addition to the emotional benefits, the Korean church community also meets wild geese mothers' practical needs.[44] Newly migrated wild geese mothers, particularly those who do not have any pre-established personal or social connections, find that Korean church networks are critical for them to smoothly settle down into the host societies, as well as to obtain educational information and resources for their children. It is important to note that, prior to migration, the majority of Korean wild geese mothers naively expected that the host society would be pretty similar to the Korean society. Accordingly, they are quite bewildered after migration as they have recognized that the system and culture of the host society are different from those of the Korean society. Consequently, many wild geese mothers cannot even start thinking about how they can effectively manage their children's education until they secure survival in the host society.

In this respect, Korean churches are very helpful, because through its networks, wild geese mothers can construct extensive social networks across the larger Korean immigrant community as well as obtain social and economic resources to solve their daily challenges in the host societies. Wild geese mothers make a number of decisions based on the information provided by the Korean church and Korean immigrant community. For example, wild geese mothers find Korean doctors to visit, Korean lawyers to consult about their legal issues, Korean realtors to find their housing, and Korean grocery markets to buy their daily necessities, based on their reputations among Korean immigrants. Some newly migrated wild geese mothers even stay at their Korean church pastor's house for several months until they find an appropriate residence. The Korean church networks are also pivotal for those who seek employment opportunities in the co-ethnic enclave stores and companies. For example, some wild geese mothers are able to find paid jobs at Korean immigrants-owned shops such as delis, laundry shops, and restaurants through their church acquaintances' referrals, despite their lack of English proficiency and/or a legitimate visa status to work.

Most importantly, wild geese mothers utilize their ethnic church networks to fulfill their educational goals. For instance, through casual conversations with their church members, wild geese mothers with older children obtain valuable educational information about the host countries' education system in general, the admission requirements for prestigious universities, and private academic institutions to help their children earn a high SAT score.[45] Furthermore, as Korean wild geese mothers are not so successful in obtaining educational information from the parents and teachers of their children's schools due to their social isolation from mainstream networks, they alternatively attempt to obtain such resources from their co-ethnic immigrant community and fulfill the role of their children's educational manager.

In particular, wild geese mothers tend to heavily rely on Korean tutors at private academic institutions in Koreatown, even if some of them did not like private academic institutions prior to migration. For example, according to Miseon, a former wild geese mother whose daughter has just graduated from one of the top universities in the United States and found a good job there, she was able to achieve her educational goals thanks to the assistance from Korean teachers at a private SAT preparation academy in Koreatown. Similar to Miseon, most wild geese mothers whose adolescent children are currently preparing for the SAT test for American college admission are likely to send (or have already sent) their children to Korean-owned private educational centers, even if their tuition is very expensive. Dambi, a wild geese mother of an eleventh grader, well explains why she has to rely on the Korean private supplementary education even after migration:

My first daughter attended a private SAT academy last year. It was a summer session costing over $3,000 for eight weeks. [. . .] It was a private academic institution owned by Koreans, although all teachers taught in English. It [sending children to commercial SAT preparation institutes] is very popular among Korean immigrant mothers here. If your children have lived in America for a long time and study hard by themselves, they don't have to go to such a private academy. However, as a wild geese mother [who migrated to America just two-and-a-half years ago], I am very anxious [about my daughter's college admission]. If your children migrated here [like mine] during their secondary school, you also might feel urgent. That's why many [wild geese] mothers send their children there [Korean cram schools]. Because I am nervous and anxious, I am willing to send her [there] again, even if it requires me to borrow money.

Parents' such dependence on private educational institutes for their children's better academic achievement is quite common among East Asian immigrant communities.[46] While they can utilize the Korean ethnic media or commercial advertisements to find appropriate Korean-owned private educational institutions, many wild geese mothers in my study tend to trust the word-of-mouth circulating in their church community as one of the most reliable sources of information. In this regard, it is even more important for wild geese mothers to maintain their membership in the Korean church community.

The informal church networks are also useful to wild geese mothers who plan to return to Korea prior to their children's completion of secondary education and thus have to keep up with the fast-changing Korean educational policies, such as terms and conditions of special admission for overseas Koreans to universities. Wild geese mothers' younger children also benefit from their church affiliation, as they make Korean American friends and attend the extracurricular activities offered by the church, such as youth orchestra, summer camp, and English classes.

In addition, wild geese mothers learn from their church networks how to communicate with their rebellious adolescent children while their husbands are physically absent (who used to or are expected to do a better job of discipline). For instance, Minhee is a wild geese mother who experienced serious confrontations with her teenage son after migration. She pressured him to study harder as she used to do in Korea, whereas her son did not follow her directions and spent a lot of time in playing online computer games. However, since she took an eight-week parent mentoring program provided by her church two years before the interview, she has changed her parenting style from pushy to communicative. She still regularly attends the weekly church parent group meetings to share with other Korean immigrant mothers her trials and errors as a sole parent in the foreign country and get some advice from them. For Minhee, her church community and her Christian belief are the critical resources that help her recover an intimate relationship with her adolescent son.

Because of many practical benefits from the Korean immigrant church community that I have described so far, not only wild geese mothers who had Christian beliefs prior to migration but also those with different or no religious beliefs have converted into Christians and regularly attend Korean immigrant churches after migration.[47] A wild geese mother named Younghwa is a good example. Younghwa used to be a Buddhist in Korea but has recently converted to a Christian as she was so grateful to, and impressed by, those who she met at the Korean immigrant church in Canada:

[After migration to Canada] I have been involved in Church. I was not Christian originally. I was Buddhist [in Korea]. When I first came here, I was under great stress. While I was really struggling here, the first person who helped me was a Christian. Thus, since then, I go to Church. Church people have really helped me a lot [to adapt to the new environment].

Many wild geese mothers also select their church affiliation primarily based on their practical needs (including their educational needs) rather than their religious matters. Hence, it is not rare to see them moving to another church if it is expected to meet their practical needs better than their current church.[48] For example, Eunji, a wild geese mother with a 13-year-old daughter, recently moved to a new Korean church that has a youth orchestra to give her daughter an opportunity to play the cello there. Nevertheless, once they have joined a church, most wild geese mothers are likely to keep remaining as part of the Korean church community, even if they move from one church to another.

Moreover, wild geese mothers who were Christians prior to migration often have become more religious after migration and deepened their attachment to their church community as time goes by. A wild geese mother named Yuna strongly believes that she has been able to overcome many practical and emotional hardships she has encountered in the host society thanks to "the blessings from the God." Reflecting on the time when she was struggling as a newly migrant, Yuna adds, "I seriously hanged on to God at that time. If I did not rely on the power of religion, I might have taken pills [to commit suicide]." Since then, Yuna has further deepened her Christian belief and organized her daily life around the Korean immigrant church. In addition to regularly going to church every Sunday, she goes to church almost every day to attend various programs, such as early morning prayer, parenting coaching programs, and Quiet Time (QT) meetings.

In sum, by becoming members and maintaining high loyalty to their immigrant church community, Korean wild geese mothers are offered emotional support and practical resources that are necessary for them to effectively perform their expected mothering roles and to achieve their educational goals.

CONSTRAINTS IN THE KOREAN IMMIGRANT COMMUNITY

While the previous section has discussed the benefits of Korean immigrant networks, this section turns its attention to the hardships that wild geese mothers undergo within their own ethnic community. In particular, this section highlights that the KPA and Korean immigrant churches do not always play positive roles in supporting wild geese mothers' lives. Interestingly, despite its disadvantages, the majority of wild geese mothers still struggle to maintain their membership in their co-ethnic community, particularly the Korean church community, because of its tremendous practical benefits to perform their role of mother and educational manager for their children.

Korean Immigrant Parents at KPA: Demanding in Unwanted Ways

While newly migrated wild geese mothers benefit from interacting with other Korean immigrant parents whom they meet through their children's schools and the KPA, these social networks are less attractive for those who have stayed in the host country for a longer period and have built other social networks within the Korean immigrant community. In fact, many wild geese mothers cease being committed to the KPA activities within a couple of years, once they have reached out to the wider Korean immigrant community.

Several reasons are addressed: (1) Some wild geese mothers explain that they have left the KPA because they are overwhelmed by its excessive educational information; (2) others do not like high competition and jealousy among Korean immigrant mothers within the organization; and (3) a few wild geese mothers even wonder why they have to follow how other KPA mothers do and/or why they have to pursue the Korean-style education and mothering practices in this new country, even though they have left Korea for something different, if not better. Hana, a wild geese mother, who served as the vice president of the KPA, reiterates such issues:

There is Korean mothers' group, known as the KPA. A woman that I met at a [Korean] Catholic church told me that I should go there to meet other Korean mothers and get some information. [. . .] If you go there, there are no one who has lived long time [in this country]. Rather, you will meet people who desperately need [educational] information [as newly migrants]. [. . .] There are various kinds of mothers [in the KPA]. Some mothers keep working hard for it. Others just disappear once they get to make some acquaintances. [. . .] I heard that lower school mothers worked very hard [for the KPA]. But, in case of high school [KPA], only [newly migrated] mothers like me are in desperate need, not mothers who have lived here for a long time and raised their children up to high schoolers, because they know what to prepare for their children's college admission. So, these mothers don't participate in the KPA which just takes their time [without benefitting them]. [. . .] Even if I served as the vice-president [of the KPA] for a year, my close friends up to now are not the ones that I have met through the KPA, but the ones through the Catholic church. Through the KPA, you can build networks to find your children's private educational institutes or private lessons. However, it does not greatly help you make truly close friends beyond some line.

Korean Immigrant Churches: Most Useful but Most Exclusive

Zhou claims in her analysis of the Korean ethnic community in LA that new Korean immigrants can benefit from its ethnic community's resources primarily based on their co-ethnicity.[49] While I agree with her that the Korean immigrant community is quite exclusive to other racial/ethnic groups, I further argue in this section that even the same-ethnic new comers cannot easily gain access to its abundant educational resources and information unless the existing community accepts them as its legitimate members.

Among various Korean immigrant communities, Korean churches are the central social organization. Zhou and Kim even claim that the Korean ethnic church is "the single most important ethnic institution" in the Korean immigrant community.[50] Therefore, the first task of newly migrated wild geese mothers who seek assistance from the Korean immigrant community is to be accepted as the legitimate members of the Korean immigrant churches. Then, the next task is to maintain their membership in order not to lose their support.

Being the central social organization of the Korean immigrant community, Korean ethnic churches are ubiquitous in wild geese mothers' everyday lives. Because Korean churches tend to have conservative perspectives on family relations and uphold patriarchal values, such as strict sexual mores,[51] Korean churches at times function like the *Panopticon*[52] that monitors and disciplines wild geese mothers. Some wild geese mothers are even ostracized if they do not seem to conform to traditional Korean values such as good mothers and faithful wives.

Sohee, a wild geese mother who appeared at the interview in fashionable short pants and a sleeveless shirt, recalls how she was annoyed and hurt when other Korean immigrants reprimanded her for wearing clothes in a supposedly unchaste way. Sohee adds:

> They criticize me not only because of what I wear. They monitor and carp at me in all aspects. So, I feel like I am a celebrity here, really. Even if I am just different from them a little bit, they blame me. Although I don't know them, they know me. It is so stressful for me.

As she stands out in her small immigrant church community, Sohee has been often misunderstood as a rude woman if she does not say hello to other Koreans whom she does not know so well. Due to the hostility and negative rumors about her, Sohee has closed her mind to others and is no longer willing to make any new friends in the immigrant community at the time of interview. She even asserts that "I now have a very pessimistic view on all human relations."

Another wild geese mother named Hyojin was divorced during the wild geese period. Then, she had to leave her church because of the church members' excessive attention to and interference in her personal life. As these two women's stories show, wild geese mothers are highly pressured by their co-ethnic church community to conform to traditional values and patriarchal norms.

To make matters worse, wild geese mothers, in general, have to tolerate even closer surveillance of their private lives than other newcomers by their church community because of their marginality in terms of family structure. Unlike so-called *normal* families in which wives and husbands live together with their children, wild geese mothers live separately from their husbands. Because of their apparent freedom from the patriarchal control of husbands who remain in Korea, wild geese mothers are now under even harsher surveillance by the Korean immigrant community that suspects wild geese mothers are prone to behave inappropriately.[53] Accordingly, some wild geese mothers who have been exhausted by the constant surveillance and discipline eventually decide to leave their Korean immigrant church communities, giving up the benefits that go along with belonging to them.

Furthermore, while Frankenberg and Espiritu have problematized *othering* between whites and nonwhites (including Asian Americans),[54] I argue that *othering* is also occurring within the same racial/ethnic immigrant community. For example, there are negative *controlling images*[55] attached to wild geese mothers, such as being perceived as exploiters who take advantage of the information and resources that other Korean Americans have strenuously built up over a long period of time and then leave after their short sojourn without making any meaningful contributions to the community.

One wild geese mother, Eunji's experience with a small Korean church in New Jersey well represents the hostility of Korean immigrants to wild geese mothers. According to Eunji, she heard some people saying sarcastically, "Oh, another wild geese mother comes again!" when she first went to the local Korean church. Others even said to her face that they did not need a wild geese mother but another person who could serve the church for a longer period. Contemplating the reasons why she was treated unfavorably, even from the first moment she joined the Korean church, Eunji points out *othering* as a main reason:

Koreans who have lived here [as permanent immigrants] view that wild geese mothers are different from them. They think wild geese mothers are those who just suck them dry and leave. So, they [Korean immigrants] don't show much affection to us.

Even though she skipped the church service only once, Eunji was severely criticized by others who believed that she did so because of her sojourner status and lack of commitment to the church community. To overcome the prejudice against her and to be accepted as a true member of her Korean church community, Eunji had to attend and serve the church more conscientiously than anyone else did. Only after that could she legitimately gain access to the church resources that had been readily available to other co-ethnic Korean immigrants. By the time of interview, Eunji has been very cautiously maintaining her good reputation within the church community in order not to lose her access to valuable educational resources.

There are other controlling images: Wild geese mothers are often branded as extravagant and/or so obsessed about their children's education that they even abandoned their husbands in Korea. Moreover, as married women without legitimate sexual partners (i.e., their husbands) being present next to them, wild geese mothers are often suspected of readily engaging in affairs with Korean immigrant men. Thus, wild geese mothers' sexual reputations are very closely monitored by their Korean immigrant community, although such monitoring of women's sexuality by the co-ethnic immigrant community is not unique to Korean immigrants.[56]

Many wild geese mothers that I interviewed have not only experienced animosity toward them but have also have internalized such negative *controlling images* about themselves. Hence, they are quite defensive about their personal lives and try hard to convince me that they are different from so-called *bad* wild geese mothers, undertaking their own *othering* process. For instance, wild geese mothers have emphasized, during their interviews, how frugal they are, criticizing other supposedly extravagant wild geese mothers who are shopping for luxury goods (e.g., CHANEL or Gucci bags) and playing golf.[57] They also stress that they are not interested in sexual relationships, as if being asexual were the prerequisite for being virtuous wild geese mothers. At the same time, they have told me of gossip they heard about some bad wild geese mothers who were flirting with men, had affairs, and even got divorced.

With their private lives under constant surveillance, some wild geese mothers, like Jiwon, have to fabricate their personal stories in order to be accepted in their immigrant community. According to Jiwon, she has not told anyone in her immigrant community that her husband has passed away. Jiwon believes that if she shares her widowed status with others, it will only result in adding one more layer of discrimination against her on top of her already stigmatized wild geese mother status. In particular, Jiwon is very concerned about the possibility that she can be seen as a potential partner for unfaithful Korean immigrant men. As she always has to be careful not to reveal her personal story to others, it is very difficult for her to make close friends. For her, the Korean ethnic community is a source of isolation and stress rather than a source of support and socializing.

In sum, while Korean immigrant social networks around Korean churches provide wild geese mothers with emotional and practical resources that help these women overcome their marginality in the host society and perform better mothering, such resources are accessible only after these women have passed the immigrant church community's strict and constant scrutiny of their private lives and are accepted as their legitimate members.

CONCLUSION

In this chapter, I have explored the changes in Korean wild geese mothers' mothering and socializing through migration. While previous literature has narrowly defined middle-class Asian women's transnational migration for their children's education as the negative outcome of patriarchal Asian culture and has focused on revealing their hardships in the host society,[58] I provide an alternative explanation: middle-class Asian women, as represented by Korean wild geese mothers, have agency and decide to migrate abroad in order to better enact the ideology of intensive mothering, which is a global *gendered* norm that pressures middle-class women across racial/ethnic backgrounds and nationalities to become devoted mothers, as Hondagneu-Sotelo and Avila have argued.[59]

I have compared how Korean wild geese mothers perform intensive mothering between Korea (prior to migration) and North America (after migration). Prior to migration, wild geese mothers' provision of physical care for their children varied by their employment status, but they were commonly enthusiastic and successful in performing the role of ambitious educational manager for their children. They even were too enthusiastic and pushy to have good relationships with their children. In contrast, after migration, most wild geese mothers can better provide emotional and physical care for their children, as intensive mothering ideology dictates, and tend to develop closer relationships with their children thanks to their relaxed mothering style. However, unexpectedly, transnational migration makes it more difficult for wild geese mothers to accomplish their educational goals, because they no longer easily gain access to the educational information and resources, which they took for granted in Korea, owing to their structural disadvantages in the host society as racial/ethnic minority women who (1) lack language fluency and cultural knowledge and (2) are isolated from mainstream social networks.

I have also described how Korean wild geese mothers are isolated from the mainstream social networks of the host society and struggle to overcome such unforeseen challenges and fulfill their intensive mothering ideology and educational goals by constructing alternative social networks within their own ethnic community. By doing so, this chapter confirms that a co-ethnic immigrant community is one of the most important sites for social resources for newly migrated minority women.[60] Thanks to the emotional and practical supports provided by the Korean immigrant community, wild geese mothers are able to overcome their frustrating experiences of being downgraded into incompetent minority migrant mothers and to achieve their educational goals.

Nonetheless, this chapter does not only highlight the positive aspects of the co-ethnic community. It also sheds light on its darker side. While the immigrant community's ethnic solidarity can be a primary resource for Asian immigrants to overcome the racial and class oppressions they encounter in the host society,[61] I add more nuanced explanations: ethnic community's resources and information are not equally available to all the co-ethnic immigrants. Usually, newcomers cannot legitimately gain access to their own ethnic community's resources and information until they have passed its scrutiny on them to be finally accepted as its members. Nonetheless, wild geese mothers are subject to even stricter monitoring of their body, sexuality, and private lives, because of their marginality in terms of their gender status and family structure (i.e., women living separately from their husbands). Even though a few wild geese mothers have resisted their immigrant community's constant surveillance of them, many others choose to maintain their membership within the Korean immigrant community rather than losing its resources that are critical for their successful mothering and survival in the host society. Wild geese mothers also tend to internalize and reproduce the prejudices against them through their own *othering* process rather than challenging them.

In conclusion, this chapter offers a nuanced explanation of the complex interplay among social class, gender, and race with regard to middle-class Asian migrant women's empowerment and hardships in the host societies, by comparing wild geese mothers' mothering practices and educational management for their children between pre-migration and after-migration periods. In particular, this chapter sheds light on the ambivalent impacts of the Korean immigrant communities on wild geese mothers' lives after migration, by comparing the advantages and disadvantages of wild geese mothers' membership in the Korean immigrant communities. Through their active involvement in the co-ethnic immigrant community, wild geese mothers obtain valuable resources to overcome the challenges in the host society and better perform their role of committed mother and effective educational manager for their children. Wild geese mothers also can enhance their domestic status within their transnational households and recover their lowered social status in the host society thanks to the varied supports from their own ethnic community. Yet, all these resources are available only if these women conform to the existing community's patriarchal family/gender norms and rules and continuously pass the community's strict monitoring on them.

NOTES

This chapter is a revised version of an article originally published as Se Hwa Lee, "Only If You Are One of Us: Wild Geese Mothers' Parenting in the Korean Immigrant Community," *Amerasia Journal* 42, no. 2 (2016): 71–94. Reprinted with permission from *Amerasia Journal*.

1. Choi, "Geese Families," 44 (in Korean); Kim, "'Downed' and Stuck," 271–311; Park and Abelmann, "Class and Cosmopolitan Striving," 534–672; Yi, "Tiger Moms," 190; Zhou and Kim, "Supplementary Education," 2–8.

2. Similar rationales were resonated in other literature on wild geese families. See Cho, "Korean Families," 163–166 (in Korean); Choi, "Geese Families," 44–45 (in Korean); Kim, "English Fever," 119–121; Kim, "'Downed' and Stuck," 283; Lee, "Kirogi Mother," 251; Lee and Koo, "Wild Geese Fathers," 541–542, 552; Park and Abelmann, "Class and Cosmopolitan Striving," 646, 650.

3. Lee, "Kirogi Mother," 253.

4. For the further discussion on the role of immigrant community's role on Asian American women, see Kibria, *Family Tightrope*, 108–143; Espiritu, *Asian American Women and Men*, 71–95; Ong and Azores, "Migration and Incorporation," 164–195.

5. Chee, "Migrating for the Children," 137–156; Huang and Yeoh, "Study Mothers," 379–400.

6. For more discussion on *intensive mothering*, see Arendell, "Conceiving and Investigating Motherhood," 1192–1207; Hays, *Cultural Contradictions of Motherhood*, 19–50.

7. Hondagneu-Sotelo and Avila, "I'm Here," 548–571.

8. Arendell, "Conceiving and Investigating Motherhood," 1192–1207; Hays, *Cultural Contradictions of Motherhood*, 19–50.

9. Choi, "Geese Families," 44 (in Korean); Kim, "'Downed' and Stuck," 271–311; Park and Abelmann, "Class and Cosmopolitan Striving," 534–672; Yi, "Tiger Moms," 190; Zhou and Kim, "Supplementary Education," 2–8.

10. Amy Chua, *Battle Hymn of the Tiger Mother* (New York: Penguin Press, 2011).

11. See Yi, "Tiger Moms," 193.

12. While Fineman shows how the ideology of intensive mothering reinforces the strict gender role division between spouses who live together in *Neutered Mother*, I further extend her argument by demonstrating an even stricter transnational gender role division among wild geese couples. See Martha Fineman, *The Neutered Mother, the Sexual Family and Other Twentieth Century Tragedies* (New York: Routledge, 1995).

13. Min Zhou, "How Neighbourhoods Matter for Immigrant Children: The Formation of Educational Resources in Chinatown, Koreatown and Pico Union, Los Angeles," *Journal of Ethnic and Migration Studies* 35, no. 7 (2009): 1153–1179.

14. Ibid.

15. Ibid.

16. Ibid.

17. Arendell, "Conceiving and Investigating Motherhood," 1192–1207; Hays, *Cultural Contradictions of Motherhood*, 19–52.

18. Chua, *Tiger Mother*.

19. See also Kim, "Wild Goose Mother," 41–59.

20. It took about an hour for Eunji to drive from her house in Ilsan (city near Seoul) to get to her daughter's school in Seoul (Capital city of South Korea). For her daughter who was a first-grade elementary school student at that time, it was quite a long distance to commute every day.

21. For self-sacrificing, devoted wild geese mothers, see Kim, "Wild Geese Family," 41–59 (in Korean).

22. Arendell, "Conceiving and Investigating Motherhood," 1192–1207; Stephanie Coontz, *The Way We Really Are: Coming to Terms with America's Changing Families* (New York: Basic Books, 1997), 51–76.

23. Chinese astronaut wives and study mothers tend to get childcare support from paid help prior to their migration. See Chang and Darlington, "Astronaut Wives," 65, 69; Huang and Yeoh, "Study Mothers," 392; Waters, "Flexible Families," 121–122.

24. Richard R. Peterson and Kathleen Gerson, "Determinants of Responsibility for Child Care Arrangements among Dual-earner Couples," *Journal of Marriage and the Family* 54 (1992): 527–536.

25. England, "Mothers, Wives, Workers," 109–122; Hochschild, *Second Shift*, 15–17; Moon, "Immigration and Mothering," 852–853; Parreñas, "Migrant Filipina Domestic Workers," 560–580.

26. It is not unique to Korean parents. Other East Asian parents like Japanese and Chinese also heavily rely on private education for their children's academic success. See Soo-young Byun and Hyunjoon Park, "The Academic Success of East Asian American Youth: The Role of Shadow Education," *Sociology of Education* 85, no. 1 (2012): 41.

27. Ibid., 40–60.

28. Annette Lareau, "Invisible Inequality: Social Class and Childrearing in Black Families and White Families," *American Sociological Review* 67 (2002): 747.

29. There are exceptions. See chapter 1 for wild geese mothers who pursue post-secondary education and/or full-time professional careers in the host societies.

30. Espiritu, *Asian American Women and Men*, 100.

31. Charles Hirschman, "The Role of Religion in the Origins and Adaptation of Immigrant Groups in the United States," *International Migration Review* 38, no. 3 (2004): 1206–1233.

32. Lareau, "Invisible Inequality," 747–776.

33. Bourdieu, *Theory of Practice*, 72–86.

34. Seoul is the capital and the largest city of South Korea.

35. As of 2015, only 3 percent of the total Korean population was foreigners, including students, white collar workers, migrant workers in low-end industries and service jobs, undocumented workers, and foreign brides. See Center for East Asian Policy Studies at Brookings, "South Korea's Demographic Changes and Their Political Impact—East Asian Policy Paper 6" (October 26, 2015), https://www.bro okings.edu/wp-content/uploads/2016/06/South-Koreas-demographic-changes-and-their-political-impact.pdf.

36. Espiritu, *Asian American Women and Men*, 99.

37. Kibria, "Migration and Vietnamese," 247–264; Hondagneu-Sotelo, *Gendered Transitions*, 72–82; Menjívar, "Family Reorganization," 223–245; Menjívar, "Transnational Parenting," 301–322; Ong and Azores, "Migration and Incorporation," 164–195.

38. Zhou, "How Neighbourhoods Matter," 1157.

39. Wild geese mothers' search of paid employment through family networks is mentioned both in chapters 1 and 6.

40. In contrast, wild geese mothers whom I interviewed in Canada did not mention about KPA. It was probably because of the differences between the research sites. One is the metropolitan New York and New Jersey area with dense Korean immigrant population, whereas the other is London in Canada, a smaller city with much fewer Korean immigrants and thus less active KPA.

41. For further discussion on the role of religion for new immigrants in the United States, see Hirschman, "Role of Religion," 206–1233; Pyong Gap Min and Jung Ha Kim, *Religions in Asian America: Building Faith Communities* (Walnut Creek, CA: AltaMira Press, 2002), 185–214.

42. Sheba Mariam George, "When Women Come First: Gender and Class and Transnational Ties among Indian Immigrants in the United States" (PhD diss., UC Berkeley, 2001), 149–165.

43. Ibid.

44. To see how other immigrant churches serve the practical needs of the immigrants, see Helen Rose Ebaugh and Janet Saltzman Chafetz, *Religion and the New Immigrants: Continuities and Adaptations in Immigrant Congregations* (New York: AltaMira Press, 2000), 45–324; Hirschman, "Role of Religion," 206–1233; Menjívar, "Liminal Legality," 1024–1025.

45. Zhou also describes the significant educational benefits of their own ethnic community for non-English speaking Korean parents in Koreatown in Los Angeles; see "How Neighbourhoods Matter," 1176.

46. See Zhou and Kim, "Supplementary Education," 7–25; Byun and Park, "Academic Success," 40–60; Grace Kao, "Parental Influences on the Educational Outcomes of Immigrant Youth," *International Migration Review* 38, no. 2 (2004): 427–449; Yongmin Sun, "The Academic Success of East-Asian American Students–An Investment Model," *Social Science Research* 27 (1998): 432–456.

47. Hurh and Kim have also noted the similar pattern. See Won Moo Hurh and Kwang Chung Kim, "Adhesive Sociocultural Adaptation of Korean Immigrants in the United States: An Alternative Strategy of Minority Adaptation," *The International Migration Review* 18, no. 2 (Summer, 1984): 189, 194–196.

48. Similar pattern is observed from Central American immigrants. See Menjívar, "Liminal Legality," 1026.

49. Zhou, "How Neighbourhoods Matter," 1153–1179.

50. Zhou and Kim, "Supplementary Education," 14.

51. Moon, "Immigration and Mothering," 840–860.

52. Michel Foucault, *Discipline and Punish: The Birth of the Prison,* translated by Alan Sheridan (New York: Pantheon Books, 1977), 200–210.

53. Guatemalan and Ecuadorian women who are left behind by their migrant husbands are similarly under close moral surveillance by their families-in-law, relatives and friends in their home country. See Cecilia Menjívar, *Enduring Violence: Latina Women's Lives in Guatemala* (Berkeley: University of California Press, 2011), 98–129; Pribilsky, "Aprendemos a Convivir," 322–333.

54. Espiritu, *Asian American Women and Men,* 97–122; Ruth Frankenberg, *White Women, Race Matters: The Social Construction of Whiteness* (Minneapolis: University of Minnesota Press, 1993), 191–235.

55. Collins, *Black Feminist Thought,* 69–96.

56. See Kibria, *Family Tightrope,* 117 for the cases of Vietnamese immigrants.

57. Golf is seen a luxury sport in Korea.

58. Chee, "Migrating for the Children," 137–156; Huang and Yeoh, "Study Mothers," 379–400.

59. Hondagneu-Sotelo and Avila, "I'm Here," 548–571.

60. Kibria, "Migration and Vietnamese," 247–264; Hondagneu-Sotelo, *Gendered Transitions,* 72–82; Menjívar, "Family Reorganization," 223–245; Menjívar, "Transnational Parenting," 301–322; Ong and Azores "Migration and Incorporation," 164–195; Zhou, "How Neighbourhoods Matters," 2009.

61. Espiritu, *Asian American Women and Men,* 71–95; Kibria, *Family Tightrope,* 108–143.

Chapter 5

Transnational Fathering and Father-Child Relationship

The paradigm of fathering has rapidly shifted over time. Fathers are now expected to be *new fathers*[1] and *equal co-parents*.[2] That is, contemporary fathers encounter heightened cultural expectations for their roles[3] and are expected to perform *responsible fathering*,[4] *involved fatherhood*,[5] and/or *intimate fatherhood*.[6] Levine and Pitt suggest two important characteristics of responsible fathering: Fathers should actively share the "continuing emotional and physical care of their children" and the "continuing financial support of their child" with mothers.[7] That is, men are defined as good fathers when they fulfill not only their traditional breadwinning role but also their new role as involved fathers who actively participate in daily childcare work and maintain close emotional relationships with their children.[8] Under this changing cultural norm of fatherhood, some middle-class Swedish men even equally share the parental leave with their wives to take care of children.[9] Furthermore, fathers' emotional and nurturing roles are emphasized regardless of whether fathers live together with their children.[10] Thus, family studies have investigated not only resident fathers but also nonresident fathers such as divorced or single fathers. However, transnational fathers who live separately from their children have been largely neglected in the family scholarship,[11] or described as atypical, abnormal, or fragile,[12] if discussed.

Compared to family studies, migration studies have paid greater attention to the fathering experiences of transnational fathers who live apart from their children,[13] reflecting the increasing significance of fatherhood. However, there are still some gaps in this growing literature on transnational fatherhood. First, similar to the family literature, fathers in transnational contexts tend to be described negatively.[14] For example, migrant fathers are portrayed as showing little concern for their children,[15] and left-behind fathers are said to neglect their roles as fathers.[16] According to Waters,[17] this negative

167

portrait of migrant men may be related to the fact that they are rarely the main object of research but "are examined only to the extent that they impact on women's lives." However, fathering behaviors of transnational men need to be explored from a more balanced perspective, given the growing diversity of transnational fathers across race/ethnicity, class, and country of origin.

Second, while maintaining familial intimacy is highly emphasized in the analysis of transnational mothering,[18] the emotional role of transnational fathers has not been appropriately addressed.[19] This is partly because of the persisting patriarchal gender expectations of parenting. While transnational mothers are expected to maintain intimate relationships with their children,[20] "fathering from a distance does not reconstitute 'normative gender behavior' in the family but instead abides by gender-ideological norms such as male breadwinning," as Parreñas has noted.[21] Therefore, scholarly research on transnational fatherhood, which is still at a nascent stage, tends to over-emphasize transnational men's breadwinner role over their nurturing one. Accordingly, transnational fathers are often assumed to be responsible fathers as long as they fulfill the breadwinning roles.[22] Indeed, breadwinning is so important for Mexican transnational fathers that they are estranged from their left-behind children if they do not fulfill economic roles.[23] However, I argue that not only economic provision but also emotional support are equally important parts of fathering even in the transnational context.

Third, transnational fathers' emotions are also under-researched.[24] In particular, migrant fathers are often assumed to be *independent* and *non-relational*[25] people who are less emotionally influenced by and suffer less from separation from their families, compared with migrant mothers.[26] However, recent studies show that transnational fathers also undergo emotional changes because of their separation from the rest of families.[27] Montes further argues that migration offers an important opportunity for men to deeply reflect on their emotional relations with family members and openly express their emotions,[28] which would not happen under normal circumstances. Given that "there is intense advocacy to recognize the connectedness of men in general to family-life,"[29] it is important to investigate transnational fathers' emotional changes to better understand how their relationships with other family members change and how their fathering patterns are re-shaped.

Finally, current migration studies have focused primarily on the experiences of working-class men who migrate abroad and have revealed little about the transnational fathering practices of middle-class fathers who remain alone in their home country.[30] Furthermore, research on Asian men's transnational fatherhood is largely missing from the existing literature.[31] Given that social class and race/ethnicity play critical roles in shaping the ways people maintain transnational ties and the resources they use,[32] the experiences of middle-class Asian fathers in transnational relationships should no longer be overlooked.

RESPONSIBLE, INVOLVED, AND INTIMATE FATHERING IN THE TRANSNATIONAL CONTEXT

This chapter seeks to fill the gap in the literature and advance the knowledge of underexplored middle-class transnational fatherhood by providing a more balanced and comprehensive analysis of transnational fathers' economic and emotional roles. For this, I employ the theoretical framework of responsible fathering,[33] which emphasizes men's continuing financial support of their children and continuing emotional and physical care of their children,[34] and analyze how Korean wild geese fathers try to be economically responsible, emotionally intimate, and physically involved fathers despite their geographical distance from their children. Specifically, I explore how wild geese fathers attempt to fulfill both components of responsible fathering (providing economic support and emotional/physical care of children), using three tools of fathering: (1) sending remittances and gifts; (2) maintaining transnational communication; and (3) having face-to-face encounters with children.

There are studies of these topics of transnational fathering. First, generally, for the families in the transnational context, fathers' economic roles tend to be highly prioritized over their emotional roles. Accordingly, transnational fathers are often deemed to be responsible fathers only if they fulfill their breadwinning role of sending remittances to their family, regardless of their maintenance of father-child intimacy.[35] However, recent studies have recognized remittances as "the currency of contact across borders"[36] and authentic ways of expressing parental love, care, and affection to children from a distance[37] rather than simply as means of fulfilling male breadwinning roles.

In contrast to substantial scholarly attention to the symbolic significance of remittances, activities that transnational fathers actually perform to take care of their children remain under-researched. Nonetheless, it has been noted that frequent and regular transnational communication is critical to maintaining intimate relationships between transnational parents and children.[38] Working-class transnational families commonly use handwritten letters, landline phones, calling cards, and old-fashioned 2G mobile phones to communicate with their families across national borders; however, unfortunately, their transnational communication is frequently interrupted because of the lack of financial and technological resources, which tends to undermine mutual understanding, particularly when transnational family separation is lengthier.[39]

Another important way of practicing involved fatherhood and reinforcing transnational parent-child emotional ties is having frequent and regular face-to-face encounters with one's children.[40] However, even less is known about specific activities transnational fathers perform during their face-to-face encounters with children. This is partly because many working-class transnational fathers cannot frequently return to their home countries because of their tight budget and undocumented legal status,[41] and partly because many transnational fathers do not provide physical care for their children but remain remote and strict disciplinarians, even when they visit or live together with their children,[42] based on patriarchal gender norms of parenting. Combined with the lack of consistent transnational communication, Filipino transnational fathers' limited involvement with their children during family visits further deteriorates their transnational emotional intimacy.[43]

Exploring fathering practices and changing father-child relationships in Korean wild geese families contributes to extending the knowledge of transnational fatherhood. On the one hand, current fathering discourse tends to negate the possibility that transnational fathers can be responsible and involved fathers, because it overly emphasizes fathers' co-presence with their children as the key component of successful fathering.[44] The ways in which wild geese fathers perform responsible fathering from a distance provides a good empirical chance to revisit the significance of men's co-presence with their children.

On the other hand, many traditional migrant fathers, such as working-class and/or Latino migrant fathers, often encounter great challenges in their efforts to practice involved and intimate fatherhood. Because of their structural marginality in the host society based on their limited economic resources and legal instability, many working-class migrant fathers find it difficult to regularly visit their children in their home countries and/or spend time together.[45] Hence, some Filipino migrant parents send age-inappropriate presents to their left-behind children,[46] and some Guatemalan and Salvadoran transnational fathers fail to recognize their children when they meet again after lengthy separation.[47] In contrast, Korean wild geese fathers have greater economic and legal resources (i.e., middle-class background, well-paid professional jobs in their home country, and legitimate visa status) to maintain transnational intimacy with their children. Thus, they may not necessarily encounter similar challenges to maintaining transnational family intimacy nor do they mainly focus on fulfilling economic roles as their working-class counterparts do.

In the following sections, I first explain the reasons why wild geese fathers remain alone in Korea rather than accompanying their family abroad. Then, I explore varied father-child relationships prior to migration and highlight transnational family separation as a turning point that re-shapes fathering practices and father-child relationships. Next, I discuss how Korean wild geese fathers practice responsible fathering (i.e., economic and emotional roles) using three tools of transnational fathering: (1) sending remittances and gifts; (2) maintaining transnational communication; and (3) having face-to-face encounters with children. Throughout this chapter, I also analyze the changes in the father-children relationships through transnational family separation. To explain the wide range of the quality of intergenerational relationships, I pay attention to various factors, such as children's age and gender, fathers' familiarity with the host society, the type of fathers' employment, wives' role as mediators, and the length of separation. The changing emotions of wild geese fathers are also discussed.

WILD GEESE FATHERS' DECISION TO REMAIN ALONE IN KOREA

For wild geese parents, it is not an option to send their children alone to a foreign country. They strongly believe that their children need parental care and guidance and that at least one parent should be accompanying their children. When asked the reasons why they have remained alone in Korea, most wild geese fathers point out their responsibility as the primary economic provider of the family. In contrast to working-class migrant fathers who do not have professional jobs in their home country and seek less-skilled low-paid jobs after migration,[48] wild geese fathers are highly educated professionals and make much more income in Korea. Therefore, if they emigrate, they would like to find the similar type and level of jobs. However, due to the difficulty in transferring their qualifications from the home country to the host country, it was not so feasible for many wild geese fathers to find good jobs commensurate with their credentials and experiences. In addition, a lack of English fluency was mentioned as one of the critical barriers to wild geese fathers' difficulty in getting any gainful jobs abroad, like Taiwanese left-behind fathers.[49] Thus, rather than risking their stable income and decent social status, many wild geese fathers, particularly those who were sole earners, decided to remain alone in Korea and continue their role as a reliable economic provider of their family.

As mentioned earlier in previous chapters, it was almost always wild geese mothers who gave up their careers (if any) and accompanied their children abroad,[50] even if some mothers earned similar income or more. This was partly because of the patriarchal ideology that dictated each parent's roles based on their gender.[51] In the accounts of both wild geese fathers and mothers I interviewed, mothers were regarded as the better nurturer by nature. Likewise, fathers were deemed to be the primary breadwinner of their households, and thus fathers' careers were more valued than wives' if both spouses were working. Accordingly, fathers were not blamed for spending little time with their children or for not providing much daily care for their children while living together with their children in Korea. Some wild geese fathers also believed that their busy work schedule and pursuit of career development and success at the price of their family time was for the sake of their family rather than for their own.

Also, prior to migration, wild geese mothers spent much more time in taking care of their children than their husbands did, regardless of their employment statuses or earning capabilities. Wild geese fathers did not question why it was not themselves but their wives (including those who were working) who had to be the primary nurturers of their children. Rather than seeing any good reasons to become good caregivers themselves, they just praised their wives as good (even ideal) mothers who were the best for their children. Furthermore, most wild geese fathers were cared for by their wives in their everyday life. Consequently, wild geese fathers did not believe that they would be able to give the necessary care to their children if they brought their children abroad without their wives.

In sum, when wild geese couples were to make the emigration decision, wild geese fathers were not even considered as the right person to accompany their children abroad and provide them with necessary physical and emotional care. Instead, wild geese fathers were expected to remain alone in Korea and continuously serve their role as a competent economic provider for their family. Korean wild geese family's transnational living arrangement in this manner is justified by and reinforces the traditional gender roles (i.e., fathers as breadwinners and mothers as caretakers). While wild geese fathers' decision to remain alone in the home country is often packaged as their sublime self-sacrifice for the family, it is basically the outcome of the patriarchal gender ideology that imposes unequal shares of caregiving responsibilities on parents.[52]

TRANSNATIONAL FAMILY SEPARATION AS A TURNING POINT

Wild geese fathers had varied quality of relationships with their children prior to transnational family separation: While a half of the fathers in my study had good relationships with children before separation, the other half tended to focus on work and neglect family life.

Dongwon, a wild geese father with a teenage son, is the one who had good relationship with his son prior to separation and keeps maintaining it even after separation. Dongwon was very enthusiastic about his son's education when he lived together with his family in Korea. He regularly met his son's teachers, observed his son at school, attended his son's performances, and served the school board committee whose members were all women except two men, including Dongwon. He used to leave his office early and gave his son a ride to ice hockey centers twice a week for seven years. He also regularly went to a stadium with his son to watch the soccer games together. He provided intensive physical and emotional care for his son with a strong belief as such:

> I see that [Korean] fathers tend to step back and entrust [everything about children] to their wives. But, I did not do that. While mother's role is important, children can do better with [their] father present.

When asked how he maintains his emotional ties with his son after family separation, Dongwon confidently responds:

> Although I meet him occasionally [after transnational family separation], I can make up [our relationship] at once. It is possible because we spent a long time together when he was younger. Because we have a strong foundational relationship, my son knows well what kind of person I am and what I have done for him. [. . .] He knows that his father pays great attention to him compared to other ordinary fathers. We also share many memories. Thus, although our relationship is sometimes unstable, it can be soon recovered. I feel that we have smoothly overcome the gaps during his adolescence, thanks to what I have done so far.

Dongwon's case supports that the pre-migration relationship with children is an asset that helps transnational fathers maintain close relationships with their children after separation.

Nonetheless, intimate father-child relationship prior to family separation is not a prerequisite for their good relationship after separation. Among the career-oriented wild geese fathers in my study, about half of them come to recognize the overlooked significance of families through transnational family separation[53] and are strongly motivated to rebuild emotional connections with their children by changing their fathering behaviors.

Sangmin, a corporate lawyer for a global company, did not like to spend much time with his young sons (elementary school student and kindergartener) when they lived together in Korea. During weekdays, he was tired from work. During weekends, although he spent just a few hours with his sons, Sangmin felt very tired and made excuses to spend less time with them:

> [When we were living together] in Korea, I always just slept after coming home. I did not want to see my children. I just said, "Good night" to them. I thought

that I did a really good job when I brought them to the park on weekends just for twenty minutes. I was just very tired.

However, after transnational family separation, he has felt deep loneliness, missed his family, and tried to reconstruct his connections with his sons by providing emotional and physical care for them whenever he visits his family abroad. He constantly tells them, "I love you." He always buys many gifts and frequently dines out with his family. He also reads many bedtime stories to his children and plays with them. He goes to museums and zoos, records every moment he spends with his children, and shares pictures and video clips with them. Sangmin emphasizes that what matters more for maintaining his transnational intimacy with his children is not his prior father-child relationship but his concerted efforts to rebuild the relationship. Sangmin says: "Really, I feel that whenever I go to America for two weeks, we spend much more time together than when we lived together in Korea. We really do."

Similar to Sangmin, many wild geese fathers in my study admit that they tended to focus on their work and overlook their family life when they lived together in Korea. They often felt bothered and tired when they had some family time with children. They grudgingly played with children occasionally on weekends not because they wanted to but because their wives asked to do so.

However, these fathers have felt deep loneliness after separation and missed their families abroad[54] regardless of them being family-oriented or not. While they do not realize how lonely they are on busy weekdays, they become particularly emotional and sad on weekends and holidays. Some fathers even suffer from severe depression and/or panic disorder, as some Latino transnational fathers do.[55]

Kyusik, a physician, explains how his panic disorder during transnational family separation has made him recognize the overlooked value of his family and has substantially changed him from a career-oriented to family-oriented man:

In the past, I tried to find happiness from external success. Thus, I tended to overlook my family. I was under high pressure as I pursued greater success outside. At that time, I was often angry at my children and my wife if things did not work well. However, since I started wild geese life, I have changed a lot. Once during my wild geese period, I had a panic disorder. After that, I have come up with an idea that my social life no longer matters. My family is most important. I used to meet many friends, drink, hang out, and play a lot, when I was in the thirties. I have learned that it is all useless. No one consoled me when I was sick and under hard time. Only my family did it. Therefore, at that time, for the first time in my life, I recognized that my family was the most valuable. So, since then, I have made a lot of efforts to be nice to my children. I also have learned how I should be changed to be a better father by attending the father school. As I have made an effort and fixed myself, my relationship with children have greatly improved and recovered. So, when I visited [my family] this time, I did not have any issues, because we have built strong trust each other.

A few wild geese fathers even cried during the interviews while explaining how heart-breaking it was to return to Korea alone after a visit to their family abroad. Loneliness after separation has greatly changed many career-oriented fathers into those who pursue intimate fatherhood as their new fathering ideology, try to approach their children and communicate with them, and derive great joy and happiness from spending time with their children. These fathers might not have had such opportunities if they continued to live with their family in Korea.[56] Changsung, a businessman with two sons, positively defines his wild geese period as this: "It is an opportunity for my family to think about each other's meanings."

In short, transnational family separation offers an important turning point to many wild geese fathers to recognize the overlooked importance of their family,[57] reflect on their family relationships, and motivate them to rebuild their family relationships. As discussed throughout this chapter, these findings are consistent with Montes's claim of migration as a critical moment that leads to a *plurality of masculinities*[58] that diverges from so-called *career masculinity*,[59] which is narrowly focused on fathers' breadwinning roles.

In the following sections, I discuss wild geese fathers' transnational fathering activities. Specifically, I explore how wild geese fathers attempt to fulfill both components of responsible fathering (i.e., providing economic support and emotional/physical care of children) in three ways: (1) sending remittances and gifts, (2) maintaining transnational communication and virtual co-presence, and (3) having face-to-face encounters. Rather than simply distinguishing remittances as economic tools and transnational communication/encounters as emotional tools, I examine the ways in which wild geese fathers utilize all three tools in their fulfillment of both economic and emotional roles and the different degrees to which they succeed in their efforts to be responsible and involved fathers in the transnational context.

TRANSNATIONAL FATHERING: REMITTANCES AND GIFTS

Given that the strict transnational parental role division is the foundation of the transnational arrangement of wild geese families, sending remittances is the single most important part of wild geese fathers' responsible fathering, as shown in previous studies on transnational fathers.[60] A wild geese father named Jaesick even asserts that economic provision is the paramount role of fathers: "I think that the ideal father is the one who makes good money. It is a lie that fathers can do something for their children even if they don't have any money."

Modes and Strategies of Sending Remittances

As noted in Introduction, wild geese fathers in my study have profitable professional jobs, and their average annual household income in Korea is about $128,000.[61] They send about $87,000 a year on average as remittances to their families abroad, which accounts for approximately 70 percent of their annual household income. While the majority of wild geese fathers send 50 percent to 100 percent of their annual income to their families abroad, substantial numbers of fathers send even more than what they actually earn, for example, by withdrawing from their savings, by selling real estate, or by getting bank loans.

Some fathers send the remittances regularly like monthly or quarterly. Other fathers put a substantial amount of money in their wives' (or joint) bank account in the host country so that their wives can use it as needed. When there is not enough money in the bank account, or when their wives ask for more money, these fathers transfer a large amount of money via online banking system. A few fathers also let their wives use their Korean credit cards for easier financial management, particularly when their family plans to stay abroad only for a short period of time (i.e., less than a year). In addition to regular remittances, wild geese fathers send money for their family's initial settlement (e.g., purchasing a house and a car), their children's education (e.g., college tuition, private SAT exam preparation services fees, and summer camp expenses), and celebration of children's important milestone events such as birthdays and graduations.

To send the maximum amount of remittances to their families abroad (sometimes even exceeding their earning capability), wild geese fathers employ two main strategies. First, most wild geese fathers have their original houses leased and then move to smaller apartments or studios. Some also choose to live with their own parents or parents-in-law. While their living with parents is primarily aimed at saving their living expenses, it also serves other goals: Some wild geese fathers frame it as their filial duty for their aged (and often sick) parents; other fathers are cared for by their parents (particularly mothers) in the absence of their wives; and a few fathers have to do so because their wives are concerned about their husbands' possible infidelity.

Second, many wild geese fathers also substantially reduce their daily living expenses and the amount of money that they spend with their own discretion, as other transnational fathers do.[62] Wild geese fathers in my study generally spend for themselves less than a thousand dollars per month. A wild geese father named Sangmin is particularly noteworthy. Although he gets a very high salary as a corporate lawyer, he lives a very frugal life. Sangmin says, "I just spend only ten dollars a day. Ten dollars a day! I use it to buy lunch! That's it!" For him, spending no more than ten dollars per day is an unavoidable decision, because he sends almost all of his income to his family abroad to pay for mortgage, auto lease, and children's schooling.

Even if most wild geese fathers in my study do not face such an impending economic difficulty like Sangmin, they still try to save spending for themselves as much as they can, because they want to be prepared for urgent situations that may occur to their family abroad. Wild geese fathers reduce nearly all spending for themselves: They do not buy their clothes; they eat meals at their company's cafeteria rather than dining out. In particular, wild geese fathers significantly decrease their entertainment and leisure expenditure. They change the type of exercises from expensive ones such as playing golf to cheaper ones such as going to a gym, walking, or hiking.

Some fathers, like Inho, also try to meet with their friends less frequently, because socializing costs money that can be otherwise used for their family. Inho is a highly ranked public official and receives a good salary. However, as he sends 90 percent of his annual income to his family abroad, the remaining 10 percent is not sufficient for Inho to make his own living and pay the mortgage bills. Thus, Inho's spending patterns have substantially changed in the way that minimizes his social life, shopping, and dining out. Inho explains:

There are big changes in my spending [after becoming a wild geese father]. For example, if I say I used to meet my friends five times before, I now meet them only once. I have just minimized socializing. It is because, if I meet my friends, I have to spend at least a hundred dollars for my roundtrip transportation, food and drink. However, if I do not go out, I do not spend even couple of dollars. Next, I don't buy my clothes. My wife buys them when she visits me here. I think that I can just wear the same clothes that I used to wear, because I don't need a good appearance to buy favors from others. I also no longer dine out because I am alone. I sometimes go to a [cheap] food court, but very rarely like once or twice [a month]. My life is now simplified around the office and I spend minimum for myself.

Interestingly, while the majority of wild geese fathers economize the spending for themselves, some men present the opposite consumption patterns during their wild geese period. They spend more money for themselves. Faced with a sudden increase of free time after separation from their family, some men do not know how to properly manage it. Furthermore, as they struggle with severe loneliness, they try to overcome it by spending more money for themselves. For example, some men develop new hobbies and spend more money for their leisure (e.g., playing golf, or riding an expensive bicycle for health). Others relieve their loneliness by meeting and drinking with people more often than before. A few men further admit that that they have abused alcohol and had extramarital relationships to relieve their loneliness, like Mexican and Honduran fathers in the transnational context.[63] A few wild geese fathers also spend more money to buy their clothes and dine out, as they no longer have wives to buy clothes and cook for them.

Financial Situations and Prospects

After becoming wild geese fathers, many of them feel insecure not only about their current finance but also about their future financial situation. One-third of wild geese fathers in my study are in debt at the time of interview, and the total amount of their liabilities has kept increasing as they take advantage of bank loans or overdrafts to make up the monthly shortage and/or pay a lump sum, for example, for their children's (college) tuition.

Fathers are anxious about imminent economic hardships. For example, Sangmin, a corporate lawyer, defines his financial situation as a crisis, "It is a little bit of crisis. Our budget is very tight every month. Too tight!" Jaesick, a wild geese father who earns high income as a vice-president of a company, laments during the interview, "All the money that we spend now comes from debts. . . . If I don't work even just for one day, we will be doomed." Inho, a public official, also expresses similar frustration about his tight budget constraint:

> I don't have any surplus. I am always in the absolute shortage [of money]. So, I have to apply for new loans again and again to make up our living expenses and pay for my children's tuition, which in turn makes me indebted growingly. As I get more loans and pay more interests, I am more concerned about our financial situation.

Some wild geese fathers plan to clear their debts with their severance pay, retirement pension, or insurance after they are retired. Nonetheless, they are not so optimistic about their future, because, even if they no longer have debts, they will not have enough deposits or financial sources to secure their elderly years after retirement. This gloomy prospect is a major source of these wild geese fathers' serious concern about their future.

Although two-thirds of wild geese fathers in my study are not in debt at the time of the interview, half of them still express a sense of financial insecurity similar to that of their indebted counterparts. While sending a huge amount of remittances (sometimes exceeding what they earn) to their families abroad, some fathers' total wealth has significantly decreased. They have sold their houses, stocks and funds, and/or have cancelled their installment savings account or life insurance plan prior to its maturity. Of course, there are some fathers whose total wealth has not decreased during their wild geese period. Nonetheless, they also feel insecure, because they have saved much smaller amounts than before and/or have not yet accumulated enough retirement savings or funds.

While some fathers think of the increased expenditure as worthy investment in their children's future, others deeply agonize whether it is overinvestment that puts their own future at risk. Thus, a few wild geese fathers discuss their current economic situation and future economic prospect with their wives abroad and ask them to save money. Dongwook is a unique wild geese father, in that he shares his financial concerns not only with his wife but also with his children abroad:

> I am so concerned about our future. I am not more affluent than others, but I am still overinvesting in my children's education beyond my ability. Thus, I tell my wife, "I am sorry, but I want you to save the remittances as much as possible. We have only this amount of assets at this moment." I also explain to my first daughter about our financial situation and tell her, "Your dad is excessively spending for your education beyond his ability. Thus, I hope you to go to the university whose tuition is cheap." Now, my daughter is applying for universities, only for universities that give scholarships.

Some fathers plan to postpone their retirement to prepare for their future. Dongwon, an architect whose wife is also working abroad, is a good example:

> We have not yet bought a house and just enjoyed our life by spending all we earned. But, we are now old and feel very insecure for our future. I don't know when I stop working. I don't know when my wife will be sick. Because we haven't prepared for such situations yet, I am very anxious about my future. So, I have to start working only for ourselves no later than about three to five years after my son becomes an adult and goes to the university.

It is important to note that not all wild geese fathers are anxious about their future. Among those who are not indebted, the other half of fathers do not express much concern about their future finance even though they send a huge amount of remittances to their families abroad. It is because these fathers have a financial safety net for their elderly period. Some fathers with a rich family background do not find much difference between the amount they used to give to their wives as living expenses in Korea and the amount they currently send to their wives abroad as remittances. They also tend to maintain their assets including a house, retirement funds, and savings. In addition, government officials and professors feel relatively safe thanks to their decent post-retirement pension plans, although they possess lesser assets than richer wild geese fathers. A few fathers also prearranged almost perfect financial planning for their wild geese period and thus do not have much unexpected expenditure beyond their budget to maintain their two transnationally split households. Even some fathers expect that their economic situation will be much better when their wives return to Korea and resume their career or start a new business.

Meaning of Sending Remittances: Economic Roles

Given all of such financial hardships and concerns that the majority of wild geese fathers experience, what does the act of sending remittances mean to wild geese fathers? It plays two important roles for them: economic and emotional roles. First of all, by sending remittances, wild geese fathers believe that they are fulfilling their economic role as fathers. Given that the strict transnational spousal role division is the foundation of wild geese families, sending remittances is certainly the most important part of wild geese fathers' responsible fatherhood. This is the case, in general, for transnational fathers,[64] but wild geese fathers manifest an even stronger sense of obligation to provide economic support for the family as if it is their paramount obligation that they should not fail. In contrast to working-class migrant fathers who often stop or delay sending remittances to their families for various reasons such as their own economic hardships,[65] discipline of their wives,[66] and discipline of their children,[67] middle-class wild geese fathers in my study do not think that they can stop or delay remittances to their family abroad for any reason. In the worst circumstances, these fathers may ask their families to return to Korea.

Behind wild geese fathers' strong sense of economic obligation are their overall high expectations for their children's future. About half of fathers admit that they have an ambitious vision of their children and want their children to be competent and cosmopolitan professionals who can work in the global market beyond the national boundaries. These fathers are also as enthusiastic in supporting their children's elite education as their wives. The other half of fathers state that they just hope their children will live freely and happily doing whatever they like. However, it is mainly because their wives are already too ambitious about education. So, this group of fathers tries not to create additional stress for their children.

In addition, as middle-class professionals, wild geese fathers in my study commonly view English fluency and college education as the minimum qualifications for their children to grow to independent adults. Thus, even if they are currently suffering from the tight budget and concerned about their uncertain future, the majority of wild geese fathers neither stop nor reduce their economic support for their children until their children finish college education (often including graduate education) and get a good job. Only after that, wild geese fathers believe that they are truly freed from their heavy burden of serving as *the father* and the economic provider of the family, that they no longer have to worry much about their children, and that they finally can start planning and managing their own future and elderly life. An account of Jaesick well represents this sentiment:

> I don't have any security for my old age. In my case, I have to choose either preparing for my elderly life or investing in my child's education. I cannot do both [because of budget constraint]. I can do this [the life of wild geese father] because I have only one child. You are crazy if you choose to become a wild geese father with two children. In my case, I choose my kid's education, although I do not expect that he will care for me later. I believe that if I invest in my kid's education now, his bright life will be possible. Then, I do not have to worry about him. I can just worry about me and my wife.

Some wild geese fathers' economic support continues even until their adult children marry and purchase a house, particularly if their adult children are sons. For example, a former wild geese father named Jiho recently bought a house for his 30-year-old son who just got married, while continuously paying college tuition for his 23-year-old son:

> My economic condition is very difficult, because I am still supporting my younger child's education. In addition, my big child got married and we bought a house for him. For that, I got a loan. So, we are in the worst [economic] situation. Yes, worst! However, how could I avoid it? In Korean society, parents' life is taken as security for children's education and marriage. It is accurate to say that our life is pledged [for children].

Woosung, a former wild geese father who will soon retire, also still economically supports his 30-year-old son who is attending a college abroad, by paying tuition and sending living expenses. Woosung justifies his prolonged economic support for his adult child, "I believe that my son will be successful, and until then, I will do my role as a father. I will support him at least until he finishes his college education. After that, he can fight his own battles."

Another wild geese father named Hojun promised to his 13-year-old daughter abroad that he would support her college education as well as her marriage expenses:

I don't have much inheritance to you. However, I will support you while you
are studying. I will pay your tuition. I will also help you when you marry. Don't
expect more than that from me! I will just help you until you graduate and get
a job.

While above wild geese fathers describe as though they are providing their
children with the minimum economic support for a limited time, it is clear
that these fathers have offered (and will continue to offer) huge economic
support to their children for a long period, because they believe that their
children are not yet competent enough to make their own independent living.

It is known that Asian and Asian American parents heavily invest in their
children's education as a family strategy to pursue their entire family's
upward social mobility, prestige, and stable future.[68] On the basis of the
Confucian belief that children will care for their elderly parents,[69] children's
educational success is also often equated with their parents' success.[70] Wild
geese fathers in my study also share the similar faith in the positive impacts of
education on the younger generation's upward social mobility, which is why
wild geese fathers eagerly offer economic support to their children until they
finish higher education and get a good job.

On the other hand, wild geese fathers in my study differ from their Asian/
Asian American counterparts in their view of children's support of their parents in return. That is, a majority of wild geese fathers do not think that their
stable elderly life can be realized through their children's success nor do they
expect that their children will care for them when they are elderly. Instead,
wild geese fathers believe that they have to live their elderly lives for themselves rather than relying on their adult children. Hongki, a wild geese father
who still economically supports his 25-year-old son studying at a doctoral
program in New York City, reiterates such sentiment:

When your children are fully grown up, they will anyway leave the nest. It is
good enough for me that my son will make his own family and live well. How
can parents rely on their children? How? I never expect my son will return what
I have invested in him. My last obligation as the father is downsizing my assets
here [in Korea] and buying my son a house there [in the United States]. Then, I
will be finally able to enjoy my own life. How other wishes do I have [from my
son]? That is not the father of my generation.

Wild geese fathers' such low expectations for returns on the investment in
their children, despite their considerable and lengthy economic support, may
reflect the Korean society's rapidly changing cultural attitudes toward the
filial duty of adult children. According to the Korea Development Institute,[71]

the percent of Koreans who think that families (i.e., adult children) should look after their parents has plummeted from 89.9 percent in 1998 to 31.7 percent in 2014, while the percent who think that parents should care for themselves has doubled from 8.1 percent in 1998 to 16.6 percent in 2014. As a part of the so-called "sandwich generation" who have to support their elderly parents but no longer expect such support from their children, many middle-aged wild geese fathers in my study claim that they will have to live their elderly lives by themselves rather than relying on their adult children.

Social class also plays a critical role in shaping wild geese fathers' strong sense of economic obligation, combined with low expectations for the return from their children. As middle-class professionals with successful careers, many wild geese fathers feel hesitant or even embarrassed to admit that they expect any economic reliance on their children in their post-retirement years. In their eyes, children are not ones whom they can rely on later but *emotionally priceless*[72] people whom they have to take care of and guide until the children become fully fledged adults. Accordingly, even though many wild geese fathers are seriously concerned about financial insecurity in their elderly years, none of them say that they expect any economic support in the future from their children.

> Basically, I think that my daughter already repaid to me by doing cute things when she was younger. I never expect anything from her. If she gives me money, I do not want to use it. I rather would like to return it to her by saving it. (Hojun, a wild geese father with one daughter)

> My children will make their own living, and I will make my own living. Eventually, I will be able to live based on my pension. That is my safety net for my old age. I console myself by the fact that I will not ask my children for money in my later years. (Inho, a wild geese father with two children)

It is important to note that such an understanding of childhood is shared by middle-class parents across race/ethnicity and culture.[73] Moreover, extended parental economic support for children is not unique among Korean parents but prevalent among middle-class parents across many cultures. For example, many American middle-class parents also provide significant financial assistance to their young adult children until they finish college education in the hope that their children will smoothly transition into adulthood with solid economic foundations.[74]

In short, by defining their children as someone they have to take care of forever rather than someone they can eventually rely on in their elderly years, wild geese fathers have maintained their masculinity and their respected status as *the father* and *the breadwinner* of their transnational households. Therefore, wild geese fathers' significant economic support of their children should be understood with an intersectional approach,[75] considering not only patriarchal gender ideology and Confucian Asian culture but also their middle-class social status.

Meaning of Sending Remittances: Emotional Roles

So far, I have discussed how Korean wild geese fathers fulfill economic roles by sending remittances to their family abroad. However, this is only a half of the story. Given that wild geese fathers' remittances are not based on the expectations of future financial support from their children later in life, further exploration of the meaning of these remittances reveals a less explored but equally important aspect of fathering: transnational fathers' fulfillment of emotional roles.

By sending remittances, wild geese fathers not only believe that they express their love, care, and attention to their children, like other transnational parents.[76] They also feel a sense of achievement, as if they are involved in the care of their children from a distance. A following story of wild geese father named Seungwon provides a good example.

Prior to transnational family separation, Seungwon, a businessman, used to be a family man who shared a large portion of daily care for his children. He attended school conferences, helped his children with school projects, gave his children a ride to extracurricular activities (e.g., tennis and youth orchestra), and watched their performances. He also enjoyed sharing housework with his wife. He vacuumed floors and washed dishes on weekends, mowed the lawn when necessary, and fixed something broken.

Since he became a wild geese father, however, Seungwon has not been able to perform such tasks for his wife and children anymore. Thus, he tries to make up for his physical absence by providing economically. Seungwon sends 100 percent of his salary as remittances to his family abroad, while he sustains his life in Korea on a small amount of activity fee offered by his company. He also bought a new car to his wife abroad so that she would not have to deal with car maintenance issues. He also tells his wife to call a repairman whenever something is broken rather than trying to fix it by herself. By sending all his income and handling his family's various economic issues from a distance, Seungwon feels that he still shares some caring and housework with his wife while expressing his continued love and attention to his family abroad.

Nevertheless, not all wild geese children notice this symbolic meaning in their fathers' remittances. Note that all wild geese fathers in my study send remittances directly to their wives, not to their children, and that most fathers do not discuss financial hardships with their children. Money is a topic discussed only between wild geese parents, as in Honduran transnational families.[77] Accordingly, although many wild geese fathers live frugally and suffer from the stress of sending huge remittances, their children often do not recognize fathers' economic sacrifices and emotional struggles, which leads to a sort of *class divide*[78] between children who maintain a comfortable middle-class life abroad and fathers who experience a lowered quality of life in Korea.

Wild geese fathers feel sad and even annoyed when their economic support and sacrifices are invisible and taken for granted by their children. A bitter description of wild geese father named Inho well shows how wild geese children are often ignorant of the harsh reality their left-behind fathers are handling in their home country:

> They [children] mostly do not recognize it [my sacrifice]. They admit only one-third of what I expected. When I sometimes tell them how [frugally] I live here, then they respond like this, "Who asked you to live like that? Spend some money for yourself!" They don't understand my mind . . . So, I don't talk about it anymore.

Even though wild geese fathers' frugal lifestyle and strong sense of economic obligation of sending as much remittances as possible are their ways of expressing love and care to their children, wild geese children often do not think the same way, and such intergenerational gaps are not unique among Korean wild geese families.[79]

To bridge the emotional gaps between fathers and children, wild geese mothers' role as mediators is critical, which is common among transnational families.[80] Many wild geese mothers in my study state that they remind children of their father's sacrifice and love for the family. Mothers tell children how their father works hard, saves money, and endures economic and emotional hardships. Mothers also ask children to express their gratitude to their father for his sacrifice and support. Through wild geese mothers' active involvement, children can better appreciate father's economic support and emotional suffering, which they would have overlooked or taken for granted otherwise. Wild geese mothers also serve as a messenger and convey their children's feelings to fathers, particularly if children are so young or adolescents that they are unable or reluctant to express their thankfulness. When families express appreciation, wild geese fathers feel that their hardships and sacrifices are worthy and rewarded, as Honduran transnational fathers do.[81]

Through wives' mediation, remittances can finally better play their emotional roles in strengthening the bond between wild geese fathers and their children across the ocean and letting fathers feel rewarded. This is consistent with existing findings that good spousal relationships are critical for transnational fathers to maintain close relationships with their children.[82] Nevertheless, many wild geese fathers in my study still cultivate intimate relationships with their children abroad without relying much on wives' involvement. It is because they actively utilize other means of fathering (i.e., sending gifts and maintaining active transnational communication), whose emotional meaning is much clearer to children, without wild geese mothers' mediation.

Meaning of Sending/Giving Gifts

Compared to remittances whose emotional impact is often mediated by wild geese mothers, gifts tend to more directly work to maintain the transnational intimate relationships between fathers and children,[83] partly because gifts go directly to children whereas remittances go to mothers. Through gifts, fathers usually can communicate with children directly, see how much their children like the gifts, and hear appreciative words from children. At the same time, children also find in the gifts strong evidence that their fathers are paying close attention to what they like and need across the ocean. Therefore, wild geese fathers never go empty-handed whenever they visit their families abroad. They often bring lots of gifts for their children. One wild geese father named Sangmin even delightfully claims, "I buy so many gifts. So, whenever I visit my family, I go broke."

Wild geese fathers feel great happiness and fulfillment when they shop what their children have asked for and bring (or send) these gifts to their family abroad, because such behaviors demonstrate that they are still communicating with their children and doing some important job as fathers even though they are not living together. For example, Minho, a businessman, monthly sends to his family abroad a gift box, filled with various kinds of snacks such as Korean ramen and crackers. Although it is not an expensive gift at all, buying and sending various snacks that his two sons like, Minho relives his longing for his children and expresses his love to them.

A wild geese father named Seungwon also greatly enjoys shopping for his children abroad. Because he is very busy during weekdays as a highly successful businessman, Seungwon usually goes shopping only on weekends. At the store, Seungwon uses his smartphone to directly show his children abroad the items that he considers buying, asks which one they like the most, and then buys the ones his children choose. By doing so, Seungwon feels great joy and fulfillment as he keeps communicating and interacting with his children.

Given that existing literature has often analyzed the meaning of gifts based on the experiences of the working-class transnational parents, my research expands its scope to the meaning of gifts for middle-class transnational fathers. For many working-class transnational parents, shopping and sending special gifts—as well as remittances—to their family is often the only way of enacting their role as responsible parents from a distance, because they cannot easily visit their family or spend much time together due to their tight budget and often undocumented legal status.[84] Furthermore, because working-class transnational fathers cannot easily find an appropriate channel to satisfy their desire for social status in the host country, shopping and sending special gifts (particularly merchandise made in the United States) to their families can be a critical and alternative means to maintain their masculinity and dominant status within their family and home communities as "successful migrants, committed husbands and attentive fathers," as Pribilsky has noted in the study of Ecuadorian transnational fathers.[85]

In contrast, for wild geese fathers, gifts are primarily a way of expressing paternal love, care, and attention to their children rather than a means of proving their masculinity or maintaining their domestic status. These middle-class fathers can regularly visit their family abroad and spend time together thanks to their stronger economic power and legitimate legal status. They also keep maintaining their stable, well-paid professional jobs in Korea so that they can send enough remittances for their family to purchase what they like or need. Accordingly, wild geese fathers do not think their domestic and social status should be (or can be) strengthened by the actions of giving gifts to their families.

Another difference is that made-in-Korea products are often preferred gifts over those made in other countries, partly because of growing global popularity of Korean pop culture among the younger generation.[86] Thus, wild geese fathers often send Korean products to their family abroad such as K-pop (Korean pop music), Korean cosmetics, Korean clothes, Korean bestsellers, Korean food and snacks, and Korean toys. Of course, electronic devices like laptops, smart phones, and game consoles are also popular gifts, even if they are not made in Korea.

In sum, gifts are wild geese fathers' critical means of performing the emotional role of responsible fatherhood rather than the breadwinning role. Through gifts, wild geese fathers can directly interact with children rather than being mediated by wives. Social class also matters, in that gifts have stronger emotional connotations among wild geese fathers than working-class transnational fathers, to whom gifts are an important means of maintaining their masculinity and status in their families.

TRANSNATIONAL FATHERING: REGULAR TRANSNATIONAL COMMUNICATION AND VIRTUAL CO-PRESENCE

In the previous section, I have discussed the functions of remittances and gifts, through which Korean wild geese fathers perform responsible fathering from far away, both financially supporting children and maintaining emotional intimacy with children during separation. While remittances and gifts enable wild geese fathers, often via wives' mediation, to provide a form of emotional support to their children, fathers' active daily transnational communication with children is more direct and effective in fulfilling their emotional roles and maintaining intimate intergenerational relationships overcoming the distance.

In this section, I discuss how wild geese fathers perform responsible fathering by regularly communicating with their children. It is known that regular communication is critical to maintain intimate relationships between migrant parents and children.[87] I also highlight how some wild geese fathers further strengthen their emotional bond with children through their virtual co-presence in children's everyday lives.

To correctly understand how wild geese fathers communicate with their children abroad, it is better to explore first what communication technologies they utilize. Wild geese fathers in my study do not use traditional handwritten letters, landline phones, or calling cards, though they are still commonly used by many working-class transnational families.[88] Furthermore, old-fashioned 2G mobile phones, through which people can just make phone calls and send text messages, are rarely used by wild geese fathers in my study, although such devices are praised as effective transnational communication methods that allow intensive parenting of working-class migrant parents from a distance.[89]

Rather, to communicate with their children abroad, wild geese fathers in my study utilize smartphones and computers and make voice/video calls, exchange instant text messages, and share photos and videos through social networking service (SNS) and emails. As middle-class professionals in South Korea, which has the fastest internet connections in the world,[90] wild geese fathers not only have ready access to high-speed internet but also are familiar with such advanced communication platforms in their everyday lives. Given that availability and accessibility of such communication technologies vary by social class and country's infrastructure, wild geese fathers' active transnational interactions with family abroad are made possible by their middle-class status and their country's advanced internet infrastructure.[91] Thus, wild geese fathers certainly have structural advantages to overcome transnational family separation and perform intimate fatherhood, compared with their working-class counterparts from less-developed countries who lack "the knowledge, experience or resources to use such technology."[92]

Hyungdon, a businessman who became a wild geese father a second time, states how technological development is a crucial factor in keeping his intimate relationship with his children during his lengthy family separation:

> When I first sent my family abroad in 2000, I used Wow-Call, which was an early PC-based internet phone [in Korea]. With that, I could only hear their voices with some disruption. However, since 2006, video calls have been possible, and I now talk with my children, watching their face via my smartphone, and interacting with them in real time. Thus, I do not feel that we live apart from each other.

Below are the discussions of the specific modes of transnational communication that wild geese fathers use and the emotional roles that wild geese fathers perform through transnational communication. The usability of communication technologies and their costs are important factors of the quality of transnational fathering practices, which is further discussed in the following sections.

Technologies for Transnational Communication

The most preferred medium of transnational communication among wild geese fathers in my study is *Kakao Talk*, which is a very popular freeware application for smartphones in Korea. Using Kakao Talk, wild geese fathers make voice calls and video calls, exchange text messages and share photos and video clips with their children abroad for free. This effective transnational communication method is possible because both wild geese fathers and their children (except for very young children) have smartphones and the internet access. While smartphones may be luxuries for working-class transnational families due to their high price, they are already essentials for wild geese families, given that 82.5 percent of Koreans use smartphones as of 2015.[93]

Furthermore, whereas working-class migrant parents often initiate transnational communication, because their left-behind children do not have financial and technological means to do so,[94] middle-class wild geese families in my study do not have such intergenerational asymmetry in transnational communication. Because both wild geese fathers in Korea and their children abroad have smartphones and computers, both sides can contact each other whenever they want.

In addition, while working-class migrant parents spend a great portion of their income for transnational communication with children,[95] wild geese parents in my study spend surprisingly less for their transnational communication, because they use smartphone application which allows them to have free-of-charge communication using Wi-Fi networks, which is not surprising given that 98.8 percent of households in Korea already have access to internet as of 2015.[96] In this respect, my study corroborates how social class[97] and the internet infrastructure play a central role in shaping the intergenerational communication patterns of transnational families.

To make international calls, wild geese fathers sometimes use landline phones, mobile phones (including smartphones), and internet phones.[98] However, these are less preferred than Kakao Talk, because all communications through Kakao Talk are free of charge, whereas international calls through landline phones and mobile phones are relatively expensive. Wild geese fathers infrequently use these expensive alternatives only when the internet connection is unstable, and thus the quality of calls through Kakao Talk is not satisfactory.

Some wild geese fathers also use internet phones to make free international calls with their families abroad. Most wild geese families in my study do not have landline phones in their homes in the destination countries. Instead, some of them bring an internet phone, which needs nothing but electricity and Wi-Fi connection. As long as both wild geese fathers in Korea and their family abroad use the internet phones from the same service provider and have the internet access, they can make free calls without limit as if both of them were in Korea. Thus, internet phones are a good alternative to Kakao Talk calls.

Nonetheless, internet phones are less preferable than Kakao Talk (and mobile phones) for two main reasons: First, internet phones are basically landline phones and thus pose the mobility issues, in that both wild geese fathers and their children must be at their respective homes concurrently; second, internet phone service providers charge monthly payment (usually a few dollars per month), which incurs additional costs for wild geese families who already use mobile phones or smartphones for their transnational communication. Thus, internet phones are less frequently used than Kakao Talk or mobile phones.

To have video calls, wild geese fathers also use Skype and Facetime, as well as Kakao Talk. Again, these are less frequently used than Kakao Talk. First, Skype is an application for computer or laptop,[99] which is less mobile than smartphone. In addition, when Wi-Fi is not available, Skype is disconnected, whereas Kakao Talk still works through the 3G or LTE network of the smartphone. Thus, Skype is less popular than Kakao Talk due to such limitations. Second, Facetime enables wild geese family members to have free video calls even when one side does not have the internet access, just like Kakao Talk. However, there is one critical constraint: Facetime requires both parties to have the Apple devices (such as iPhone or iPad). Because most wild geese fathers in my study use smartphones of Korean brands (e.g., Samsung and LG) due to Apple's lower popularity in Korea, Facetime is not very commonly used for video calls between wild geese fathers and their families abroad.

Many wild geese fathers also use Kakao Talk to exchange instant text messages with their children abroad at no cost. Some fathers open a group chatting room in Kakao Talk for all family members. Wild geese family members like this method of text-based communication for its ease of use. They can exchange insignificant messages anytime of the day without considering much. For example, they can just send text messages to one another, even when they are doing something else, and do not need to consider the time lags between Korea and their families abroad to make sure that the other side is available. Wild geese fathers also like the fact that they can organize their thoughts more clearly and logically in their text messages than talking on the phone. This is particularly useful when wild geese fathers want to give some useful instructions to their children or when they want to calm down and talk to their children in dispute. Some reserved fathers find it easier to express their love and affection to their children through text messages rather than voice calls or video calls. Also, text messages are useful for memory so that wild geese families use text messages to arrange meetings (from important events to just chats) with each other.

Emotional Connections through Voice Calls, Video Calls, and Text Messages

Using voice calls, video calls, and text messages, wild geese fathers try to maintain frequent and regular communications with children abroad. For example, a wild geese father named Inho talks with his children at least once a day, in addition to exchanging several text messages. Another wild geese father, Suman, finishes his day by having a short video call with his children every night. For these fathers, frequent daily transnational communication with children is as important as the action of sending remittances, even if the content shared is trivial, because the daily nature of their rituals demonstrates that they are still emotionally connected with their children so that all family members maintain a sense of coherence as a family despite separation.[100]

Through active daily transnational communication, many wild geese fathers perform intensive parenting[101] and provide emotional support and practical care for children from a distance and fulfill an important component of responsible fathering, which is very well depicted in the following stories of three wild geese fathers:

First, Jihwan, a public official, always says, "I love you" whenever he has calls with his two teenage children abroad. As faithful Christians, Jihwan and his children also have Quiet Time (QT; time for prayer) daily and share what they have prayed for. Jihwan gives educational advice to his children whenever he feels necessary or is asked any questions. When his daughter once sent a picture of the first paycheck from her part-time job to him via Kakao Talk, Jihwan expressed how deeply he was grateful for her small but meaningful financial support to the family economy.

Second, Minho, a businessman, maintains his intimate relationship with his two sons, who are elementary school students, by playing online computer games frequently with them and having fun conversations with them. Minho checks daily how much his sons have improved their swimming skills through the video clips sent by his wife, and whenever he finds some improvement from his sons' performance, Minho highly praises them. Minho, as mentioned in an earlier part of this chapter, also figures out the kinds of Korean snack that his children want to have through daily casual communication with them and sends the right snacks in his monthly gift box, which his children always look forward to.

Last, Dongwook, a government official, well explains how technological development helps him maintain the intergenerational intimacy and serve as a discussant and counselor for his two teenage daughters during his second phase of wild geese lives. When he first became a wild geese father, he mostly relied on international phone calls when communicating with his family abroad. Back then, because international phone calls costed a lot, he could not make phone calls frequently, or, when he made a phone call, it had to be a short conversation just to check something important. Since the end of their first phase of transnational separation, Dongwook has witnessed huge technological development that significantly lowered the cost of transnational communication.

Now, Dongwook communicates much more frequently and longer with his daughters abroad than before, without being concerned about the communication cost. Dongwook, for example, discusses diverse topics with his daughters via Kakao Talk, ranging from daily issues, such as playdates and sleepovers, to academic issues, including schoolwork, grades and exams, to social issues, such as LGBT rights. He also exchanges pictures with his daughters daily and quickly picks up on their moods, which greatly helps him perform his role as a mediator between his wife and his adolescent daughters:

I call my [first] daughter very often. I ask her in Kakao Talk. While talking with her, I can figure out her mood of the day based on her voice from the phone call or from the content of her Kakao Talk [message and profile]. One day, she was very depressed, because she had a quarrel with her mom. If that happens, I try to placate her right away. Although I cannot physically be there to be with her, I let her know that I am on her side and I deeply understand her position. I encourage her and advise her to well resolve the disputes [with her mom]. Then, after one night, she sends me a good text message. I think that I am proactively intervening in my children's issues.

Like Dongwook, many wild geese fathers in my study define themselves as friendly fathers who are close to their children despite the distance. They also serve as counselors for their children and mediators between mothers and children. They further want to serve as role models for their children.

Interestingly, however, none of the wild geese fathers in my study include being a strict disciplinarian in their definition of ideal fatherhood, in contrast to working-class Filipino[102] and Mexican transnational fathers.[103] Wild geese fathers generally put much more emphasis on maintaining friendship with their children rather than asserting the authority as fathers. Some men want to comfort their children, because their wives are strict and disciplinary enough. Other fathers are afraid to be a strict disciplinarian and be estranged from their children during the separation. Thus, when there is a dispute between their wives and children, wild geese fathers try to arbitrate between them rather than unilaterally scolding their children. Wild geese fathers' such rejection of conventional authoritative fatherhood demonstrates that the patterns of masculinity and fatherhood are quite diverse across social classes.[104] It also reflects the emerging Korean fathering paradigm that increasingly values friendly and communicative fathering practices as integral parts of *good fatherhood*.[105]

Among the wild geese fathers who maintain strong emotional connections with their children abroad through frequent and regular communication, Seungwon, a businessman, is an exceptional performer of involved transnational fatherhood through his virtual co-presence and active involvement in his children's everyday lives. He provides routine care and micro-management of his children's everyday lives as if he is living together with them, exceeding the degree to which Filipina migrant mothers perform intensive mothering from a distance.[106] He turns on Skype 24 hours a day and let his life in Korea deeply mingled with his family's life abroad:

I install the Skype right in front of my bed. [. . .] I act according to what I would have done if I were in America. I try to do whatever I can do [for my children] from here. I wake up my children at 6:00 am Eastern time, which is 8:00 pm in Korean time. Then, my children wake up, wash their faces, and go to school at 6:30 am. When my wife gives them a ride and comes back home, it is 9:00 pm in Korea. After that, she and I have conversations until midnight [in Korean time]. Then, I go to bed. When I wake up about 6:00 am here [in Korea], it is 4:00 pm [in the United States] when my wife returns home with our children picked up from school. Then, I ask my children how their school was and what they have done that day. I also check their homework and help them do it. When my wife tells me she has gotten a package or a bill that day, I make a phone call to check it.

Emotional Connections through SNS and Emails

In addition to voice calls, video calls, and text messages that I have described so far, some wild geese fathers further communicate with their children abroad through SNS such as Facebook, Band, Kakao Story and Daum Café, the last three of which are Korean social media. Transnational communication through SNS may be less instantaneous compared to voice calls, video calls, and text messages. Nonetheless, it also gives wild geese fathers a valuable means to share their everyday lives with their families abroad, perform their role as responsible fathers from a distance, and build and strengthen emotional bond with their children.

Some wild fathers create an online community for the family in SNS and serve the role of a private tutor for their children abroad. Kanghyuk, a teacher, provides a detailed description of how he has used SNS to help his two daughters with their homework for five years of separation:

> When they first left, we made a Daum Café together and four of us [Kanghyuk, his wife and two daughters] became its members. [. . .] In the beginning, my daughters' English was not so good. So, whenever they had a homework assignment like writing an essay, I, an English teacher [in Korea], helped them a lot. If they posted their English essays on the [online] Café, I downloaded it, checked their grammars, corrected some errors, and then posted the edited ones. Particularly, for the first two years, I helped their homework a lot, as they continuously asked for my help. [. . .] While reviewing their homework, I could tell what they were learning. It was really fun to me. Then, as their [English] level went up, they asked fewer questions to me.

According to Kanghyuk, he no longer uses SNS to offer academic consultations to his daughters. He admits that his two daughters, who are now college students in Canada, have excelled him in English proficiency. He expresses mixed feelings on this. On the one hand, he is so proud of his children. On the other hand, he feels a little sad that he is not his daughters' teacher any longer and is less useful to them now. Now, this online Café, which once used to be online private academy, has been transformed into a virtual locus of family socializing where all his family members including relatives and extended family interact and share their milestones.

Another wild geese father, Hojun, also greatly performs his role as an involved father through various transnational communication platforms and even strengthens his emotional bond with his 13-year-old daughter abroad. He and his daughter have a video chat every night through Skype and share their daily lives. His daughter also talks behind her mother's back (Hojun's wife) when she has some complaints about her mother. Hojun also actively interacts with his daughter through Band, a popular social media platform in Korea. In Band, when he writes his thoughts and feelings on its online bulletin board, his daughter and wife add their comments. When he sees beautiful scenery or has some delicious Korean food, Hojun takes pictures and uploads them to share his joyful moments with family. Upon his daughter's milestone events, such as birthday celebrations, graduations, contests or performances, which Hojun cannot attend, his wife video-records the events and shares them with him via the family Band. For Hojun, the family Band is a critical locus like a *diary* where all his family members record their daily lives and share them instantaneously. In addition, Hojun frequently visits his daughter's Facebook page and keeps up with her on her recent interests so that he can buy some surprise gifts that she likes. Hojun reads his daughter's postings on her Facebook page, observes how much his daughter has grown into a mature adolescent during separation, and accordingly adjusts his fathering practices as well as gifts to match her physical and mental growth. Through active daily transnational communication, Hojun successfully performs intimate fatherhood and reinforces transnational emotional ties with his daughter. Hence, Hojun is certain that he is still "very close" to his daughter despite the four years of transnational separation. In short, SNS is a very effective way of strengthening the intergenerational ties. However, only a few wild geese families actively use it. It is probably because it needs a lot of efforts and time to maintain such a virtual family community.

Emails are also used by small numbers of wild geese fathers for communication with their children abroad. However, emails are not so frequently used, owing to the availability of other (and better) communication methods such as voice calls, video calls, and text messages. To upload pictures and videos, wild geese fathers prefer SNS to emails for its merit of easily sharing with family members. While emails have been welcomed by the working-class transnational families as a cheaper means than phone calls,[107] wild geese fathers do not find many merits of emails as they can use smartphones for free voice calls, video calls, and text messages with their family members abroad.

Other Factors of Transnational Father-Child Communication and Intimacy

Thus far, I have discussed how wild geese fathers daily and routinely utilize advanced communication technologies and attempt to fulfill the emotional aspect of responsible and involved fatherhood despite a distance from children. This finding challenges the negative portrait of transnational fathers as those who perform only the breadwinner roles and remain absent from their children's lives. Their close and intimate relationships with children abroad are achieved thanks to wild geese fathers' active utilization of various communication mediums including voice calls, video calls, text messages, SNS, and emails.

While the importance of communication technology in shaping transnational family relationships is acknowledged by the literature,[108] the specific usages of each medium by transnational families, particularly by middle-class ones, have rarely been discussed.[109] While previous studies have described how working-class families' transnational communication is restricted by their lack of resources,[110] my study explores the patterns and the meanings of transnational communications between wild geese fathers and children and contributes to a better understanding of the roles of social class and technology in shaping the transnational fathering practices of middle-class families.

Nevertheless, I also would like to point out that technology does not "automatically guarantee a smooth flow of transnational communication" as Parreñas[111] has argued. Even though all wild geese fathers in my study have a similar level of technological resources, their achievement in maintaining or improving transnational intimacy widely varies. On one extreme, there are wild geese fathers like Seungwon and Hojun who are virtually co-present in their children's everyday lives and strengthen their emotional ties with children. On the other extreme, there are some fathers who communicate mostly with their wives, but hardly with their children.

A wild geese father named Kangsan was a workaholic when he lived together with his family in Korea. He also enjoyed socializing with his colleagues rather than having family time. Thus, he went to work very early in the morning and came back home around midnight after having drink with his friends. Because he was not so interested in communicating with his children, he was not so close to his children prior to the transnational family separation. After becoming a wild geese father, neither his communication pattern nor his intergenerational relationship with his children abroad has changed much:

> I haven't done much fathering [for my children]. [. . .] I sometimes call them to hear their voices. However, because I don't know specifically what they are doing there, I just ask such insignificant questions. Then, they also give me such banal answers. After having a very short conversation composed with just two or three sentences, then they toss the phone to their mom.

As Kangsan's case shows, technology is not a magic tool that suddenly improves intergenerational intimacy that did not exist. Rather, communication technologies can have meaningful impacts on transnational family intimacy only if family members are willing to utilize such technologies and try to avail themselves of frequent transnational communications.

There are also other important factors that influence the quality of transnational communication and father-child relationships. First, father-child relationship prior to separation is important. As described earlier, in my study, wild geese fathers who were close to their children prior to separation tend to make more efforts to communicate with their children and thus maintain more intimate intergenerational relationships after separation.

Second, child's age matters. Previous studies argue that the negative impacts of separation on intergenerational relationships are greater for younger children than older ones, because younger children do not have clear memories of their parents and need to rely on other adults to communicate with their transnational parents, whereas older children have more vivid memories of their parents and can directly communicate with their parents abroad.[112] In contrast, wild geese fathers in my study tend to maintain more intimate relationships with younger children than older adolescent children and feel it easier to recover their emotional ties (if damaged) with the younger ones than older ones.

Third, children's gender is also important in shaping transnational father-child interactions and their relationships. According to wild geese fathers with adolescent children, they tend to have more frequent intergenerational conflicts and confrontations with sons than with daughters. While adolescent wild geese children's challenges to their parents are not easy for many wild geese fathers to handle from a distance, these fathers still find it relatively easier to overcome the problems with adolescent daughters than the problems with adolescent sons. It is because wild geese fathers tend to maintain closer relationships with their adolescent daughters than with sons, by having more frequent transnational communications and exchanging affections and attentions more comfortably with their daughters than with sons. Indeed, stronger emotional ties with daughters provide wild geese fathers with greater leverage to recover their relationships when they encounter intergenerational conflicts. Seunghyun, a wild geese father with a 22-year-old son and a 17-year-old daughter, describes the difference between his daughter and son:

My older [son] is a little passive and silent, different from the younger [daughter]. My younger [daughter] approaches me and is friendly with me, but not the older one does so. It is more fun to raise my younger [daughter]. That is the reason why father needs a daughter. But, regarding my son, he seems to fend for himself.

Fourth, as discussed in next section, wild geese fathers in my study tend to have more troubles with children who migrated at a younger age and/or have been separated for a longer period, unless they maintain active transnational communication during family separation, often due to increasing cultural gaps between Korea and the host countries. Given this, lengthy separation exerts negative influences on the transnational father-child relationships.[113]

Lastly, wild geese fathers who have prior experiences of living together with their family in the host society tend to experience less cultural conflict with their children and cultivate intimate intergenerational relationships more easily. For example, a wild geese father named Dongwook explains how his prior experience of living together with his family in the United States helps him maintain his emotional ties with them despite the lengthy separation:

> If I had just sent my family abroad and I stayed here, emotional ties with my family might have weakened. [. . .] However, I first lived there with my family for a year. And this time, I stayed there together with them for two years. Thus, when we talk each other, we are neither hesitant nor uncomfortable. When we talk, we easily understand what each other means to say. They tell me where they have been today and whom they have met. They tell me how delicious the food they had today, "Dad, you know this food which we ate together." Although we cannot physically be together, we have a sense of coherence.

TRANSNATIONAL FATHERING: REGULAR FACE-TO-FACE ENCOUNTERS

This section highlights the importance of regular face-to-face encounters. Though many wild geese fathers in my study maintain emotional connections with their children and overcome the distance through frequent and regular transnational communication, there are still information gaps among wild geese family members during the separation, because they no longer easily "share all the nonsignificant daily events or thoughts in life,"[114] as Şenyürekli and Detznera have noted.

It is known that some transnational parents are greatly embarrassed by the mismatch between children in their mind and their children's actual appearance with great maturity when they actually meet their children in person after lengthy separation.[115] Likewise, despite their regular transnational communication, many wild geese fathers in my study tend to view their children as young as when they first separated and fail to acknowledge how much their children have grown into mature adolescents during the separation.

Jaehoon, a businessman, has just reunited with his wife and a 13-year-old daughter after three years of transnational separation. He still vividly remembers how he was surprised when he met his daughter at the airport one year after they had separated, because she had grown much more than he had imagined. He even wondered, "Oh, is this the girl that I know?" He also felt a sense of loss, because he suddenly recognized that transnational family separation robbed him of the valuable time that he could have made many wonderful memories with his young fast-growing daughter.

In addition, some wild geese parents practice censorship on the information they share with their families. Wild geese fathers tend to hide their current economic hardships and concerns about the future from their wives and children abroad. Wild geese mothers tend to show only their adolescent children's positive aspects to their husbands in order not to worry or disappoint them. Because of censorship practiced by both sides of wild geese families,[116] frequent transnational communications do not always allow wild geese family members to have a good understanding of one another during separation.[117]

Furthermore, when there are some conflicts or misunderstandings with family members abroad, many wild geese fathers find it more difficult to resolve such issues while separated than when they lived together, because one side across the ocean can easily refuse to have transnational communication. For example, a wild geese father named Hojun, still points out a weakness of transnational communication, even if he actively communicates with his family abroad:

Although I always communicate with my family, [. . .] when we have some troubles, then they can last for two or three days [longer than usual from Hojun's standard], because one side refuses to communicate with another. [. . .] Though we eventually have a conversation, it is possible that our communication completely stops. [. . .] When we lived together in Korea, we had to see each other no matter what. But, we can now just live without any communication [unless we make an effort to communicate]. This is what I am concerned about.

Given this, while frequent and regular transnational communication is very helpful to maintain transnational family intimacy, face-to-face encounters are still important and beneficial, particularly when separation is lengthier. Existing literature also shows that transnational father-child emotional ties can be further reinforced when fathers' virtual co-presence is accompanied by the "moments of physical co-presence."[118] Therefore, in this section, I discuss how wild geese fathers attempt to perform involved and intimate fatherhood through frequent and regular face-to-face encounters and maintain or further strengthen their relationship with children living abroad. I also suggest that transnational fathers' relationships with children are highly influenced not only by the quantity of their face-to-face encounters with families but also by the quality of their specific fathering activities during those encounters.

Overseas Visits: Frequency, Length, and Cost

Wild geese fathers generally meet their children more often and spend a longer time with them than do working-class Latino transnational parents who cannot frequently visit their children in home countries because of their tight budget and/or undocumented immigrant status.[119] Out of thirty-three wild geese fathers interviewed, four wild geese fathers meet their families about eight to twelve times per year and spend about three to seven days together each visit, as their families reside in one of the closest Asian countries, such as Singapore, the Philippines, and China. The other twenty-nine wild geese fathers, whose families are residing in farther countries, such as the United States, Canada, and Australia, still meet their families 2.5 times a year on average. Specifically, among these twenty-nine fathers, four of them meet their families less than once a year; seven fathers once a year; fifteen fathers two to four times a year; and three fathers five to seven times a year despite the long distance.

It is usually wild geese fathers who fly to the other side. It is a practical decision to save travel costs: They decide whether to buy just one flight ticket (for father) or multiple tickets (for mother and children) to achieve the same outcome, a family reunion. This strategy helps wild geese families to increase the frequency of family reunions within the tight travel budget. Indeed, most wild geese fathers spend a lot of money for airfares. If their families live closer, they pay cheaper airfares but buy more of flight tickets; if their families live farther away, they have to pay more per flight ticket so purchase fewer of them. Because many wild geese fathers, prior to separation, did not expect that they would spend such a huge amount of money for international transportation, they often describe this as "throwing money away in the air." Nonetheless, wild geese fathers still regard it as the requisite costs for maintaining intimate relationships with their family abroad.

The length of stay per visit is another matter of strategic decision. Wild geese fathers in my study stay with their families in the host countries about forty days per year on average. They present interesting variations not only in their number of visits but also in their length of visit by the type of employment. On the one extreme, there are some wild geese fathers who spend only about a week or two with their families each year. Particularly, in case of wild geese fathers who are businessmen or public officials, their lengthy vacations are not easily approved by their employers. This is partly because of their busy work schedule, and partly because of the organizational culture in Korea, where supervisors do not like to allow their subordinates to have a long break.[120] Note that Koreans are even designated as "the world's most vacation deprived workers," as they spend only six days off out of the given fifteen days of the annual paid leaves.[121] Given this, it is not surprising that wild geese fathers in my study stay only a week or two when they visit their family abroad. Thus, in order to stay longer with their families abroad, these wild geese fathers strategically combine their vacation time with one of the two biggest Korean holidays (i.e., Korean New Year's Day and Korean Thanksgiving Day). Or, they stop by their families when they go to or come from international business trips.

On the other extreme, there are some wild geese fathers who are professors, teachers, and business owners (including doctors and architects). These fathers not only visit their families abroad more often but also stay longer during each visit than the other wild geese fathers. For example, professors and teachers can stay with their families abroad about a month or two per visit during the summer or winter breaks, even though they can stay only about a week or two per visit during the regular semesters. Sometimes professors can take sabbaticals to live with their families abroad for about a year or two.

Besides, it should not be overlooked that wild geese children and their mothers also go back to Korea to meet their fathers. They make much less frequent visits (e.g., once a year) than their fathers, but stay much longer per visit. Wild geese mothers and children tend to visit Korea during the summer breaks and stay about one to three months.

In sum, most wild geese fathers in my study spend at least two weeks per year with families, and about one-fourth of fathers even stay with their families about three to five months per year, combining their visits abroad and their family's visits to Korea. Such frequent transnational face-to-face encounters among wild geese family members certainly indicate that social class and legal status are critical resources for transnational families to stay connected and overcome the physical distance.

Quality of Visits

As much as it is difficult and costly to visit their children abroad, wild geese fathers strive to effectively spend the precious time with their children. During family visits, wild geese fathers try to fulfill their economic role of responsible fathers by spending extra money in dining out, buying gifts that their children have asked for, and traveling with their children. Interestingly, a domestic trip with their families is a must for each visit, even if the visit is as short as only a week.

Family visits also enable many wild geese fathers to overcome the traditional gender role division of parenting and provide emotional and physical care for their children, thereby filling the emotional gaps that might have occurred during lengthy transnational separation. For instance, fathers joy-fully drive their children to school and other extracurricular activities during visits. They express affection to their children by directly saying "I love you" in person and/or by hugging them. Many fathers try to engage in physical activities with children, such as basketball, soccer, tennis, golf, bowling, box-ing, biking, or walking. Some fathers gladly cook for their children, even if cooking is a typically female-typed task they previously avoided, considering it their wives' exclusive domain.[122]

A few fathers further participate in their children's school activities during visits. They attend educational sessions for parents, PTA meetings, and confer-ences at their children's school. Some fathers arrange one-to-one consultations with their children's teacher to catch up about their children. Other fathers become a member of private gatherings and socialize with local parents when-ever they visit their family abroad. A couple of fathers also volunteer to serve as a classroom helper or give a guest lecture to their children's class during visits.

It is important to note that such active involvement in children's school community is shown by some exceptional wild geese fathers who have much higher educational zeal than other fathers and have prior experiences of liv-ing in the host countries with their family. Thus, they know the people and the system in the host countries. The rest of wild geese fathers in my study hardly engage in their children's schools during visits, even if many of them actively provide emotional and physical care for children. They are neither confident of their English proficiency nor familiar with the education system of the host countries. Accordingly, these fathers tend to entrust their wives with children's education and school-related activities.

In addition to engaging in various activities for and with their children, wild geese fathers try to have many conversations with their children during visits. If wild geese fathers share the same hobbies or cultural interests with their children, such as music, TV programs, movies, or books, it is much easier for them to have conversations with their children without feeling much discomfort or awkward despite lengthy separation.

A wild geese father named Kanghyuk intentionally listens to Korean pop music (K-pop) that his two adolescent daughters like. He also brings Korean bestsellers to his family abroad so that he can have some common topics to discuss with his daughters. During his visits, he also watches popular Korean music shows, TV programs, or movies that his wife has carefully selected and enjoys talking about them with the family. When his daughters visit him in Korea, he goes to popular singers' concerts with them. By discussing and experiencing together what his children like, Kanghyuk can maintain emo-tional connections with them and overcome the spatial and temporal distance. Kanghyuk also makes it clear that his current intimate relationship with his children is the outcome of his intentional and endless efforts:

If I do not consciously make such efforts, I will be a total stranger to them. [. . .] By approaching my children with the same hobbies and movies, I can maintain the [emotional] bond and communicate with them. Otherwise, if I meet them once in a while [without making such efforts], although I can just watch TV and have meals together, I no longer have the ties with them. [. . .] Yes, I am still intimate with them. But it is now the outcome of my intentional efforts, while it was natural intimacy beforehand [prior to separation].

Such involved and intimate parenting practices presented by wild geese fathers during their family visits are certainly outside of the narrow scope of fathers' traditional breadwinning role and offer evidence to counterbalance the dominant description of transnational fathers as being largely absent from their children's lives.[123]

A following story of wild geese father named Youngtae suggests that both transnational communication and family encounters are equally important means of transnational fathering, with which wild geese fathers can maintain (and even improve) intimate father-child relationships despite lengthy family separation. Youngtae has been separated from his family for ten years. Nonetheless, Youngtae confidently asserts that he is still very close to his two teenage children, particularly to his daughter, to the extent that she can comfortably share with him about her physical changes of puberty.

Youngtae thinks that his deep emotional connections with his daughter can be achieved thanks to his constant transnational communication and frequent face-to-face encounters with her. Youngtae has conversations with his daughter several times a day to share each other's unimportant and important moments of life. He also meets his family three to four times a year: He goes abroad two to three times a year on Korean holidays and stay there about ten days each time, while his children come to Korea every summer break and stay two months. During their stays in Korea, Youngtae lives as a family man:

I make frequent phone calls. I also spend relatively . . . no . . . absolutely longer time with my children than other [wild geese fathers]. I stay together with my children in fact more than three months per year. [. . .] They are in Korea for two months and I go there, too. While they are staying in Korea, I leave my office at 6:00 pm[124] and get home at 7:00 pm. I don't drink at all, and just spend all my time with them. I don't think that my children feel that they grow apart from me.

However, unfortunately, not all wild geese fathers are successful in performing the role of intimate fathers during their family encounters. It is certain that face-to-face encounters are extremely beneficial to strengthen the intergenerational relationships, if wild geese fathers have maintained intimate relationships with their children through constant daily transnational communication. In contrast, face-to-face encounters may not greatly help wild geese fathers, if they have lacked such active transnational communication with their children.

A few wild geese fathers even feel lonely and isolated during their family visits. Because these fathers have not maintained consistent transnational communication with their children, they are likely to plan their family visits without having a good understanding of their families' schedules in the host countries. These fathers also tend to expect that they will be greatly welcomed by their families upon their arrival and that their wife and children will re-organize all their schedules for the father. In contrast to these fathers' expectations, wild geese families abroad often rejoice only a few days at their fathers' arrival and then return to their ordinary life, even if their fathers have made the visit after a long time of transnational family separation.

Woosung is a former wild geese father who neglected regular transnational communication with his children for his eleven years of transnational family separation. Woosung gives a detailed explanation of his frustration and awkwardness as an unwelcomed visitor when he first went to meet his family in Canada:

> When I went there by taking a flight for a long time, I had high expectations that they would treat me well and I would spend a lot of time with my children. I thought that everything would be organized centered on me. But, [when I got there] my children just said, "Hello, Dad," and went to their room. [During my stay in Canada] I did not have much conversation with my children, and just felt awkward. [. . .] In the morning, my wife gave the children a ride and I stayed home alone. While watching TV, I did not understand what people said. [. . .] Then I watched a Korean video that my son borrowed. When my wife returned home, she gave me lunch. After lunch, I read a book [. . .] and then went to the park with a dog. Or I did some exercise [alone].

Among the wild geese fathers who have lacked regular transnational communication with their children during lengthy separation, a few men even experience serious confrontations with their children during family encounters. Oftentimes, the father-child tension is likely to be dormant or disguised during the period of separation, because of their lack of transnational communication. Nonetheless, when wild geese family members gather together through their face-to-face encounters, the father-child tension is likely to surface again. Children in a foreign culture have grown to understand less and less of Korean-style authoritative fathers, whereas Korean fathers happen to find their teenage children have become more rebellious and disrespectful.

Sangho, a wild geese father whose two adult children still live in Canada, well shows the changes in his intergenerational relationships over the last thirteen years of transnational family separation. According to Sangho, his children were quickly acculturated into the host society. Thus, whenever he visited his family in Canada, he was not treated as the respected father with authority but a bigot who was continuously reproached by his children for his cultural ignorance.

For example, when Sangho had a seat at a restaurant before being seated, and when he talked loudly in a public space, his children scowled at him and hurt his feelings. When he tried to give educational advice to his children, his children disrespected him and said, "Don't intervene it without knowing [the system]." He thought that his children talked to and treated him very impolitely and rudely. However, whenever Sangho tried to discipline his children for their inappropriate attitudes, they stopped him by pointing out that he talked too loud and intemperately. With such constant conflicts over time, Sangho has been very upset about his children, no longer wanted to talk with them, and even questioned for what he had sacrificed his life during those thirteen years.

Jaeman, a wild geese father in his fifth year of transnational separation, also mentions the similar kinds of intergenerational conflict with his three sons. He strongly believes that his sons would never have shown such defiant attitudes toward him, if they had continuously lived together with him in Korea. Furthermore, Jaeman recognizes that he has been gradually isolated and excluded from his children even during his visits. In Jaeman's first annual visit to Canada, his children willingly went out with him for shopping and provided necessary English interpretation for him. In the second annual visit, his children seemed to be ashamed when Jaeman negotiated the price with a clerk at the mall as he had done in his first visit, and thus refused to interpret for him despite his several requests. So, they had a severe quarrel at the mall. In his third annual visit, his children no longer wanted to go out with Jaeman, because they felt uncomfortable to do so. Consequently, Jaeman could no longer get along with his children during his visit. Mixed with frustration, anger, and a sense of betrayal, Jaeman told his children as below, when he returned to Korea after his third and last visit:

I will never come back [to see you]. [. . .] I have sent you here the money that I have earned very strenuously. How can you treat me like this! I am so annoyed. You will see if I ever come back!

While his wife tried to mediate the conflict between him and his children, Jaeman felt that his wife was totally on his children's side.

Since his last visit to Canada, Jaeman's discontent has kept accumulating and his transnational family relationship has not been recovered yet. Jaeman even bitterly admits that after confrontation with his children, he is no longer happy to send remittances to his family abroad, even if he has not stopped sending money. While Mexican migrant fathers are estranged from their children when they cannot send remittances,[125] Jaeman's case indicates that wild geese fathers tend to send remittances even if they are estranged from their family.

CONCLUSION

This chapter analyzes the transnational fathering practices of wild geese fathers, focusing on how these men attempt to fulfill both components of responsible fathering (i.e., providing economic support and emotional/physical care for children) in the transnational context. My study corroborates that transnational fathers fulfill their breadwinning roles by sending remittances and gifts to their children who live apart.

Yet, I further suggest that sending remittances and gifts also serves an emotional role, as if it does for transnational mothers. This framework is beneficial to better understanding transnational fathers' economic provision beyond the simple male-breadwinner framework. In addition, I delve into the mechanisms that remittances and gifts differently shape transnational father-child intimacy: While remittances' emotional impact is often managed by mothers, gifts tend to more directly affect transnational intimacy between fathers and children.

I consider social class of transnational families and discuss the different meanings of sending remittances and gifts between working-class transnational families and middle-class transnational families. I further confront the existing theory's tendency to view Asian and Asian American parents' educational zeal as something primarily based on patriarchal Asian culture and alternatively suggest that it may be common among middle-class families across cultures.

Next, I have analyzed how wild geese fathers fulfill their emotional roles through transnational communication with their children. My study confirms that frequent and regular transnational communication is critical to maintaining intimate relationships between migrant parents and children and overcoming the geographical and temporal distance. Through transnational communication, wild geese fathers not only express their love, care, and attention to their children but also play diverse roles such as tutors, mediators, counselors, and role models. In so doing, friendship is highly emphasized in wild geese fathers' definition of ideal fatherhood.

I also demonstrate that communication technologies play a pivotal role in transnational fathers' efforts to improve the transnational father-child relationships.[126] At the same time, I cautiously note that technology does not wield magical power to abruptly create intergenerational intimacy where it does not exist.[127]

Finally, I have shown that face-to-face encounters are also crucial to enhance intergenerational intimacy among transnational family members. There has not been much knowledge on transnational fathers' fathering activities during face-to-face encounters, partly because many transnational fathers do not care for their children, even when they visit or live together with their children based on the gendered expectations on parenting. However, by describing wild geese fathers' diverse parenting activities during their family visits, I demonstrate that some transnational fathers actually cross the strict *gender boundaries*[128] and provide emotional and physical care for their children at least during their encounters. My analysis of wild geese fathers' emotions also contributes to producing the better understanding of transnational fathers, who have been previously perceived as unemotional.

This chapter makes significant contributions to existing literature of transnational fatherhood. First, it sheds light on the largely overlooked subject of middle-class Asian fatherhood in transnational settings. It revisits the one-dimensional and economically deterministic descriptions of transnational fathers and documents wild geese fathers' growing emotional work and expressions of affection toward their children from a distance, in addition to the emotional and symbolic implications of their remittances. It also demonstrates that fathers' co-presence with children may not be a prerequisite for the enactment of involved fathering, because some transnational fathers, like wild geese fathers, are successful involved fathers.

This chapter also suggests that emotional and physical care is an essential element of contemporary middle-class transnational fatherhood and is not less important than economic provision. Indeed, the fact that there is a substantial variation in intergenerational intimacy between wild geese fathers and their children, although all wild geese fathers fulfill their economic roles, indicates that emotional components are the key to successful enactment of contemporary middle-class transnational fathering, as much as they are to successful transnational mothering.

Second, this chapter demonstrates that transnational fathers do not always passively obey but actively interpret and renegotiate patriarchal gender norms. Substantial numbers of wild geese fathers, who were far from being family-oriented men before family separation, transgress the gendered boundary of parenthood (i.e., father as breadwinner and mother as caretaker) and become more affectionate, expressive, nurturing, and involved fathers through separation. This finding corroborates that transnational family separation is a significant turning point and enables many transnational fathers to recognize the overlooked value of their families and pursue more intimate and friendly relations as their new approach to fatherhood rather than remaining traditional breadwinners and strict remote disciplinarians.

Furthermore, many wild geese fathers regard themselves as good fathers only if they successfully accomplish their emotional roles as well as their economic roles. Given their concerted effort to combine the traditional role of breadwinners with the new role of emotional and physical caretakers, wild geese fathers are among the new fathers who actively embrace more flexible concepts of masculinity and implement new ideologies of involved and intimate fatherhood in their fathering practices to overcome their physical separation from children.

Lastly, this chapter suggests that an intersectional approach, combining race/ethnicity, social class, and legality, can produce more nuanced explanations of the diverse patterns of transnational fatherhood. Whereas existing literature has primarily focused on describing how difficult it is for undocumented working-class transnational fathers to perform responsible and involved fatherhood because of their lack of resources, this chapter alternatively highlights how substantial numbers of wild geese fathers renegotiate many elements of the patriarchal parenting ideology and maintain/strengthen transnational father-child intimacy, by drawing on their middle-class status, including economic, technological, and legal resources. It also cautions against simple generalizations of Asian fatherhood based exclusively on a father's race/ethnicity or so-called patriarchal Asian culture, as my findings indicate that Asian fatherhood is quite diverse and changes dynamically in response to social, political, and technological changes.

NOTES

This chapter is a revised version of an article originally published online as Se Hwa Lee, ""I Am Still Close to My Child": Middle-Class Korean Wild Geese Fathers' Responsible and Intimate Fatherhood in a Transnational Context," in the *Journal of Ethnic and Migration Studies*. DOI: https://doi.org/10.1080/1369183X.20 19.1573662. Reprinted with permission from the *Journal of Ethnic and Migration Studies*.

1. Brittany McGill, "Navigating New Norms of Involved Fatherhood: Employment, Fathering Attitudes, and Father Involvement," *Journal of Family Issues* 35, no. 8 (2014): 1089–1106.

2. Elizabeth H. Pleck and Joseph H. Pleck, "Fatherhood Ideals in the United States: Historical Dimensions," in *The Role of the Father in Child Development*, 3rd ed., ed. Michael E. Lamb (New York: Wiley, 1997), 33–48.

3. Lucas Gottzén, "Involved Fatherhood? Exploring the Educational Work of Middle-class Men," *Gender and Education* 23, no. 5 (2011): 619–634.

4. William J. Doherty, Edward F. Kouneski, and Martha F. Erickson, "Responsible Fathering: An Overview and Conceptual Framework," *Journal of Marriage and the Family* 60 (1998): 277–292.

5. Glenda Wall and Stephanie Arnold, "How Involved Is Involved Fathering? An Exploration of the Contemporary Culture of Fatherhood," *Gender & Society* 21, no. 4 (2007): 508–527.

6. Esther Dermott, *Intimate Fatherhood: A Sociological Analysis* (London: Routledge, 2008), 3.

7. James A. Levine and Edward W. Pitt, *New Expectations: Community Strategies for Responsible Fatherhood* (New York: Families and Work Institute, 1995), 6.

8. Dermott, *Intimate Fatherhood*, 43–75; Michael Lamb, "The History of Research on Father Involvement," *Marriage & Family Review* 29, nos. 2–3 (2000): 23–42; McGill, "Navigating New Norms," 1089–1106; Wall and Arnold, "How Involved," 508–527.

9. Thomas Johansson, "The Construction of the New Father: How Middle-Class Men Become Present Fathers," *International Review of Modern Sociology* 37, no. 1 (2011): 121–136.

10. Levine and Pitt, *New Expectations*.

11. For an exception, see Jenna Nobles, "Parenting from Abroad: Migration, Nonresident Father Involvement, and Children's Education in Mexico," *Journal of Marriage and Family* 73 (2011): 729–746.

12. Dermott, *Intimate Fatherhood*, 114–120.

13. Dreby, "Honor and Virtue," 32–59; Parreñas, "Transnational Fathering," 1063–1064; Jason Pribilsky, "Consumption Dilemmas: Tracking Masculinity, Money and Transnational Fatherhood between the Ecuadorian Andes and New York City," *Journal of Ethnic and Migration Studies* 38, no. 2 (2012): 323–343; Schmalzbauer, "Temporary and Transnational," 211–226; Waters, "Flexible Families," 117–134.

14. See the critique of Karlijn Haagsman and Valentina Mazzucato, "The Quality of Parent-Child Relationships in Transnational Families: Angolan and Nigerian Migrant Parent in the Netherlands," *Journal of Ethnic and Migration Studies* 40, no. 11 (2014): 1677–1696.

15. Brenda S. A. Yeoh and Katie Willis, "'Heart' and 'Wing,' Nation and Diaspora: Gendered Discourses in Singapore's Regionalisation Process," *Gender, Place and Culture* 6 (1999): 355–372.

16. Rhacel Salazar Parreñas, *Children of Global Migration: Transnational Families and Gendered Woes* (Stanford, CA: Stanford University Press, 2005), 98–103.

17. Johanna L. Waters, "Becoming a Father, Missing a Wife: Chinese Transnational Families and the Male Experience of Lone Parenting in Canada," *Population, Space and Place* 16, no. 1 (2009): 66.

18. Dreby, "Honor and Virtue," 32–59; Ehrenreich and Hochschild, "Introduction," 1–13; Fresnoza-Flot, "Migration Status," 252–270; Hondagneu-Sotelo and Avila,

"I'm Here," 559–560; Madianou and Miller, "Mobile Phone Parenting," 457–470; Parreñas, "Long Distance Intimacy," 317–336.

19. For exceptions, see Montes, "Role of Emotions," 469–490 and Schmalzbauer, "Temporary and Transnational," 211–226.

20. Dreby, "Honor and Virtue," 32–59; Hondagneu-Sotelo and Avila, "I'm Here," 559–560; Parreñas, "Long Distance Intimacy," 317–336.

21. Parreñas, "Transnational Fathering," 1057.

22. Dreby, "Honor and Virtue," 32–59; Hondagneu-Sotelo, "Overcoming Patriarchal Constraints," 393–415; Lee and Koo, "Wild Geese Fathers," 533–553; McKay, "Sending Dollars Shows Feeling," 175–194; Parreñas, "Transnational Fathering," 1063–1064; Pribilsky, "Aprendemos a Convivir," 313–334.

23. Dreby, "Honor and Virtue," 32–59.

24. See critique of Jørgen Carling, Cecilia Menjívar, and Leah Schmalzbauer, "Central Themes in the Study of Transnational Parenthood," *Journal of Ethnic and Migration Studies* 38, no. 2 (2012): 191–217 and Montes, "Role of Emotions," 469–490.

25. Kilkey, Plomien, and Perrons, "Migrant Men's Fathering," 179.

26. Dreby, "Honor and Virtue," 32–59.

27. Schmalzbauer, "Temporary and Transnational," 211–226; Paula A. Worby and Kurt C. Organista, "Alcohol Use and Problem Drinking among Mexican and Central American Immigrant Laborers: A Review of the Literature," *Hispanic Journal of Behavioral Sciences* 29, no. 4 (2007): 413–455.

28. Montes, "Role of Emotions," 469–490.

29. Kilkey, Plomien, and Perrons, "Migrant Men's Fathering," 179.

30. Lee and Koo, "Wild Geese Fathers," 533–553 for exception.

31. See Parreñas, "Transnational Fathering," 1063–1064 and Waters, "Becoming a Father," 63–74 for exceptions.

32. Carling, Menjívar, and Schmalzbauer, "Transnational Parenthood," 191–217; Patricia Landolt and Wei Wei Da, "The Spatially Ruptured Practices of Migrant Families: A Comparison of Immigrant Families from El Salvador and the People's Republic of China," *Current Sociology* 53, no. 4 (2005): 625–653; Menjívar, "Family Reorganization," 223–245; Parreñas, "Long Distance Intimacy," 317–336; Saskia Sassen, "Two Stops in Today's New Global Geographies: Shaping Novel Labor Supplies and Employment Regimes," *American Behavioral Scientist* 52, no. 3 (2008): 457–496.

33. Doherty, Kouneski, and Erickson, "Responsible Fathering," 277–292.

34. Levine and Pitt, *New Expectations*, 6.

35. Dreby, "Honor and Virtue," 32–59; Parreñas, "Transnational Fathering," 1063–1064; Pribilsky, "Aprendemos a Convivir," 313–334.

36. Joanna Dreby and Timothy Adkins, "Inequalities in Transnational Families," *Sociology Compass* 4, no. 8 (2010): 680.

37. Horst, "Blessings and Burdens," 143–159; Kilkey, Plomien, and Perrons, "Migrant Men's Fathering," 178–191; McKay, "Sending Dollars Shows Feeling," 175–194; Zentgraf and Chinchilla, "Transnational Family Separation," 345–366.

38. Carling, Menjívar, and Schmalzbauer, "Transnational Parenthood," 191–217; Haagsman and Mazzucato, "Parent-Child Relationships," 1677–1696; Louise Ryan

et al., "Family Strategies and Transnational Migration: Recent Polish Migrants in London," *Journal of Ethnic and Migration Studies* 35, no. 1 (2009): 61–77; Schmalzbauer, "Temporary and Transnational," 211–226; Zentgraf and Chinchilla, "Transnational Family Separation," 345–366.

39. Carling, Menjívar, and Schmalzbauer, "Transnational Parenthood," 191–217; Haagsman and Mazzucato, "Parent-Child Relationships," 1677–1696; Horst, "Blessings and Burdens," 143–159; Madianou and Miller, "Mobile Phone Parenting," 457–470; Parreñas, "Transnational Fathering," 1063–1064; Şenyürekli and Detznera, "Communication Dynamics," 807–824; Andrea Smith, Richard N. Lalonde, and Simone Johnson, "Serial Migration and Its Implications for the Parent-Child Relationship: A Retrospective Analysis of the Experiences of the Children of Caribbean Immigrants," *Cultural Diversity and Ethnic Minority Psychology* 10, no. 2 (2004): 107–122; Raelene Wilding, "'Virtual' Intimacies? Families Communicating across Transnational Contexts," *Global Networks* 6, no. 2 (2006): 125–142; Zentgraf and Chinchilla, "Transnational Family Separation," 345–366.

40. Esben Leifsen and Alexander Tymczuk, "Care at a Distance: Ukrainian and Ecuadorian Transnational Parenthood from Spain," *Journal of Ethnic and Migration Studies* 38, no. 2 (2012): 219–236; John Urry, "Social Networks, Travel and Talk," *British Journal of Sociology* 54, no. 2 (2003): 155–175.

41. Menjívar, "Family Reorganization," 223–245; Pribilsky, "Consumption Dilemmas," 323–343; Zentgraf and Chinchilla, "Transnational Family Separation," 345–366.

42. Parreñas, "Transnational Fathering," 1063–1064; Yeoh and Willis, "'Heart' and 'Wing,'" 355–372; see Nobles, "Parenting from Abroad," 729–746 for exception.

43. Parreñas, "Transnational Fathering," 1063–1064.

44. Doherty, Kouneski, and Erickson, "Responsible Fathering," 277–292; Juliana Sobolewski and Valarie King, "The Importance of the Coparental Relationship for Nonresident Fathers' Ties to Children," *Journal of Marriage and Family* 67 (2005): 1196–1212.

45. Dreby, "Honor and Virtue," 32–59; Menjívar, "Transnational Parenting," 301–322; Pribilsky, "Consumption Dilemmas," 323–343.

46. Madianou and Miller, "Mobile Phone Parenting," 457–470.

47. Menjívar, "Family Reorganization," 233.

48. Pribilsky, "Consumption Dilemmas," 323–343; Schmalzbauer, "Temporary and Transnational," 211–226.

49. Chee, "Migrating for the Children," 137–156.

50. There are two gender role reversed case out of sixty-four wild geese parents in my study.

51. Carling, Menjívar, and Schmalzbauer, "Transnational Parenthood," 191–217; Dreby, "Honor and Virtue," 32–59; Hondagneu-Sotelo and Avila, "I'm Here," 548–571; Menjívar, "Transnational Parenting," 301–322; Parreñas, "Long Distance Intimacy," 317–336.

52. Ibid.

53. Dreby, "Honor and Virtue," 32–59; Lee, "Closer or Estranged," 503–533; Montes, "Role of Emotions," 469–490.

54. See Schmalzbauer, "Temporary and Transnational," 211–226 for Mexican guest workers' emotions.

55. Dreby, "Honor and Virtue," 32–59; Schmalzbauer, *Striving and Surviving*, 68–69; Schmalzbauer, "Temporary and Transnational," 211–226.

56. Montes, "Role of Emotions," 469–490.

57. Dreby, "Honor and Virtue," 32–59.

58. Montes, "Role of Emotions," 486.

59. Johansson, "Construction of the New Father," 124.

60. Dreby, "Honor and Virtue," 32–59; Kilkey, Plomien, and Perrons, "Migrant Men's Fathering," 178–191; McKay, "Sending Dollars Shows Feeling," 175–194; Menjívar, "Transnational Parenting," 301–322; Nobles, "Parenting from Abroad," 729–746; Parreñas, "Transnational Fathering," 1063–1064; Pribilsky, "Aprendemos a Convivir," 313–334; Pribilsky, "Consumption Dilemmas," 323–343.

61. Throughout the chapter, I have changed the currency from Korean on to United States dollar in all accounts.

62. Kilkey, Plomien, and Perrons, "Migrant Men's Fathering," 178–191; Pribilsky, "Consumption Dilemmas," 323–343.

63. Dreby, "Honor and Virtue," 32–59; Schmalzbauer, *Striving and Surviving*, 69.

64. Dreby, "Honor and Virtue," 32–59; McKay, "Sending Dollars Shows Feeling," 175–194; Nobles, "Parenting from Abroad," 729–746; Parreñas, "Transnational Fathering," 1063–1064; Pribilsky, "Consumption Dilemmas," 323–343.

65. Dreby, "Honor and Virtue," 32–59.

66. Pribilsky, "Aprendemos a Convivir," 313–334.

67. Kilkey, Plomien, and Perrons, "Migrant Men's Fathering," 178–191.

68. Huang and Yeoh, "Study Mothers," 379–400; Lee and Koo, "Wild Geese Fathers," 533–553; Zhou and Kim, "Supplementary Education," 2–8.

69. Kibria, *Family Tightrope*, 131–132.

70. Choi, "Geese Families," 37–65 (in Korean); Yi, "Tiger Moms," 190–195.

71. Korea Development Institute (KDI), "Role of the Family, Government and Society to Protect the Elderly Life," *KDI Issue Focus Report* (Korea: Korea Development Institute, March 30, 2015), 1–8 (in Korean).

72. Viviana A. Zelizer, *Pricing the Priceless Child: The Social Value of Children* (New York: Basic Books, 1994), 209.

73. Annette Lareau, *Unequal Childhoods: Class, Race, and Family Life* (Berkeley: University of California Press, 2003), 294–296.

74. Sallie Mae, "How America Pays for College 2016: Sallie Mae's National Study of College Students and Parents" (2016), accessed August 17, 2017, http://news.salliemae.com/files/doc_library/file/HowAmericaPaysforCollege2016FNL.pdf; Robert F. Schoeni and Karen Ross, "Material Assistance from Families during the Transition to Adulthood," in *On the Frontier of Adulthood: Theory, Research, and Public Policy*, ed. Richard Settersten, Jr., Frank Furstenberg, and Ruben Rumbaut (Chicago: University of Chicago Press, 2005), 396–416.

75. Collins, "Toward a New Vision," 25–45.

76. Horst, "Blessings and Burdens," 143–159; Kilkey, Plomien, and Perrons, "Migrant Men's Fathering," 178–191; McKay, "Sending Dollars Shows Feeling," 175–194.

77. Schmalzbauer, "Family Divided," 329–346.

78. Ibid., 332.

79. See Schmalzbauer, "Family Divided," 329–346; Zentgraf and Chinchilla, "Transnational Family Separation," 345–366 for other cases.

80. Doherty, Kouneski, and Erickson, "Responsible Fathering," 277–292; Parreñas, "Long Distance Intimacy," 317–336; Pribilsky, "Aprendemos a Convivir," 313–334.

81. Schmalzbauer, "Family Divided," 329–346.

82. Dreby, "Honor and Virtue," 32–59; Kilkey, Plomien, and Perrons, "Migrant Men's Fathering," 178–191.

83. Dreby, "Honor and Virtue," 32–59; Kilkey, Plomien, and Perrons, "Migrant Men's Fathering," 178–191; Leifsen and Tymczuk, "Care at a Distance," 219–236; Pribilsky, "Aprendemos a Convivir," 313–334; Pribilsky, "Consumption Dilemmas," 323–343.

84. Dreby, "Honor and Virtue," 32–59; Parreñas, "Long Distance Intimacy," 317–336; Pribilsky, "Aprendemos a Convivir," 313–334; Pribilsky, "Consumption Dilemmas," 323–343.

85. Pribilsky, "Consumption Dilemmas," 336.

86. Michael Fuhr, *Globalization and Popular Music in South Korea: Sounding Out K-Pop* (New York and London: Routledge, 2016), 6–8.

87. Carling, Menjívar, and Schmalzbauer, "Transnational Parenthood," 191–217; Haagsman and Mazzucato, "Parent-Child Relationships," 1677–1696; Kilkey, Plomien, and Perrons, "Migrant Men's Fathering," 178–191; Madianou and Miller, "Mobile Phone Parenting," 457–470; Parreñas, "Transnational Fathering," 1063–1064; Ryan et al., "Family Strategies," 61–77; Schmalzbauer, "Family Divided," 329–346; Schmalzbauer, "Temporary and Transnational," 211–226; Smith, Lalonde, and Johnson, "Serial Migration," 107–122; Zentgraf and Chinchilla, "Transnational Family Separation," 345–366.

88. Horst, "Blessings and Burdens," 143–159; Madianou and Miller, "Mobile Phone Parenting," 457–470; Orellana et al., "Transnational Childhoods," 572–591; Parreñas, "Long Distance Intimacy," 317–336; Pribilsky, "Aprendemos a Convivir," 313–334; Wilding, "Virtual Intimacies," 125–142.

89. Horst, "Blessings and Burdens," 143–159; Madianou and Miller, "Mobile Phone Parenting," 457–470; McKay, "Sending Dollars Shows Feeling," 175–194; Şenyürekli and Detznera, "Communication Dynamics," 807–824; Wilding, "Virtual Intimacies," 125–142.

90. Akamai, "State of the Internet," in *Q3 2015 Report*, 1–56, accessed March 7, 2016, https://www.akamai.com/us/en/multimedia/documents/report/q3-2015-soti-connectivity-final.pdf.

91. As of 2017, Korean adults show 96 percent of internet users (highest in the world), 96 percent of smartphone owners (highest in the world), and 69 percent of social networking sites users (one of the top five in the world). See Pew Research Center, "Social Media Use Continues to Rise in Developing Countries, but Plateaus across Developed Ones," 10, 14, 16, accessed November 1, 2019, https://www.pew research.org/global/wp-content/uploads/sites/2/2018/06/Pew-Research-Center-Globa l-Tech-Social-Media-Use-2018.06.19.pdf.

92. Zentgraf and Chinchilla, "Transnational Family Separation," 353.

93. As of 2015, smartphone users in Korea include 79.6 percent among the six to nineteen years old, 99.9 percent among the twenties, 99.7 percent among the thirties, 98.6 percent among the forties, and 89.9 percent among the fifties. See Korea Internet and Security Agency, "2015 Survey on the Internet Usage Executive Summary," (December 31, 2015) (in Korean), accessed March 7, 2016, http://www.msip.go.kr/web/msipContents/contentsView.do?cateId=mssw311&artId=1289520.

94. Carling, Menjívar, and Schmalzbauer, "Transnational Parenthood," 191–217; Madianou and Miller, "Mobile Phone Parenting," 457–470; Parreñas, "Long Distance Intimacy," 317–336; Pribilsky, "Aprendemos a Convivir," 313–334.

95. Madianou and Miller, "Mobile Phone Parenting," 457–470.

96. Korea Internet and Security Agency, "2015 Survey."

97. Carling, Menjívar, and Schmalzbauer, "Transnational Parenthood," 191–217.

98. Internet phones are landline phones, connected exclusively through the Wi-Fi network.

99. At the time of interview, Skype was an application for laptops or computers, while it is now available for smartphone.

100. Carling, Menjívar, and Schmalzbauer, "Transnational Parenthood," 191–217; Haagsman and Mazzucato, "Parent-Child Relationships," 1677–1696; Madianou and Miller, "Mobile Phone Parenting," 457–470.

101. Arendell, "Conceiving and Investigating Motherhood," 1192–1207.

102. Parreñas, "Transnational Fathering," 1063–1064.

103. Schmalzbauer, "Temporary and Transnational," 211–226.

104. Johansson, "Construction of the New Father," 121–136; Lareau, "Invisible Inequality," 748–749; Park, "Public Fathering, Private Mothering," 563–586.

105. Young In Kwon and Kevin M. Roy, "Changing Social Expectations for Work and Family Involvement among Korean Fathers," *Journal of Comparative Family Studies* 38, no. 2 (2007): 286.

106. Madianou and Miller, "Mobile Phone Parenting," 457–470.

107. Orellana et al., "Transnational Childhoods," 572–591; Wilding, "Virtual Intimacies," 125–142.

108. Horst, "Blessings and Burdens," 143–159; McKay, "Sending Dollars Shows Feeling," 175–194; Wilding, "Virtual Intimacies," 125–142.

109. See Orellana et al., "Transnational Childhoods," 572–591; Parreñas, "Long Distance Intimacy," 317–336 for a comparison of transnational communication between working-class and middle-class transnational families.

110. Carling, Menjívar, and Schmalzbauer, "Transnational Parenthood," 191–217; Sarah Mahler, "Engendering Transnational Migration: A Case Study of Salvadorans," *American Behavioral Scientist* 42, no. 4 (1999): 690–719; Sassen, "Two Stops," 457–496; Schmalzbauer, "Searching for Wages," 1323–1324; Schmalzbauer, "Family Divided," 329–346; Şenyürekli and Detznera, "Communication Dynamics," 807–824.

111. Parreñas, "Long Distance Intimacy," 329.

112. Carling, Menjívar, and Schmalzbauer, "Transnational Parenthood," 191–217; Haagsman and Mazzucato, "Parent-Child Relationships," 1677–1696; Schmalzbauer, "Searching for Wages," 1323–1324.

113. Carling, Menjívar, and Schmalzbauer, "Transnational Parenthood," 191–217; Fresnoza-Flot, "Migration Status," 252–270; Haagsman and Mazzucato, "Parent-Child Relationships," 1677–1696; Menjívar, "Family Reorganization," 223–245; Parreñas, "Transnational Fathering," 1063–1064; Smith, Lalonde, and Johnson, "Serial Migration," 107–122; Waters, "Becoming a Father," 63–74.

114. Şenyürekli and Detznera, "Communication Dynamics," 816.

115. For Filipino transnational parents, see Rhacel Salazar Parreñas, *Servants of Globalization: Women, Migration and Domestic Work* (Stanford, CA: Stanford University Press, 2001). For Guatemalan and Salvadoran transnational parents, see Menjívar, "Family Reorganization," 223–245.

116. For other immigrant groups, see Şenyürekli and Detznera, "Communication Dynamics," 807–824; Zentgraf and Chinchilla, "Transnational Family Separation," 345–366.

117. For other immigrant groups, see Madianou and Miller, "Mobile Phone Parenting," 457–470; Schmalzbauer, "Family Divided," 329–346.

118. Urry, "Social Networks," 156.

119. Menjívar, "Family Reorganization," 223–245; Pribilsky, "Aprendemos a Convivir," 313–334; Pribilsky, "Consumption Dilemmas," 323–343; Zentgraf and Chinchilla, "Transnational Family Separation," 345–366; For exceptions, see Mexican guest worker fathers in Schmalzbauer, "Temporary and Transnational," 211–226.

120. Korea Culture & Tourism Institute, "A Study on the Improvement Plans of Leave System for Increase Domestic Tourist Demand" (2012) (in Korean), accessed March 13, 2016, https://www.kcti.re.kr/03_1.dmw?method=view&reportSeq=863 &reportId=2.

121. Expedia, "2015 Vacation Deprivation Study" (2015), accessed March 13, 2016, https://viewfinder.expedia.com/news/expedia-s-2015-vacation-deprivation-stu dy-europe-leads-world-in-paid-vacation-time-while-americans-and-asians-lag/.

122. See South and Spitze, "Housework," 327–347 for gender-typed housework.

123. Parreñas, "Transnational Fathering," 1063–1064; Pribilsky, "Consumption Dilemmas," 323–343; Yeoh and Willis, "'Heart' and 'Wing,'" 355–372. See Park, "Public Fathering, Private Mothering," 563–586 for changing Asian transnational fatherhood.

124. Given that Koreans have the second-longest working hours among the thirty-four OECD member countries as of 2015, it is surprisingly early to leave office at 6:00 pm for many businessmen in Korea. See Korea Times, "Koreans Work Second Longest Hours in OECD" (November 3, 2015), accessed March 18, 2016, http://www .koreatimes.co.kr/www/news/biz/2015/11/488_190167.html.

125. Dreby, "Honor and Virtue," 32–59.

126. Horst, "Blessings and Burdens," 143–159; McKay, "Sending Dollars Shows Feeling," 175–194; Wilding, "Virtual Intimacies," 125–142.

127. Parreñas, "Long Distance Intimacy," 317–336.

128. Parreñas, "Transnational Fathering," 1070.

Chapter 6

After Family Reunification

In my study, nineteen out of sixty-four wild geese parents are former wild geese parents who have completed their transnational family separation and reunited with their families in Korea by the time of the interview. A majority of them started their transnational life when their children were still young, such as kindergartners or elementary school students, with a hope to maximize the educational benefits from a short sojourn in foreign countries. With respect to the timing of family reunification, two different patterns are found. When children were younger and still are elementary or middle-school students, wild geese mothers returned to Korea with their children as they had originally planned. On the other hand, when children were high school students, wild geese mothers tended to extend their sojourn in the host countries until their children (particularly the oldest child) would finish the high school education abroad and enter a university, which at times escalated unexpected spousal conflicts due to extended family separation and increased economic burdens.

Former wild geese parents in my study tend to evaluate their success of migration and family separation primarily based on their children's educational outcomes (i.e., enhanced English fluency or admission to the prestigious universities). Nonetheless, they still share with me various other issues that have occurred to their lives after family reunification, as well as during family separation.

In this chapter, I examine the various outcomes of transnational family separation, including gender and social status, spousal relationships, children's education in the host country, and re-adaptation to Korean society. The stories of former wild geese families provide valuable insights into the long-term and complex effects of transnational family separation.

GENDER PATHS AFTER REUNIFICATION
BY MOTHERS' EMPLOYMENT AND
CHILDREN'S EDUCATION

In previous chapters, I have highlighted how wild geese mothers' employment and their children's educational achievement are closely related to these women's bargaining power and gender status within their transnational households. In this section, I explore the long-term impact of wild geese mothers' employment and their children's educational accomplishment, for which I examine the empowerment patterns of former wild geese mothers after family reunification. I have found that the positive impact of wild geese mothers' official employment, combined with their children's educational success, lasts even after their family reunification, because they are more likely to have new (even better) employment in their home country. On the other hand, former wild geese mothers with informal employment have lost much of their enhanced sense of social power and autonomy after family reunification, as they have returned to their prior position, the full-time homemaker. Such difference is well illustrated by the stories of two former wild geese mothers: Minkyung and Youngmi.

Minkyung's Story

Minkyung was in her mid-fifties at the time of the interview. Her case shows the positive impacts of wild geese mothers' stable legal status and income, combined with their children's educational success, on their domestic and social statuses after family reunification.

Before marriage, Minkyung was a businesswoman. She worked for more than five years in a global corporation where she had daily communications in English with her foreign colleagues and clients. After getting married to a doctor and having the first child, Minkyung quit her job and lived as a full-time homemaker. She was an enthusiastic educational manager for her two children. Interestingly, Minkyung's parents and relatives were immigrants who had migrated to the United States long time ago and became U.S. citizens. Thanks to her own family ties, Minkyung frequently visited her parents and relatives in the United States when her children were younger, which motivated her children to study in the United States, as they were greatly attracted to American education. Minkyung's children migrated to the United States as international students and then, two years later, Minkyung joined them when she acquired permanent residency through her parents' sponsorship. Five years after her migration, Minkyung further acquired U.S. citizenship. She finally returned to Korean after her younger child entered a university and her older child was studying at the graduate school in the United States.

According to Minkyung, her life as a migrant was much more stable than other wild geese mothers. Thanks to the support from her parents and relatives who were citizens of the host country, she was able to make many new friends, build extensive immigrant social networks across her children's school, Korean immigrant church, and American neighborhood, and deal with her daily issues without many difficulties. Her extensive familial and immigrant social networks, combined with her legitimate and stable legal statuses (first as a legal permanent resident and then as a U.S. citizen), allowed Minkyung to successfully run a small family business in the Korean ethnic enclave. It is certain that Minkyung was increasingly empowered through migration, as she effectively utilized her resources, such as stable legal status, own business, and her familial and immigrant networks in the host society.

Children's educational success is also another important resource for Minkyung's empowerment. At the time of the interview, both her children graduated from prestigious universities in the United States and were working as professionals in the United States. In particular, the fact that her older child graduated from an IVY league university and became a doctor was regarded as Minkyung's own success as a mother, which in turn greatly strengthened her domestic status not only during her migration period but also after her family reunification.

With her increased confidence and autonomy that grew during the transnational spousal separation, Minkyung refused to return to her prior full-time homemaker position when she finally returned to Korea. Rather, she opened a new business based on her entrepreneurship experiences in the United States. Minkyung also has developed a very active social life as a leader of the local business community and religious community. Meanwhile, Minkyung has built more egalitarian conjugal relationship. For example, while her husband did not share housework before separation, he now shares a significant portion of housework with her. Minkyung and her husband also frequently dine out to reduce their burden of cooking and cleaning.

In short, Minkyung's continued work and social activities, during migration and after reunification, as well as her children's educational success, have served as a critical leverage for Minkyung to successfully renegotiate with her husband to the extent that, as she proudly states, she now has the *equal* power with her husband. She also delightfully describes her enhanced bargaining power, borrowing her husband's comment:

My husband sometimes tells me, "My wife gets scarier," because my voice gets higher to him. If husband says something wrong, even if it is minor issue, I tell him, "Don't think like that." Then, my husband weakens and accepts my advice.

Youngmi's Story

Youngmi was in her late forties at the time of the interview. Her case reveals how wild geese mothers' loss of job, combined with their children's unsatisfactory educational outcomes, has an adverse impact on their gender status after family reunification. Youngmi was a 1.5 generation U.S. immigrant and met her husband when he was studying in the United States. Youngmi and her husband came to Korea when their first child was three years old. During her marriage in Korea, Youngmi was a full-time homemaker, while her husband was a successful entrepreneur. She migrated again to the United States when her older child was a fifth grader and her younger child was a first grader, as she wanted her children to enhance their English fluency. After several years of sojourn in the United States, she finally returned to Korea with her children who were teenagers.

Youngmi was similar to Minkyung in many aspects. As a 1.5 generation U.S. immigrant, Youngmi was equipped with critical resources for her successful mothering, such as U.S. citizenship, family networks, familiarity with the host society's system, and English fluency. She was also easily able to find a part-time job at a laundry shop in the Korean immigrant community, which gave her a heightened sense of economic and emotional autonomy from her husband during their separation:

> [Thanks to my citizenship], I was able to find a part-time job easily. Even if my husband sent me a lot of money, I still wanted to have some extra money that I could use at my discretion without telling him how I used it. Of course, I also wanted to relieve his burden, [laugh]. So, I told him about my job much later. I just told him that I was working just one or two days a week without giving him any further information. [. . .] As I made all the decisions [how to spend the money] by myself rather than discussing with my husband, I felt freer.

However, unlike Minkyung, Youngmi did not think her educational goal was achieved through migration. Unlike Minkyung's children, Youngmi's children migrated to the United States mainly because of their parents' educational zeal rather than their own. Youngmi's older child, in particular, had a very hard time both during migration and after family reunification, because he failed to adapt to the changing environment. During migration, he was exposed to bullying from other boys. Moreover, his introverted personality further prevented him from improving his English fluency and making any new friends. Unfortunately, even after returning to Korea, Youngmi's son was still struggling, because he, this time, could not catch up with the extremely competitive and fast-paced Korean education. As a result, he now prepares to apply for colleges in the United States. Because of her teenage son's struggles, Youngmi (as well as her husband) not only regrets the decision of transnational family separation but also feels her weakened status within the family, as she did not successfully fulfill her expected role of educational manager for her children.

> I think that my children should have migrated [abroad] when they wanted, not when their parents decided. Then, they could have done much better. I believed that my children would be able to do a good job. However, it was not the case. Only after returning to Korea, I have learned that my son is not a type of person who can do well both here [Korea] and there [United States] . . . As I have been getting through all the struggles with him, I have come up with a regretful conclusion that my son should have not returned to Korea. It might be much better if he kept staying there [United States]. I am very sorry for him . . .

Furthermore, Youngmi's work experiences as a part-time employee at a local laundry shop did not transfer to Korea. After her return to Korea, Youngmi no longer pursued paid employment, which has deprived her of enhanced autonomy she used to enjoy during transnational spousal separation. As a result, Youngmi has resumed her prior patriarchal life as a good housewife and filial daughter-in-law who cares and serves her husband and parents-in-law while performing all the household labor by herself. Youngmi recalls her changed status after family reunification in Korea:

> When I was alone with children [in the United States], it was a liberating time! I was released from my in-law related stress, as I was physically separated from them across the Pacific Ocean. I also felt freer, because I no longer had to take care of my husband . . . [After return to Korea] The downside is that I have just come back to my original [status] . . . I again should take care of all the trifle and minor matters for my husband and family-in-law. . . . While my husband was good at doing housework [during family separation], since I returned, he has no longer done any housework, and we have no conversation about it . . .

GENDER PATHS AFTER REUNIFICATION BY MOTHERS' ADDITIONAL EDUCATION

In previous chapters, I have explained that wild geese mothers' additional education in the host societies increases their employability in both host and home countries and promotes their leverage not only during transnational separation but also after family reunification. In this section, I explore a case that shows the long-term positive impacts of wild geese mothers' additional education on their empowerment.

Miseon's Story

Miseon was a former wild geese mother in her late forties when I met her in Korea for an interview. Miseon first migrated to the United States to accompany her husband who was an international student, and then returned to Korea when her husband achieved a doctoral degree. Then, Miseon migrated again to the United States when her husband had an opportunity to work there as a visiting scholar. At the time of the second migration, her daughter was in her high school. After one year of stay in the United States, Miseon's husband returned to Korea, whereas Miseon and her daughter stayed back. Miseon extended her stay and supported her daughter's continued education as she was a gifted student. Miseon delightfully returned to Korea when her daughter was admitted with scholarship to one of the most prestigious universities in the United States. At the time of the interview, her daughter has recently graduated and started working for a global company in New York City.

Until she became a wild geese mother, Miseon had maintained a husband-and-child-centered life as a full-time housewife and devoted mother. However, during the period of her transnational spousal separation, Miseon not only supported her daughter's education but also studied hard for herself and achieved a TESOL (Teachers of English to Speakers of Other Languages) certificate.

After returning to Korea, Miseon was able to find a good teaching position at a private English Institute thanks to her TESOL certificate. Soon after, she was promoted to an assistant director. Miseon is a very popular teacher, not only because she has a highly valued American TESOL certificate but also because Miseon provides her students and their parents with high-quality consultation services based on her unique experiences of successfully educating her own child abroad at a top university. Miseon defines her migration and additional education in the host society as a "turning point" that has led to many positive changes in her life. Miseon says:

> Migration was a great opportunity to me, because I was able to study English and achieve a TESOL certificate. [During my migration] I wanted to spend my time more effectively. I did not want to waste my time because I wanted to find a job after returning to Korea. So, I studied hard. After return [to Korea], I applied for a teaching job at a private educational institute, and since then I have kept working. I was promoted to an assistant director, because I was renowned and scouted [by my current institute]. [. . .] In conclusion, it [migration] offered me a turning point in my life and I greatly appreciate that I could find a job. While my family had a hard time at that time [during family separation], when I look back, I think that hard time turned into a good opportunity.

Using her enhanced social status and income from her employment, combined with her child's educational success which is equated to her own success as a mother, Miseon has built a more egalitarian relationship with her husband after family reunification. Miseon has also accomplished the more equal division of household labor with her husband:

> [Prior to separation] If my husband came home earlier than me, he never prepared dinner but just played with his computer until I came home. However, [after family reunification] particularly recently, he increasingly helps me prepare for dinner. [. . .] And, in the past [prior to separation], when I came home late, he used to be really mad at me. However, when I now come home late, he no longer complains but just follows me and helps me do the work [housework]. So, these days, we spend more time together. He also helps me a lot do other housework.

In addition, Miseon's husband is quite supportive of her career and increasingly expresses his gratitude for her contribution to the family economy, which in turn makes Miseon more pleased with her new life after family reunification. In short, Misoen's story indicates that education is one of the key resources that empower migrant women both socially and domestically not only during their migration but also after their family reunification in the home countries.

SEXUAL INTIMACY AFTER REUNIFICATION

Previous chapters have noted that sexual intimacy is an important issue for many wild geese mothers and fathers but in different ways. Wild geese fathers are much more likely than wild geese mothers to relate their marital satisfaction with sexual intimacy with their wives and express a higher level of dissatisfaction with a decreased frequency of sexual relations. On the other hand, wild geese mothers tend to worry about their husbands' discontent with the reduced number of sexual relations with them, while emphasizing their lack of sexual desire as if lack of it were an essential virtue of wifehood. Nonetheless, the following stories of two former wild geese parents indicate that decreased spousal sexual intimacy can be a serious issue that lowers both husbands' and wives' marital satisfaction when they are reunited and live together.

Inkuk's Story

Inkuk, a former wild geese father in the early fifties, was a professor at the prestigious university in Korea at the time of the interview. He has recently reunited with his wife after ten years of transnational separation. Inkuk's two children who migrated to the United States when they were elementary and middle-school students are both attending prestigious universities in the United States, particularly the younger one in an IVY League university. Inkuk highly appreciates his wife as she has successfully performed the role of competent educational manager for his two children.

Nonetheless, Inkuk admits that he was gradually estranged from his wife during lengthy spousal separation to the extent that he even casted a doubtful question to himself, "Are we truly a married couple?" Interestingly, he rather became more comfortable after he gave up sexual relationship with his wife. Therefore, when he finally reunited with his wife in Korea, he felt very awkward to be with his wife, although it gets better over time. Inkuk recalls:

> When she returned, I no longer felt intimate to her. . . . It was just so awkward to be together. Such uncomfortableness lasted more than two months [after reunification]. During that time, we did not even hold hands together, not to mention we didn't sleep together.

Sowon's Story

Sowon was the wife of one of the two couples whose gender roles were reversed. That is, Sowon remained in Korea while her husband and two children migrated to Canada for two years. It was not her husband but Sown who was left behind, because Sowon, a banker, earned much more money than her husband who was a small business owner in Korea. At the time of the interview, Sowon was in the early forties, and two years have passed since her family reunification.

Sowon is, in general, highly satisfied with her family's migration. She likes that her children were exposed to a new society, different culture, and diverse groups of people and thoughts. Sowon is also happy as she had greater free time for herself so that she could use it for her own leisure as well as her self-development such as learning a foreign language and getting multiple certificates of appreciation. Besides, Sowon highly praises her husband who provided good care for their children during family separation:

> He fed our children much better than other wild geese mothers do. He always prepared kids' lunch box. I didn't know how well he cooked [before his migration], because he did not cook during our marriage in Korea. After going there [Canada], he prepared high-quality food. He even made kimchi, even if [it is difficult to make and thus other] Korean mothers bought kimchi.

Notwithstanding many benefits from her family's migration, when asked her if there are any changes in her life through transnational family separation,

Sowon directly points out the reduced number of sexual relations with her husband after family reunification as the biggest and worst change she has encountered. However, because of the patriarchal gender norms that mandate spousal sexual relations as wives' marital obligation rather than their right to pursue, Sowon has not yet discussed this issue openly with her husband:

> Frankly speaking, we have much fewer spousal life [sexual intercourse] compared to the pre-migration time. [. . .] Even if it is a big problem to us, we don't talk about it. I do not want to hurt his pride as a man. I do not want to be seen as a prurient woman, either. [. . .] It [sexlessness] is a hot potato. Should I touch it or not? He may have the same idea.

In short, the two stories above indicate that spousal sexual intimacy, once it has been reduced during lengthy separation, cannot be easily recovered after family reunification, which in turn lowers the reunited wild geese couples' marital satisfaction, even if they are highly satisfied with other outcomes of their transnational life, such as children's education.

LEADERSHIP AND THE DIVISION OF HOUSEWORK AFTER REUNIFICATION

In previous chapters, I have presented how wild geese parents have renegotiated their patriarchal gender roles and gradually moved toward more egalitarian relationships during their lengthy transnational spousal separation. However, in many cases, such changes have not accomplished without spousal confrontations. Furthermore, some spousal tension can be even intensified after family reunification, if wild geese couples have failed to successfully rearrange their changed roles: wild geese mothers do not want to relinquish their enhanced status, while their husbands want to recover their dominance as the leaders of the household. Here, I explore how spousal conflict over the leadership of the household and the division of household labor can be exacerbated after family reunification, by examining the story of a former wild geese mother, Minji.

Minji's Story

Minji was a former wild geese mother in the mid-fifties at the time of the interview. She migrated to the United States with her two children when the older one was in the high school and the younger one in elementary school. She wanted to give a new opportunity to her older son who was struggling in his school. Minji and her children stayed in the United States for seven years and returned to Korea, because her older son had to fulfill his mandatory military service. At the time of the interview, the older son was working as a businessman and the younger son was in college in Korea.

Prior to migration, Minji was a full-time housewife and obedient to her husband who was running a successful business. However, after migration, Minji unexpectedly expanded her roles from a homemaker to a student and worker, and successfully performed her new roles. While Minji was initially enrolled in the ESL program so that her children could have free public education, she later pursued her own dream and majored arts in a local community college. Meanwhile, because of sudden economic hardship that severely hit her husband's business, Minji jumped around multiple under-the-table part-time jobs within Korean immigrant community, including grocery store, video shop, sandwich shop, department store, and hamburger place, and earned a substantial amount of income that accounted for half of their living expenses in the United States. In addition, while managing her extremely busy work and study schedules, Minji gradually lost her interests in doing housework. Minji recalls her migration period as a time that she struggled for survival with her two children in the foreign country:

Reflecting that time, it is more accurate to say that I was fighting there, rather than just living. It was miraculous that I could return [to Korea] instead of dying there. I was adventurous. Further, I was not scared of doing any work there, because I was a mother, yes, because I was a mother of two children.

Her experiences in the host society turned Minji into an assertive, confident, and autonomous woman. Therefore, after her return to Korea, Minji refuses to return to her prior full-time homemaker position. Instead, Minji, as an artist, has become even busier with her new professional and social life. Nonetheless, Minji's husband, who still undergoes many financial problems in his business, is not so happy about Minji's changes and wants to reinstate their patriarchal relationship. Above all, Minji's husband expects her to perform all the housework again, which ends up in confrontations and conflict and substantially lowers their marital quality after reunification.

When I lived in America, I had a very active social life. After return [to Korea], I have extended such a pattern of life. Thus, I no longer eagerly perform housework as I used to do [prior to separation]. I no longer find any joy from doing housework. Nonetheless, my husband tremendously expects that I do all the housework. Because of that we have fought a lot since I returned [to Korea].

CHILDREN'S EDUCATIONAL OUTCOMES AND RE-ADAPTATION AFTER REUNIFICATION

As previous chapters have noted, wild geese parents endure lengthy family separation mainly for the sake their children. Therefore, if their children present satisfactory educational outcomes (i.e., enhancement of English fluency or admission to prestigious universities), wild geese parents evaluate that their goal of transnational family separation is achieved. On the other hand, if their children present unsatisfactory educational outcomes, many wild geese parents, particularly fathers, do not only feel greatly disappointed but also tend to regard their transnational family separation as a failure, which causes serious spousal conflict.

The following stories of two former wild geese fathers, Dongkun and Woosung, demonstrate how wild geese parents' evaluation of their transnational family separation can widely vary by children's educational achievement and re-adaption to Korean society.

Dongkun's Story

Dongkun was a former wild geese father in his mid-forties at the time of the interview. He was a banker and living with a full-time homemaker wife. Dongkun's wife and his two children migrated to the United States when they were lower graders in the elementary school. They stayed in the United States for two years and later returned to Korea three months prior to the interview. Dongkun defines his family's migration to the United States as a "big success" for two main reasons. First, his two children substantially enhanced their English fluency during their short sojourn in the United States.

> [After migration] My children were extremely well adapted [to American education] to the extent that their teachers even said that they had never seen students like my children who were so quickly adapted. My son was very shy in Korea and never talked [to me or to my wife] about his teachers. But, there, he said to his mom, "I like my teachers . . . I like my school . . . I want to buy some gifts for my teachers." Seeing his positive changes, I felt that I made the right decision [of becoming a wild geese family] . . . Also, even if two years might not be enough [for my children] to achieve English fluency like native speakers, my children have still improved their English a lot. Frankly, when my children have conversation [with each other in English], I cannot understand. Their English has enhanced much more than I expected.

Second, Dongkun is also greatly pleased that his two children have been successfully re-adapted to the Korean education since their return to Korea.

Dongkun proudly talks about the academic performance of his sixth grade son and third grade daughter:

> After return [to Korea], my children have been much better adapted [to Korean education] than I expected. They took assessment test [right after return to Korea] at school. My daughter took math and Korean tests, and she got perfect scores except one wrong. My son got perfect scores in math and English, while getting 80 in Korean and 60 in social studies. But, I told him "Don't worry. It is rather weird if you get the perfect scores [in Korean and social studies], given that you were abroad for the last two years." [. . .] I feel so far so good. My daughter was applauded by her new English teacher [at school] and classmates because of her good [English] pronunciation. [laugh]

Dongkun's high satisfaction with his family's migration is attributed to the following factors: his children's tender age at the time of migration, his children's short stay in the host society and return to Korea as planned, his children's excellent educational outcomes, and his children's successful re-adaptation to Korean education after reunification.

Woosung's Story

A story of former wild geese father named Woosung highlights how children's maladaptation to both host and home countries, combined with their unsuccessful educational outcomes, makes wild geese parents regret their decision of transnational family separation. Woosung was a teacher in his early sixties at the time of the interview. Woosung's wife and his two sons migrated to Canada when his older son was a high school student and his younger son was in his middle school. Woosung's wife migrated with a work permit and his two sons migrated with a study permit, and they aimed for permanent immigration to Canada. While Woosung stayed in Korea and sent remittances to his family abroad, he also planned to join his family after his retirement.

Nonetheless, after eleven years of transnational family separation, while both sons were attending Canadian colleges, his family suddenly had to return to Korea due to two issues: Their petition for Canadian permanent residency was finally rejected after a series of unfruitful applications and both his sons had to fulfill the mandatory military service before it was too late. By law, all Korean adult men (but only a small number who meet the exemption criteria, including those with serious disabilities and Olympic medalists) are mandated to complete the military service (for —eighteen to twenty-four months) until the age of thirty.[1]

Interestingly, because of their age gap, Woosung's two sons had different experiences both in Canada and Korea. During migration, his older son had difficulties in adapting to the Canadian society (partly because of language barriers), and it took much longer for him to complete his high school education than expected. On the other hand, his younger son did a better job and completed middle school and high school on time.

After return to Korea, unfortunately, Woosung's two sons struggled again to re-adapt to Korean society but in different ways. His younger son did not have any social networks in Korea to help him succeed, because he joined middle school in Canada and completed his graduation. His older son had many old friends and social networks that could help him re-adjust in Korea, but he could not find a suitable job in Korea without a bachelor's degree, as he had not completed his college education when he returned to Korea. Consequently, his older son has recently re-migrated alone to Canada to attend a college, and his younger son is also preparing to migrate to Canada to pursue employment there. Woosung describes his sense of frustration as he watches his two adult sons' struggles in both countries, particularly in Korea:

> It is heartbreaking that we could not fulfill our goal of migration. After they unexpectedly came back, my sons had to go to [mandatory] military service when they were too old. My first son went to Canada when he was a high school student and my second son went there when he was a middle-school student. In Korea, the importance of old school ties and regionalism cannot be dismissed. After returning, the elder one was better off. Because he left Korea at an older age, he could easily recover his old friendship network at school and at church. But the younger one had a difficult time. It was difficult for him to rebuild his friendship network and socialize with other Koreans. If we got residency [in Canada], my children would have graduated college and found jobs there. Then I could join them later after my retirement. But, because our residency was rejected, my children had to return to Korea and enter military service. It was so difficult for them to re-adapt to Korean society, as they lost friend networks that I mentioned earlier.

Woosung's dissatisfaction with his family migration is related to the following factors: his children's older age at the time of migration, children's long stay in the host country, children's unsuccessful educational outcomes, and children's maladaptation to both host and home countries.

CONCLUSION

This chapter explores what former wild geese parents have experienced in Korea after family reunification and how they evaluate the period of transnational family separation. I discuss their experiences based on important aspects, including wild geese mothers' empowerment through employment and education, sexual intimacy between wild geese couples, the division of housework, and children's educational outcomes and re-adaptation in Korea. Because my sample includes only nineteen former wild geese parents, this chapter is organized in the way of contrasting the different experiences of the selected individuals. The variations in wild geese families' experiences can help clarify the long-term effects of transnational family separation and provide useful insights into the lives of contemporary migrant families and their members both in the host and home societies.

NOTE

1. For detailed information, see Korean Military Manpower Administration (in Korean), accessed May 30, 2020, http://www.mma.go.kr/index.do.

Conclusion

Several years have passed since the time when I met wild geese parents in the United States, Canada, and Korea for interviews. As of 2021, people around the world undergo an unprecedently difficult time due to the COVID-19 pandemic. This is particularly challenging for transnational families, including wild geese families, as they no longer freely meet their loving ones across the borders. Ironically, the current pandemic situation gives us a chance to learn again how important it is to have regular and frequent transnational communication for intimate transnational family relationships during lengthy physical separation. Since the COVID-19 pandemic, wild geese families also encounter many new (or more difficult) challenges in North America because many of them hold temporary visas and live with school-aged children under more restrictive immigration policies on temporary migrants and international students.

Recently, I happened to meet Yejin, one of wild geese mothers in my study. While Yejin originally planned to return to Korea after her children would graduate high school, Yejin still stays in the United States during this pandemic with her children who are young adults now. It has been almost a year since Yejin and her children met her husband last time. Before the pandemic, Yejin's husband regularly visited his family twice a year. However, he no longer can do so because of the two weeks quarantine rule for international travelers in both countries, where non-essential travel is highly discouraged. Consequently, Yejin's family no longer enjoys the benefits of frequent face-to-face encounters. Yejin still shares her everyday life with her husband in Korea through active transnational communication, which is the only way available to them now and has become an essential part of their lives through quasi-permanent family separation over ten years.

I would like to share with readers the final comments my interview participants provided at the end of their interviews. First, even if they planned for just a short family separation, unforeseen circumstances often turned it into a lengthier separation, for example, more than ten years. One of their common suggestions for potential wild geese families is to prepare for a lengthy transnational family separation, as their separation can be much longer no matter how carefully a family plans for it. Second, many wild geese families have spent much more than their initial budget plan, which has become a new source of serious transnational spousal conflict. They suggest that transnational family separation costs more than any careful initial plans. Third, many wild geese parents highlight having regular and frequent transnational communication as a key to successfully maintain intimate family relationship during separation. It is also critical to openly share emotions as well as trivial moments of daily lives among family members rather than just discussing big issues like budget and/or hiding each other's hardships or concerns. Fourth, those with adolescent children note that middle-school students and high-school students may find it more challenging than younger ones to adapt to the host society during migration and/or re-adapt to the home society after reunification. Because adolescent children may face with more costs than benefits from their wild geese period, their own willingness to study abroad can be an important consideration. Finally, while transnational migration certainly gives many wild geese families new opportunities and a turning point, it also involves unexpected hardships and changes in their lives and their family relationships. Many wild geese parents emphasize that the choice of legal status (or visa category) critically determines the quality of their transnational lives. Additionally, wild geese mothers' employment and additional education in the host society are also noted as crucial resources to lead to positive changes not only during transnational family separation but also after family reunification.

Discussions in this book are built upon rich in-depth interview data and provide sociological insights into the experiences of Korean wild geese families. Plus, their unique experiences offer readers of the book valuable venues to better understand the lives of increasingly diverse transnational families in North America.

Appendix
Research Design

I gathered the data for this book by conducting qualitative in-depth interviews with sixty-four Korean wild geese parents in the course of a year at three main research sites: (1) Tenafly and surrounding areas, New Jersey, the United States, (2) London, Ontario, Canada, and (3) Seoul, South Korea. Specifically, I interviewed thirty-one wild geese mothers (twenty-three current and eight former) and thirty-three wild geese fathers (twenty-two current and eleven former).

RECRUITMENT OF CURRENT AND FORMER WILD GEESE MOTHERS

To recruit current wild geese women in the United States, I started with an initial purposive sample of wild geese mothers in New Jersey, which was one of the most popular destinations in the Eastern coast among wild geese families[1] and accordingly had a large pool of potential research subjects. I recruited a few initial participants from one of the largest Korean churches in the metropolitan New Jersey-New York area, who referred to other wild geese mothers later.

The recruitment of the initial sample took longer than expected, because many wild geese mothers were hesitant to participate. That is related to the fact that wild geese women are a stigmatized group among Korean immigrants[2] despite their higher social and class positions than other Koreans. Because many wild geese mothers in my sample knew such prejudices very well and/or already had experienced animosity against them, they were quite defensive and reluctant to share their personal experiences with anyone outside of their group.

Fortunately, after having interviewed the initial participants, I was able to recruit a number of wild geese mothers faster through a snowball sampling procedure.[3] Indeed, referrals from the wild geese mothers whom I had already interviewed was probably the most effective way of recruiting other wild geese mothers, because most of who were living in the same local community and hardly interacted with anyone outside of their own networks. Because I successfully built rapport and trust with the initial interview participants, many of them were willing to refer to others. Plus, those who were recruited through referrals often trusted me even before meeting me. My identity as a mother with a young child and my academic degree from a prestigious university in Korea also helped me build rapport with wild geese mothers and thus improve the quality of interviews with them.

Wild geese mothers in Canada were also recruited through snowball sampling, as one wild geese mother of the United States sample referred to another wild geese mother in Canada, who was willing to participate and refer to other wild geese mothers in her community. Considering many similarities between the United States and Canada, as well as their geographic proximity, I was advised to revise the initial data collection plan and include wild geese mothers in Canada. Retrospectively, Canadian cases greatly enriched my data and highlighted the differences in the immigration and settlement policies between the United States and Canada.

In order to recruit former wild geese mothers in Korea, I first drew on my personal networks, including my family and academic networks. After having obtained the initial sample, I gathered a number of former wild geese mothers through snowball sampling. Like wild geese mothers in the United States and Canada, many former wild geese mothers in Korea expressed their satisfaction with the interviews and willingly referred me to other wild geese mothers.

Some women were so satisfied with their interviews that they asked their husbands to participate even before I asked for any referrals. However, their husbands often rejected the interview. Out of five spousal referrals arranged by wild geese mothers, only one interview was successfully accomplished. Accordingly, only one couple was included in my sample.

RECRUITMENT OF CURRENT AND
FORMER WILD GEESE FATHERS

To recruit the initial sample of wild geese fathers in Korea, I started from my personal networks, including my family, professional, academic, and religious networks, and then gathered more wild geese fathers through snowball sampling. In contrast to the recruitment of wild geese mothers, it took much longer to recruit wild geese fathers, because they did not know many other wild geese fathers. Wild geese fathers did not live in the same residential area with other wild geese fathers, whereas wild geese mothers tended to belong to the same locality, such as Koreatown or the Korean immigrant church community. They did not socialize with other wild geese fathers, either, as some wild geese fathers even tried to minimize their socialization with anyone else.

COMPENSATIONS

Research subjects were compensated for participating in qualitative in-depth interviews. Because cash remuneration was less appropriate in Korean culture, I provided a $15 (or 15,000 Korean won) gift card (for Starbucks or other vendors) at the time of each interview. Some people refused to receive it, as they were concerned about my budget. This refusal mostly happened when participants thought that I travelled a long distance (and thus paid a large amount for transportation) to have an interview with them. However, in the end, all participants received gift cards with pleasure. Providing financial compensation was critical, not simply as a method of encouraging participation but also as an effective way of expressing my gratitude to them for sharing their personal experiences and valuable time with me.

DATA COLLECTION: IN-DEPTH INTERVIEWS

Korean is my mother tongue and I am very familiar with Korean culture and society, as I grew up in Korea. Most interviews were conducted in Korean, while both Korean and English were used for a few interviews. Interviews were conducted in a setting that was mutually agreeable to the participant and me in order to maximize privacy and a sense of comfort. Interviews with wild geese mothers were held either in their houses or cafés near their houses, and interviews with wild geese fathers were mostly held in their offices or cafés near their offices. Only one wild geese father was interviewed in his house.

I interviewed most wild geese parents during weekdays. Wild geese mothers preferred to meet me during the daytime on weekdays because of their busy schedule with their children during the weekends. Wild geese fathers preferred to meet me during or after their work in or near their office to save time. Some wild geese fathers also changed the interview schedule many times because of unexpected changes in their work schedule. I also sometimes had to wait up to an hour for wild geese fathers in their offices or nearby cafés when they were too busy to meet me on time.

It took about two hours or more to conduct each interview with most wild geese mothers. Sometimes, it took more than three hours, when wild geese mothers had many issues to talk. On the contrary, interviews with wild geese fathers took an hour and a half on average, while some interviews lasted longer than three hours.

Interviews were conducted based on semi-structured guides with open-ended questions. In addition to the prepared questions, I improvised some questions during the interview and probed for additional information. I audio-recorded all my interviews and transcribed them later. After each interview, I also added extensive field notes and an analytic summary to the interview transcript, based on which I kept updating the interview guide.

During the interview, I was very careful to inquire about sensitive topics, such as spousal relationships. I was also cognizant of my female gender identity when interviewing wild geese fathers, as Arendell has pointed out earlier.[4] I had obtained and internalized the skills of overcoming such difficulties and building rapport with interview participants via thorough methodological training and rich research experiences, including my past study of Korean international male students and their wives.[5] I found that the expression of my empathy to the interviewees was particularly useful to successfully build rapport and effective research partnership. I also used probing questions effectively in order to extract candid and vivid accounts about *markers*.[6] Through these various techniques, I produced rich data not only from wild geese mothers but also from wild geese fathers.[7]

I also tried to ensure maximum validity of interviews. As Weiss mentions, I cannot assume that the interviewees have told me "the whole truth nor the precise truth" but "richly detailed accounts of vividly remembered events are likely to be trustworthy."[8] I believe that I established good research partnership with participants, which was especially helpful for me to extract more concrete and rich accounts, which in turn helped ensure the validity of the interview findings.

DATA MANAGEMENT AND ANALYSIS

All interview data were audio-recorded in a digital recorder and then transcribed verbatim on my personal computer. Since most of the interviews were conducted in Korean according to interview participants' preference, I translated parts of the transcripts in English that were quoted in my book.

My qualitative data include personal information, by which research subjects may be identifiable. In order to safeguard the data from an unauthorized access, I saved my audio files and field notes in locked files and protected the computer with passwords. I also substituted codes for personal identifiers and maintained code lists and data files separately in secure locations without internet connection. Pseudonyms are used in all transcripts to protect confidentiality of the research subjects. The entire process of the research was done following the guidelines from the Institutional Review Board (IRB) of the University at Albany, State University of New York, which reviewed and approved this research.

NOTES

1. Kim, "Wild Goose Mother," 41–59 (in Korean).

2. Ibid.

3. Snowball sampling refers to "a method for generating a field sample of individuals possessing the characteristics of interest by asking initial contacts if they could name a few individuals with similar characteristics who might agree to be interviewed." See John Lofland et al., *Analyzing Social Settings: A Guide to Qualitative Observation and Analysis*, 4th ed. (Belmont, CA: Wadsworth Publishing Company, 2006), 43.

4. Terry Arendell, "Reflections on the Researcher-Researched Relationship: A Woman Interviewing Men," *Qualitative Sociology* 20, no. 3 (1997): 341–368.

5. Lee, "Bifurcated Statuses," 135–156.

6. Markers refers to "a passing reference made by a respondent to an important event or feeling state." See Robert S. Weiss, *Learning from Strangers: The Art and Method of Qualitative Interview Studies* (New York: Free Press, 1994), 77.

7. Weiss says that "(G)ood interviewers remain good interviewers irrespective of the sex of the respondent. Also, it has seemed to me, the great majority of respondents can form a good research partnership with an interviewer of either sex." See Weiss, *Learning from Strangers*, 140.

8. Ibid., 148, 150.

Bibliography

Akamai. "State of the Internet." *Q3 2015 Report*, 1–56. Accessed March 7, 2016. https://www.akamai.com/us/en/multimedia/documents/report/q3-2015-soti-conne ctivity-final.pdf.

Arendell, Terry. "Conceiving and Investigating Motherhood: The Decade's Scholarship." *Journal of Marriage and the Family* 62, no. 4 (2000): 1192–1207.

———. "Reflections on the Researcher-Researched Relationship: A Woman Interviewing Men." *Qualitative Sociology* 20, no. 3 (1997): 341–368.

Aye, Alice M. M. M. T. and Bernard Guerin. "Astronaut Families: A Review of Their Characteristics, Impact on Families and Implications for Practice in New Zealand." *New Zealand Journal of Psychology* 30, no. 1 (2001): 9–16.

Bianchi, Suzanne M., Melissa A. Milkie, Liana C. Sayer, and John P. Robinson. "Is Anyone Doing the Housework? Trends in the Gender Division of Household Labor." *Social Forces* 79, no. 1 (2000): 191–228.

Bloemraad, Irene. "Becoming a Citizen in the United States and Canada: Structured Mobilization and Immigrant Political Incorporation." *Social Forces* 85, no. 2 (2006): 667–695.

Bosniak, Linda. "Citizenship Denationalized." *Indiana Journal of Global Legal Studies* 7 (2000): 447–492.

Bourdieu, Pierre. *Outline of a Theory of Practice*. New York: Cambridge University Press, 1977.

Brines, Julie. "Economic Dependency, Gender, and the Division of Labor at Home." *American Journal of Sociology* 100 (1994): 652–688.

Bureau of Labor Statistics. "American Time Use Survey – 2019 Results." Washington, DC. Accessed November 25, 2020. https://www.bls.gov/news.release/atus.nr0.htm.

Byun, Soo-young and Hyunjoon Park. "The Academic Success of East Asian American Youth: The Role of Shadow Education." *Sociology of Education* 85, no. 1 (2012): 40–60.

Carling, Jørgen, Cecilia Menjívar, and Leah Schmalzbauer. "Central Themes in the Study of Transnational Parenthood." *Journal of Ethnic and Migration Studies* 38, no. 2 (2012): 191–217.

Center for East Asian Policy Studies at Brookings, "South Korea's Demographic Changes and Their Political Impact—East Asian Policy Paper 6." October 2015. http://www.brookings.edu/~/media/research/files/papers/2015/10/south-korea-demographic-changemoon/south-koreas-demographic-changes-and-their-political-impact.pdf.

Chang, Man Wai and Yvonne Darlington. "Astronaut Wives: Perceptions of Changes in Family Roles." *Asian and Pacific Migration Journal* 17, no. 1 (2008): 61–77.

Chee, Maria W. L. "Migrating for the Children: Taiwanese American Women in Transnational Families." In *Wife or Worker? Asian Women and Migration*, edited by Nicola Piper and Mina Roces, 137–156. New York: Rowman and Littlefield, 2003.

Cherlin, Andrew. *The Marriage-Go-Round: The State of Marriage and the Family in America Today*. New York: Knopf, 2009.

Cho, Uhn. "세계화 최첨단에 선 한국의 가족: 신글로벌 모자녀 가족사례 연구" [Korean Families on the Forefront of Globalization]. 경제와 사회 [*Economy and Society*] 64 (2004): 148–171 (in Korean).

Choi, Yang-Suk. "부부분거경험의 성별차이를 중심으로 본 기러기 가족 현상" [The Phenomenon of "Geese Families": Marital Separation between Geese-fathers and Geese-mothers]. 가족과 문화 [*Family and Culture*] 18, no. 2 (2006): 37–65 (in Korean).

Chong, Kelly H. "Negotiating Patriarchy: South Korean Evangelical Women and the Politics of Gender." *Gender & Society* 20, no. 6 (December, 2006): 697–724.

Chua, Amy. *Battle Hymn of the Tiger Mother*. New York: Penguin Press, 2011.

Collins, Patricia Hill. *Black Feminist Thought: Knowledge, Consciousness, and the Politics of Empowerment*. 2nd ed. New York: Routledge, 2000.

———. "Toward a New Vision: Race, Class, and Gender as Categories of Analysis and Connection." *Race, Sex & Class* 1, no. 1 (1993): 25–45.

Coltrane, Scott. "Research on Household Labor: Modeling and Measuring the Social Embeddedness of Routine Family Work." *Journal of Marriage and the Family* 62 (2000): 1208–1233.

Coontz, Stephanie. *The Way We Really Are: Coming to Terms with America's Changing Families*. New York: Basic Books, 1997.

Coutin, Susan. "Denationalization, Inclusion, and Exclusion: Negotiating the Boundaries of Belonging." *Indiana Journal of Global Legal Studies* 7 (2000): 585–591.

Coverman, Shelly. "Explaining Husbands' Participation in Domestic Labor." *Sociological Quarterly* 26 (1985): 81–97.

Department of Homeland Security. "Curricular Practical Training (CPT)." Accessed February 6, 2015. http://www.uscis.gov/working-united-states/students-and-exchange-visitors/students-and-employment.

———. "Optional Practical Training (OPT)." Accessed February 10, 2015. http://www.ice.gov/doclib/sevis/pdf/opt_policy_guidance_042010.pdf.

Dermott, Esther. *Intimate Fatherhood: A Sociological Analysis*. London: Routledge, 2008.

Doherty, William J., Edward F. Kouneski, and Martha F. Erickson. "Responsible Fathering: An Overview and Conceptual Framework." *Journal of Marriage and the Family* 60 (1998): 277–292.

Dreby, Joanna. *Everyday Illegal: When Policies Undermine Immigrant Families.* Oakland: University of California Press, 2015.

———. "Honor and Virtue: Mexican Parenting in the Transnational Context." *Gender & Society* 20, no. 1 (2006): 32–59.

Dreby, Joanna and Timothy Adkins. "Inequalities in Transnational Families." *Sociology Compass* 4, no. 8 (2010): 673–689.

Ebaugh, Helen Rose and Janet Saltzman Chafetz. *Religion and the New Immigrants: Continuities and Adaptations in Immigrant Congregations.* New York: AltaMira Press, 2000.

Ehrenreich, Barbara and Arlie Russell Hochschild. "Introduction." In *Global Woman: Nannies, Maids, and Sex Workers in the New Economy*, edited by Barbara Ehrenreich and Arlie Russell Hochschild, 1–13. New York: Metropolitan Books, 2003.

England, Kim. "Mothers, Wives, Workers: The Everyday Lives of Working Mothers." In *Who Will Mind the Baby: Geographies of Child Care and Working Mothers*, edited by Kim England, 109–122. New York: Routledge, 1996.

England, Paula. "Marriage, the Costs of Children, and Gender Inequality." In *Ties that Bind: Perspectives on Marriage and Cohabitation,* edited by Linda Waite, Christine Bachrach, Michelle Hindin, Elizabeth Thomson, and Arland Thornton, 320–342. New York: Aldine de Gruyter, 2000.

Espiritu, Yen Le. *Asian American Women and Men: Labor, Laws, and Love.* 2nd ed. Thousand Oaks, CA: Sage Publications, 2008.

Expedia. "2015 Vacation Deprivation Study." 2015. Accessed March 13, 2016. https ://viewfinder.expedia.com/news/expedia-s-2015-vacation-deprivation-study-eu rope-leads-world-in-paid-vacation-time-while-americans-and-asians-lag/.

Eyou, Mei Lin, Vivienne Adair, and Robyn Dixon. "Cultural Identity and Psychological Adjustment of Adolescent Chinese Immigrants in New Zealand." *Journal of Adolescence* 23 (2000): 531–543.

Fineman, Martha. *The Neutered Mother, the Sexual Family and Other Twentieth Century Tragedies.* New York: Routledge, 1995.

Fix, Michael and Wendy Zimmermann. "All Under One Roof: Mixed-Status Families in an Era of Reform." *International Migration Review* 35, no. 2 (2001): 397–419.

Foucault, Michel. *Discipline and Punish: The Birth of the Prison.* Translated by Alan Sheridan. New York: Pantheon Books, 1977.

Frankenberg, Ruth. *White Women, Race Matters: The Social Construction of Whiteness.* Minneapolis: University of Minnesota Press, 1993.

Fresnoza-Flot, Asuncion. "Migration Status and Transnational Mothering: The Case of Filipino Migrants in France." *Global Networks* 9, no. 2 (2009): 252–270.

Fuhr, Michael. *Globalization and Popular Music in South Korea: Sounding Out K-Pop.* New York and London: Routledge, 2016.

George, Sheba Mariam. "When Women Come First: Gender and Class and Transnational Ties among Indian Immigrants in the United States." PhD diss., UC Berkeley, 2001.

Glenn, Evelyn Nakano. "From Servitude to Service Work: The Historical Continuities of Women's Paid and Unpaid Reproductive Labor." *Signs: Journal of Women in Culture and Society* 18, no. 1 (1992): 1–44.

———. "Split Household, Small Producer and Dual Wage Earner: An Analysis of Chinese-American Family Strategies." *Journal of Marriage and Family* 45, no. 1 (1983): 35–46.

Gottzén, Lucas. "Involved Fatherhood? Exploring the Educational Work of Middle-Class Men." *Gender and Education* 23, no. 5 (2011): 619–634.

Government of Canada. "Student Work Permit–Work on Campus." Accessed July 14, 2014. http://www.cic.gc.ca/english/study/work-oncampus.asp.

Government of Canada. "Work or Live in Canada after You Graduate." Modified March 17, 2021. https://www.canada.ca/en/immigration-refugees-citizenship/services/study-canada/work/after-graduation.html.

Grahame, Kamini Maraj. "'For the Family': Asian Immigrant Women's Triple Day." *Journal of Sociology & Social Welfare* 30, no. 1 (2003): 65–90.

Gupta, Sanjiv. "The Effects of Transitions in Marital Status on Men's Performance of Housework." *Journal of Marriage and Family* 61 (1999): 700–711.

Haagsman, Karlijn and Valentina Mazzucato. "The Quality of Parent-Child Relationships in Transnational Families: Angolan and Nigerian Migrant Parent in the Netherlands." *Journal of Ethnic and Migration Studies* 40, no. 11 (2014): 1677–1696.

Hattery, Angela. *Women, Work and Family: Balancing and Weaving.* Thousand Oaks, CA: Sage, 2001.

Hays, Sharon. *The Cultural Contradictions of Motherhood.* New Haven, CT: Yale University Press, 1996.

Hirschman, Charles. "The Role of Religion in the Origins and Adaptation of Immigrant Groups in the United States." *International Migration Review* 38, no. 3 (2004): 1206–1233.

Ho, Elsie. "Chinese or New Zealanders? Differential Paths of Adaptation of Hong Kong Chinese Adolescent Immigrants in New Zealand." *New Zealand Population Review* 21, nos. 1 & 2 (1995): 27–49.

Ho, Elsie and Richard Bedford. "Asian Transnational Families in New Zealand: Dynamics and Challenges." *International Migration* 46, no. 4 (2008): 41–62.

Hochschild, Arlie, with Anne Machung. *The Second Shift.* New York: Viking Press, 1989.

Hondagneu-Sotelo, Pierrette. *Gendered Transitions: Mexican Experiences of Immigration.* Los Angeles: University of California Press, 1994.

———. "Overcoming Patriarchal Constraints: The Reconstruction of Gender Relations among Mexican Immigrant Women and Men." *Gender & Society* 6, no. 3 (1992): 393–415.

Hondagneu-Sotelo, Pierrette and Ernestine Avila. "'I'm Here, But I'm There': The Meaning of Latina Transnational Motherhood." *Gender & Society* 11, no. 5 (1997): 548–571.

Horst, Heather A. "The Blessings and Burdens of Communication: Cell Phones in Jamaican Transnational Fields." *Global Networks* 6, no. 2 (2006): 143–159.

Huang, Shirlena and Brenda S. A. Yeoh. "Transnational Families and Their Children's Education: China's 'Study Mothers' in Singapore." *Global Networks* 5, no. 4 (2005): 379–400.

Hurh, Won Moo and Kwang Chung Kim. "Adhesive Sociocultural Adaptation of Korean Immigrants in the U.S.: An Alternative Strategy of Minority Adaptation." *The International Migration Review* 18, no. 2 (Summer, 1984): 188–216.

Johansson, Thomas. "The Construction of the New Father: How Middle-class Men Become Present Fathers." *International Review of Modern Sociology* 37, no. 1 (2011): 121–136.

Kao, Grace. "Parental Influences on the Educational Outcomes of Immigrant Youth." *International Migration Review* 38, no. 2 (2004): 427–449.

Kibria, Nazli. *Family Tightrope: The Changing Lives of Vietnamese Americans.* Princeton, NJ: Princeton University Press, 1993.

———. "Migration and Vietnamese American Women: Remaking Ethnicity." In *Women of Color in U.S. Society*, edited by Maxine Zinn and Bonnie Dill, 247–264. Philadelphia, PA: Temple University Press, 1994.

Kilkey, Majella, Ania Plomien, and Diane Perrons. "Migrant Men's Fathering Narratives, Practices and Projects in National and Transnational Spaces: Recent Polish Male Migrants to London." *International Migration* 52, no. 1 (2014): 178–191.

Kim, Bok-Rae. "The English Fever in South Korea: Focusing on the Problem of Early English Education." *Journal of Education & Social Policy* 2, no. 2 (2015): 117–124.

Kim, Jeehun. "'Downed' and Stuck in Singapore: Lower/Middle Class South Korean Wild Geese (Kirogi)." *Research in the Sociology of Education* 17 (2010): 271–311.

Kim, Minjeong. "'Forced' into Unpaid Carework: International Students' Wives in the United States." In *Global Dimensions of Gender and Carework*, edited by Mary K. Zimmerman, Jacquelyn S. Litt, and Christine E. Bose, 162–175. Stanford, CA: Stanford University Press, 2006.

Kim, Seonmi. "재미 국제 장기 분거가족 전업주부의 일상적 삶과 정체성 유지에 관한 연구:'기러기엄마'되기 과정" ["A Qualitative Study on the Life Experience and Identity Maintenance of the Full-Time Housewives of the Korean Wild Geese Family in U.S.A."]. 한국가족자원경영학회지 [*Journal of Korean Home Management Association*] 11, no. 4 (2007): 171–189 (in Korean).

———. "기러기엄마로 살기: 일상생활의 구성 그리고 관계맺기" ["A Qualitative Study on the Wild Goose Mother's Everyday Life, Family Relationship and Social Networking"]. 한국가족자원경영학회지 [*Korean Family Resource Management Association*] 13, no. 1 (2009): 41–59 (in Korean).

Kim, Sung-Sook. "기러기아빠의 생활 변화와 적응 문제" ["The 'Kirogi' Fathers' Changes of Lives and Adaptation Problems"]. 한국가족자원경영학회지 [*Journal of Korean Home Management Association*] 24, no. 1 (2006): 141–158 (in Korean).

Kim, Young-Hee, Myung-Seon Choi, and Jee-Hang Lee. "뉴질랜드 거주 기러기 어머니의 생활 실태 연구" ["Actual State of Korean 'Geese Mothers' in New Zealand"]. 대한가정학회지 [*Journal of the Korean Home Economics Association*] 43, no. 11 (2005): 141–152 (in Korean).

Kim, Yang Hee and On Jeong Chang. "장기 분거 가족에 관한 탐색적 연구 –기러기 가족에 초점을 맞추어" ["Issue of Families That Run Separate Households for a Long Time: The So-called 'Wild Geese Family'"]. 한국가족관계학회지 [*Korea Association of Family Relations*] 9, no. 2 (2004): 1–23 (in Korean).

King, Valarie and Juliana M. Sobolewski. "Nonresident Fathers' Contributions to Adolescent Well-Being." *Journal of Marriage and Family* 68 (2006): 537–557.

Korea Culture & Tourism Institute. "A Study on the Improvement Plans of Leave System for Increase Domestic Tourist Demand" 2012 (in Korean). Accessed March 13, 2016. https://www.kcti.re.kr/03_1.dmw?method=view&reportSeq=863 &reportId=2.

Korea Development Institute (KDI). "노후보장을 위한 가족, 정부, 사회의 역할" ["Role of the Family, Government and Society to Protect the Elderly Life"]. *KDI Issue Focus Report*. Korea: Korea Development Institute, March 30, 2015, 1–8 (in Korean).

Korea Internet and Security Agency. "2015 Survey on the Internet Usage Executive Summary." December 31, 2015 (in Korean). Accessed March 7, 2016. http://www .msip.go.kr/web/msipContents/contentsView.do?cateId=mssw311&artId=1289 520.

Korea Times. "Koreans Work Second Longest Hours in OECD." November 3, 2015. Accessed March 18, 2016. http://www.koreatimes.co.kr/www/news/biz/2015/11/4 88_190167.html.

Korean Educational Development Institute (KEDI). "2005 Educational Statistics Analysis" (in Korean). Accessed August 10, 2012. http://cesi.kedi.re.kr/index .jsp.

———. "2017 Educational Statistical Analysis" (in Korean). Accessed June 27, 2018. http://cesi.kedi.re.kr/.

Korean Military Manpower Administration (in Korean). Accessed May 30, 2020. http://www.mma.go.kr/index.do.

Korean Ministry of Education (in Korean). Accessed June 27, 2018. https://www .moe.go.kr/.

Korean National Law Information Center, "Act on the Punishment of Arrangement of Commercial Sex Acts" (in Korean). Accessed May 28, 2020. https://www.law .go.kr/법령/성매매알선등행위의처벌에관한법률.

———. "Korean Educational Public Official Law" (in Korean). Accessed May 28, 2020. http://www.law.go.kr/법령/교육공무원법.

Korean Statistical Office. "2015 Korean Household Finance and Welfare Survey Result" (in Korean). Accessed July 7, 2018. http://kostat.go.kr/portal/korea/ko r_nw/2/4/4/index.board.

Kwon, Young In and Kevin M. Roy. "Changing Social Expectations for Work and Family Involvement among Korean Fathers." *Journal of Comparative Family Studies* 38, no. 2 (2007): 285–305.

Kyle, David. *Transnational Peasants: Migrations, Networks, and Ethnicity in Andean Ecuador*. Baltimore, MD: Johns Hopkins University Press, 2000.

Lamb, Michael. "The History of Research on Father Involvement." *Marriage & Family Review* 29, nos. 2–3 (2000): 23–42.

Landolt, Patricia and Wei Wei Da. "The Spatially Ruptured Practices of Migrant Families: A Comparison of Immigrant Families from El Salvador and the People's Republic of China." *Current Sociology* 53, no. 4 (2005): 625–653.

Lareau, Annette. "Invisible Inequality: Social Class and Childrearing in Black Families and White Families." *American Sociological Review* 67 (2002): 747–776.

———. *Unequal Childhoods: Class, Race, and Family Life.* Berkeley: University of California Press, 2003.

Lee, Doohyoo. "기러기아빠의 교육적 희망과 갈등 연구" ["A Study of Kiroghee Fathers' Hopes and Struggles about Children's Education"]. 교육문제연구 [*Research in Educational Issues*] 32 (2008): 21–46 (in Korean).

Lee, Hakyoon. "'I Am a Kirogi Mother': Education Exodus and Life Transformation among Korean Transnational Women." *Journal of Language, Identity & Education* 9, no. 4 (2010): 250–264.

Lee, Se Hwa. "The Bifurcated Statuses of the Wives of Korean International Students." In *Koreans in North America: Twenty-First Century Experiences*, edited by Pyong Gap Min, 135–156. Lanham, MD: Lexington Books, 2013.

———. "Closer or Estranged: Transnational Spousal Relationships between Korean Wild Geese Parents." In *Companion to Korean American Studies*, edited by Rachael Joo and Shelley Lee, 503–533. Boston, MA: Brill, 2018.

———. "'I Am Still Close to My Child': Middle-Class Korean Wild Geese Fathers' Responsible and Intimate Fatherhood in a Transnational Context." *Journal of Ethnic and Migration Studies* (2019). https://doi.org/10.1080/1369183X.2019.15 73662.

———. "Only If You Are One of Us: Wild Geese Mothers' Parenting in the Korean Immigrant Community." *Amerasia Journal* 42, no. 2 (2016): 71–94.

Lee, Yean-Ju and Hagen Koo. "'Wild Geese Fathers' and a Globalised Family Strategy for Education in Korea." *International Development Planning Review* 28, no. 4 (2006): 533–553.

Leifsen, Esben and Alexander Tymczuk. "Care at a Distance: Ukrainian and Ecuadorian Transnational Parenthood from Spain." *Journal of Ethnic and Migration Studies* 38, no. 2 (2012): 219–236.

Levine, James A. and Edward W. Pitt. *New Expectations: Community Strategies for Responsible Fatherhood.* New York: Families and Work Institute, 1995.

Lim, In-Sook. "Korean Immigrant Women's Challenge to Gender Inequality at Home: The Interplay of Economic Resources, Gender, and Family." *Gender & Society* 11, no. 1 (1997): 31–51.

Lofland, John, David A. Snow, Leon Anderson, and Lyn H. Loafland. *Analyzing Social Settings: A Guide to Qualitative Observation and Analysis.* 4th ed. Belmont, CA: Wadsworth Publishing Company, 2006.

Madianou, Mirca and Daniel Miller. "Mobile Phone Parenting: Reconfiguring Relationships between Filipina Migrant Mothers and Their Left-Behind Children." *New Media & Society* 13, no. 3 (2011): 457–470.

Mahler, Sarah. "Engendering Transnational Migration: A Case Study of Salvadorans." *American Behavioral Scientist* 42, no. 4 (1999): 690–719.

Man, Guida. "From Hong Kong to Canada: Immigration and the Changing Family Lives of Middle-Class Women from Hong Kong." In *Family Patterns, Gender Relations*, edited by Bonnie J. Fox, 420–440. New York: Oxford University Press, 2001.

Manalansan, Martin F., IV. "Queer Intersections: Sexuality and Gender in Migration Studies." *International Migration Review* 40 (2006): 224–249.

McGill, Brittany. "Navigating New Norms of Involved Fatherhood: Employment, Fathering Attitudes, and Father Involvement." *Journal of Family Issues* 35, no. 8 (2014): 1089–1106.

McKay, Deirdre. "'Sending Dollars Shows Feeling': Emotions and Economies in Filipino Migration." *Mobilities* 2, no. 2 (2007): 175–194.

Menjívar, Cecilia. *Enduring Violence: Latina Women's Lives in Guatemala*. Berkeley: University of California Press, 2011.

———. "Family Reorganization in a Context of Legal Uncertainty: Guatemalan and Salvadoran Immigrants in the United States." *International Journal of Sociology of the Family* 32, no. 2 (2006): 223–245.

———. "Liminal Legality: Salvadoran and Guatemalan Immigrants' Lives in the United States." *American Journal of Sociology* 111, no. 4 (January 2006): 999–1037.

———. "Transnational Parenting and Immigration Law: Central Americans in the United States." *Journal of Ethnic and Migration Studies* 38, no. 2 (2012): 301–322.

Min, Pyong Gap. "Changes in Korean Immigrants' Gender Role and Social Status, and Their Marital Conflicts." *Sociological Forum* 16, no. 2 (2001): 301–320.

Min, Pyong Gap and Jung Ha Kim. *Religions in Asian America: Building Faith Communities*. Walnut Creek, CA: AltaMira Press, 2002.

Montes, Veronica. "The Role of Emotions in the Construction of Masculinity: Guatemalan Migrant Men, Transnational Migration, and Family Relations." *Gender & Society* 27, no. 4 (2013): 469–490.

Moon, Seungsook. "Immigration and Mothering: Case Studies from Two Generations of Korean Immigrant Women." *Gender & Society* 17, no. 6 (2003): 840–860.

Nam, Jung Mi. "The Changing Role of English in Korea: From English as a Tool for Advancement to English for Survival." *Pan-Pacific Association of Applied Linguistics* 9, no. 2 (2005): 227–240.

Nobles, Jenna. "Parenting from Abroad: Migration, Nonresident Father Involvement, and Children's Education in Mexico." *Journal of Marriage and Family* 73 (2011): 729–746.

O'Connor, Allison and Jeanne Batalova. "Korean Immigrants in the United States." Migration Policy Institute. April 10, 2019. Accessed October 1, 2020. https://www.migrationpolicy.org/article/korean-immigrants-united-states-2017.

OECD. "Society at a Glance 2016: A Spotlight on Youth." October 5, 2016. Accessed July 10, 2018. http://www.oecd.org/korea/sag2016-korea.pdf.

Ong, Paul and Tania Azores. "The Migration and Incorporation of Filipino Nurses." In *The New Asian Immigration in Los Angeles and Global Restructuring*, edited by Paul Ong, Edna Bonacich, and Lucie Cheng, 164–95. Philadelphia, PA: Temple University Press, 1994.

Orellana, Marjorie Faulstich, Barrie Thorne, Anna Chee, and Wan Shun Eva Lam. "Transnational Childhoods: The Participation of Children in Process of Family Migration." *Social Problems* 48, no. 4 (2001): 572–591.

Overseas Korean Education Portal. "Guideline for Overseas Koreans' College Admission" (in Korean). Accessed October 1, 2020. http://okep.moe.go.kr/html/page.do?htmlId=18&menu_seq=21.

Park, Juyeon. "Public Fathering, Private Mothering: Gendered Transnational Parenting and Class Reproduction among Elite Korean Students." *Gender & Society* 32, no. 4 (2018): 563–586.

Park, Se-il. "The Labor Market Policy and Social Safety Net in Korea: After the 1997 Crisis." The Brookings Institution: Washington, DC, September 1, 1999. Accessed July 21, 2018. https://www.brookings.edu/research/the-labor-market-policy-and-social-safety-net-in-korea-after-the-1997-crisis/.

Park, So Jin and Nancy Abelmann. "Class and Cosmopolitan Striving: Mothers' Management of English Education in South Korea." *Anthropological Quarterly* 77, no. 4 (2004): 645–672.

Parreñas, Rhacel Salazar. *Children of Global Migration: Transnational Families and Gendered Woes.* Stanford, CA: Stanford University Press, 2005.

———. "Long Distance Intimacy: Class, Gender, and Intergenerational Relations between Mothers and Children in Filipino Transnational Families." *Global Networks* 5, no. 4 (2005): 317–336.

———. "Migrant Filipina Domestic Workers and the International Division of Reproduction." *Gender & Society* 14, no. 4 (2000): 560–580.

———. *Servants of Globalization: Women, Migration and Domestic Work.* Stanford, CA: Stanford University Press, 2001.

———. "Transnational Fathering: Gendered Conflicts, Distant Disciplining and Emotional Gaps." *Journal of Ethnic and Migration Studies* 34, no. 7 (2008): 1057–1072.

Pe-Pua, Rogelia, Colleen Mitchell, Stephen Castles, and Robyn Iredale. "Astronaut Families and Parachute Children: Hong Kong Immigrants in Australia." In *The Last Half Century of Chinese Overseas*, edited by Elizabeth Sinn, 279–298. Hong Kong: University of Hong Kong Press, 1998.

Pessar, Patricia R. "The Linkage between the Household and Workplace in the Experience of Dominican Immigrant Women in the United States." *International Migration Review* 18 (1984): 1188–1211.

———. "On the Homefront and in the Workplace: Integrating Women into Feminist Discourse." *Anthropological Quarterly* 68, no. 1 (1995): 37–47.

———. "The Role of Gender in Dominican Settlement in the United States." In *Women and Change in Latin America,* edited by June Nash and Helen Safa, 273–294. South Hadley, MA: Bergin and Garvey, 1986.

———. "The Role of Households in International Migration and the Case of U.S.-Bound Migration from the Dominican Republic." *International Migration Review* 16 (1982): 342–364.

Peterson, Richard R. and Kathleen Gerson. "Determinants of Responsibility for Child Care Arrangements among Dual-Earner Couples." *Journal of Marriage and the Family* 54 (1992): 527–536.

Pew Research Center. "Social Media Use Continues to Rise in Developing Countries, but Plateaus Across Developed Ones." Accessed November 1, 2019. https://ww w.pewresearch.org/global/wp-content/uploads/sites/2/2018/06/Pew-Research-Ce nter-Global-Tech-Social-Media-Use-2018.06.19.pdf.

Pleck, Elizabeth H. and Joseph H. Pleck. "Fatherhood Ideals in the United States: Historical Dimensions." In *The Role of the Father in Child Development*. 3rd ed., edited by M. E. Lamb, 33–48. New York: Wiley, 1997.

Portes, Alejandro and Rubén G. Rumbaut. *Immigrant America: A Portrait.* 3rd ed. Berkeley: University of California Press, 2006.

Pribilsky, Jason. "'Aprendemos a Convivir': Conjugal Relations, Co-parenting, and Family Life among Ecuadorian Transnational Migrants in New York City and the Ecuadorian Andes." *Global Networks* 4, no. 3 (2004): 313–334.

———. "Consumption Dilemmas: Tracking Masculinity, Money and Transnational Fatherhood Between the Ecuadorian Andes and New York City." *Journal of Ethnic and Migration Studies* 38, no. 2 (2012): 323–343.

Ryan, Louise, Rosemary Sales, Mary Tilki, and Bernadetta Siara. "Family Strategies and Transnational Migration: Recent Polish Migrants in London." *Journal of Ethnic and Migration Studies* 35, no. 1 (2009): 61–77.

Sallie Mae. "How America Pays for College 2016: Sallie Mae's National Study of College Students and Parents." 2016. Accessed August 17, 2017. http://news.sal liemae.com/files/doc_library/file/HowAmericaPaysforCollege2016FNL.pdf.

Sassen, Saskia. "Two Stops in Today's New Global Geographies: Shaping Novel Labor Supplies and Employment Regimes." *American Behavioral Scientist* 52, no. 3 (2008): 457–496.

Schmalzbauer, Leah. "Family Divided: The Class Formation of Honduran Transnational Families." *Global Networks* 8, no. 3 (2008): 329–346.

———. "Searching for Wages and Mothering from Afar: The Case of Honduran Transnational Families." *Journal of Marriage and Family* 66, no. 5 (2004): 1317–1331.

———. *Striving and Surviving: A Daily Life Analysis of Honduran Transnational Families.* New York: Routledge, 2005.

———. "Temporary and Transnational: Gender and Emotion in the Lives of Mexican Guest Worker Fathers." *Ethnic and Racial Studies* 38, no. 2 (2015): 211–226.

Schoeni, Robert F. and Karen Ross. "Material Assistance from Families during the Transition to Adulthood." In *On the Frontier of Adulthood: Theory, Research, and Public Policy*, edited by Richard Settersten, Jr., Frank Furstenberg, and Ruben Rumbaut, 396–416. Chicago: University of Chicago Press, 2005.

Şenyürekli, Ayşem R. and Daniel F. Detznera. "Communication Dynamics of the Transnational Family." *Marriage & Family Review* 45, nos. 6–8 (2009): 807–824.

Shim, Rosa Jinyoung. "Englishized Korean: Structure, Status, and Attitudes." *World Englisher* 13, no. 2 (1994): 225–244.

Smith, Andrea, Richard N. Lalonde, and Simone Johnson. "Serial Migration and Its Implications for the Parent-Child Relationship: A Retrospective Analysis of the Experiences of the Children of Caribbean Immigrants." *Cultural Diversity and Ethnic Minority Psychology* 10, no. 2 (2004): 107–122.

Sobolewski, Juliana and Valarie King. "The Importance of the Coparental Relationship for Nonresident Fathers' Ties to Children." *Journal of Marriage and Family* 67 (2005): 1196–1212.

South, Scott and Glenna Spitze. "Housework in Marital and Nonmarital Households." *American Sociological Review* 59 (1994): 327–347.

Sun, Yongmin. "The Academic Success of East-Asian American Students– An Investment Model." *Social Science Research* 27 (1998): 432–456.

Tsuda, Takeyuki. *Strangers in the Ethnic Homeland: Japanese Brazilian Return Migration in Transnational Perspective*. New York: Columbia University Press, 2003.

Urry, John. "Social Networks, Travel and Talk." *British Journal of Sociology* 54, no. 2 (2003): 155–175.

Wall, Glenda and Stephanie Arnold. "How Involved Is Involved Fathering? An Exploration of the Contemporary Culture of Fatherhood." *Gender & Society* 21, no. 4 (2007): 508–527.

Waters, Johanna L. "Becoming a Father, Missing a Wife: Chinese Transnational Families and the Male Experience of Lone Parenting in Canada." *Population, Space and Place* 16, no. 1 (2009): 63–74.

———. "Flexible Families?: 'Astronaut' Households and the Experiences of Lone Mothers in Vancouver, British Columbia." *Social and Cultural Geography* 3 (2002): 117–134.

———. "Transnational Family Strategies and Education in the Contemporary Chinese Diaspora." *Global Networks* 5, no. 4 (2005): 359–377.

Weiss, Robert S. *Learning from Strangers: The Art and Method of Qualitative Interview Studies*. New York: Free Press, 1994.

West, Candace and Don H. Zimmerman. "Doing Gender." *Gender & Society* 1, no. 2 (1987): 125–151.

Wilding, Raelene. "'Virtual' Intimacies? Families Communicating across Transnational Contexts." *Global Networks* 6, no. 2 (2006): 125–142.

Worby, Paula A. and Kurt C. Organista. "Alcohol Use and Problem Drinking among Mexican and Central American Immigrant Laborers: A Review of the Literature." *Hispanic Journal of Behavioral Sciences* 29, no. 4 (2007): 413–455.

Yeoh, Brenda S. A. and Katie Willis. "'Heart' and 'Wing', Nation and Diaspora: Gendered Discourses in Singapore's Regionalisation Process." *Gender, Place and Culture* 6 (1999): 355–372.

Yeoh, Brenda S. A. and Louisa-May Khoo. "Home, Work and Community: Skilled International Migration and Expatriate Women in Singapore." *International Migration* 36, no. 2 (1998): 159–184.

Yi, Joseph. "Tiger Moms and Liberal Elephants: Private, Supplemental Education among Korean-Americans." *Society* 50 (2013): 190–195.

Zelizer, Viviana A. *Pricing the Priceless Child: The Social Value of Children*. New York: Basic Books, 1994.

Zentgraf, Kristine M. "Immigration and Women's Empowerment: Salvadorans in Los Angeles." *Gender & Society* 16, no. 5 (2002): 625–646.

Zentgraf, Kristine M. and Norma Stoltz Chinchilla. "Transnational Family Separation: A Framework for Analysis." *Journal of Ethnic and Migration Studies* 38, no. 2 (2012): 345–366.

Zhou, Min. "How Neighbourhoods Matter for Immigrant Children: The Formation of Educational Resources in Chinatown, Koreatown and Pico Union, Los Angeles." *Journal of Ethnic and Migration Studies* 35, no. 7 (2009): 1153–1179.

Zhou, Min and Susan S. Kim. "Community Forces, Social Capital, and Educational Achievement: The Case of Supplementary Education in the Chinese and Korean Immigrant Communities." *Harvard Educational Review* 76, no. 1 (2006): 1–29.

Index

About the Author

Se Hwa Lee is a visiting scholar and research scientist at the University at Albany, State University of New York. She earned her PhD degree in sociology at the University at Albany and worked as a visiting assistant professor at Dickinson College. She is interested in the topics of gender, family, immigration, race/ethnicity, social inequality, public policy, and Asians/Asian Americans. Her articles have appeared in the *Journal of Ethnic and Migration Studies, Amerasia Journal,* and *Journal of Women, Politics, and Policy,* as well as in collected volumes.